How to Think Like
a Philosopher

Also by Julian Baggini from Granta Books

The Godless Gospel

How the World Thinks: A Global History of Philosophy

Freedom Regained: The Possibility of Free Will

The Virtues of the Table: How to Eat and Think

The Ego Trick

*Should You Judge This Book by Its Cover?: 100 Fresh
Takes on Familiar Sayings and Quotations*

*Do They Think You're Stupid?: 100 Ways of Spotting Spin
& Nonsense from the Media, Pundits & Politicians*

Welcome to Everytown: A Journey into the English Mind

*The Pig That Wants to be Eaten: And 99
Other Thought Experiments*

What's It All About? – Philosophy and the Meaning of Life

By Julian Baggini and Jeremy Stangroom

Do You Think What You Think You Think?

HOW TO THINK LIKE A PHILOSOPHER

Essential Principles for Clearer Thinking

Julian Baggini

GRANTA

Granta Publications, 12 Addison Avenue, London W11 4QR
First published in Great Britain by Granta Books, 2023

A CIP catalogue record for this book
is available from the British Library.

1 3 5 7 9 10 8 6 4 2

ISBN 978 1 78378 851 4 (hardback)
ISBN 978 1 78378 980 1 (trade paperback)
ISBN 978 1 78378 854 5 (ebook)

Typeset in Janson by M Rules
Printed and bound by CPI Group (UK) Ltd, Croydon, CR0 4YY

www.granta.com

MIX
Paper | Supporting
responsible forestry
FSC® C171272

CONTENTS

INTRODUCTION

It is in just such stupid things clever people are
most easily caught. The more cunning a man
is, the less he suspects that he will be caught
in a simple thing. The more cunning a man is,
the simpler the trap he must be caught in.

FYODOR DOSTOEVSKY, *Crime and Punishment*

Has humanity lost its reason, or did we never have it in the first place? In every age we hear laments of decline, but today they seem to be louder, more frequent, more despairing. However, it is hard to think of any previous era in which it has been significantly easier to reason well. Imagine trying to think rigorously when you were much more likely to be illiterate than able to read; when what was published was strictly controlled by the church or state and books were prohibitively expensive; when heresies political or religious could get you hung from a noose; and when our scientific knowledge was minimal and spurious theories reigned supreme. As recently as fifty years ago, most people's main sources of information were highly partisan newspapers and a handful of television and radio channels. Public libraries were the Wikipedia of their time, but much less well stocked and harder to search.

The cognoscenti have always been tempted to declare their own age to be one of exceptional decadence or irrationality, but philosophers are well placed to see that our failures of reason are permanent and legion. There is indeed an urgent need to think better right now, but only because it is always necessary to think better and it is always now. Our present abundance of crooked thinking needs setting straight as much as the past's. Follies that were on the fringes have moved centre stage: conspiracy theories, climate-change denial, vaccine scepticism, quack remedies, religious extremism. At the same time, the once-respected mainstream appears to be clueless. The Queen of the United Kingdom never looked more like the representative of her people than when she asked discomfited economists why they had not seen the 2008 financial crisis coming. As the Swedish teenager Greta Thunberg has shown, it takes no great expertise to point out that the world's leaders have been rearranging the deckchairs while a climate catastrophe unfolds in front of their very eyes. In numerous educated, wealthy, industrialised countries, such as the USA, Brazil and Hungary, millions have given up on mainstream politics and voted for hateful populist demagogues.

More hopefully, we also have plenty of examples of what happens when good thinking prevails. We have seen numerous signs of human ingenuity and intelligence, such as the rapid development of vaccines against Covid-19; massive reductions of people living in poverty, and deeper understanding about the irrationality and harm of racism, misogyny and homophobia.

If we want to promote better reasoning, we can learn a lot from the philosophers who have been specialists in sound thinking for millennia. In an age which fetishizes novelty and innovation, there is a need to relearn the greatest lessons from the past and appreciate that what is timeless is always timely. Of course, not every philosopher will agree with all I have to say, because philosophers disagree even – *especially* – on fundamental matters. Nor does philosophy have a monopoly on rigorous reasoning, and nor is it immune to sloppy thought. But it is uniquely focused on the need to think straight, above all else. Every other discipline has something more concrete to rely on. Scientists have experiments, economists data, anthropologists participant observation, historians documents, archaeologists artefacts, and so on. Philosophers have no special store of information. Their unique skill is the ability to think without a safety net. If we want to know how to think better, without resort to specialist knowledge, it is hard to find better models.

However, standard outlines of the principles of philosophical reasoning leave out what is most important. Students of philosophy learn the rules of logical deduction, lists of fallacies to avoid, explanations of the difference between inductive and abductive reasoning, and so forth. These are all important, but by themselves they are not enough. It's like driving. Most motorists know how to change gears, what the speed limits are and so on. The difference between good and bad drivers is not primarily a matter of principles and techniques. It's the *attitude* they have to their driving which is essential: how much care and attention they pay, how motivated they are to drive properly, how thoughtful they are to other road users. Similarly, thinking is about attitudes as well as techniques.

Having the right attitudes is philosophy's own X-factor – call it the P-factor. It's what elevates the best philosophers above those who have all the logical chops but lack insight. Like the elusive X-factor, the P-factor defies precise definition. It is a kind of virtue, by which I do not mean eating organic oat bran or doing good works. Virtue, in the Ancient Greek philosophical sense, simply means the habits, attitudes and character traits that are conducive to living – and thinking – well. The approach to reasoning known as virtue epistemology (epistemology meaning the theory of knowledge) holds that good reasoning requires certain habits and attitudes of thought, not simply mastery of formal procedures that could be programmed into a computer. The importance of epistemic virtue has been more appreciated in academic philosophy in recent decades, but still not enough, and word has not yet got out. It's time it was granted its proper place at the heart of good thinking.

Over more than thirty years of studying, reading, writing and talking about philosophy, often with philosophers, I have become convinced that without the P-factor of 'epistemic virtue', critical-thinking skills are little more than highbrow party tricks which give users the ability to impress with the dexterity of their thoughts and to rip the arguments of others to shreds. I want to identify what sets genuinely good reasoning apart from mere cleverness. Clever thinkers who lack the P-factor are tiresome, boring and cannot help with philosophy's historical mission to enable us to understand the world and each other better.

My interest is not only in what makes for a good philosopher, but what makes for good thinking about anything. So this book does not just aim to provide insights into philosophical problems and how philosophers have thought about them. I also want to show how philosophical habits of thought apply in politics, general problem-solving, self-care and making sense of the world.

I will draw on dozens of interviews I have conducted for magazine articles and books with some of the world's leading philosophers and thinkers over many years. I have found that many have made asides or tangential comments about how they work which are more revealing than those that come out of overt discussion of philosophical method. I also refer to many of the great philosophical works of all time. Most of my examples will come from the tradition of Western philosophy in which I was educated, but the principles are universal, as the more occasional references to the rest of the world's philosophies remind us. Historically, women have not been given as much voice as men in philosophy, so although I will cite many brilliant female philosophers, inevitably the cast list is skewed towards the patriarchy.

I will be looking at the many traps that await the would-be skilled reasoner. Like any tool, reasoning can be misapplied and misused, even with the best of intentions. One feature of virtue epistemology is the need for vigilance and modesty. Beware of anyone who believes they are a brilliant thinker: true geniuses are rarely dazzled by their own reflections.

Another thing that I hope distinguishes this book from other 'smart thinking' tomes is that I do not shy away from the sheer difficulty of thinking well. An invitation to think like a philosopher would be disingenuous if it disguised the challenge of the task. When sugar-coating goes too far, you end up with sickly confectionery and no nourishment. In our time-poor attention economy we are seduced by the promise of hacks. We want shortcuts, time savers, cognitive accelerators. But thinking reaches limits of efficiency very quickly and every corner cut comes at a cost. We need to hack off the hacks, not find more of them; to stop trying to make thinking easier than it is and to do it properly.

We get better at thinking by practice, so if this book is not at times a vigorous mental workout it is useless. The epigrams from Fyodor Dostoevsky at the start of each chapter should be taken as opportunities to engage in a little such intellectual exercise. They are not to be read like social media memes, distilled wisdom that you can nod at approvingly, share and move on. I invite the reader to decide for themselves their relevance and meaning in the context of the chapter they introduce.

Although I am an advocate for philosophy, I'm suspicious of the claim that philosophers are *always* the best purveyors of 'transferable thinking skills', as many university departments, including Cambridge, boast.[1] It's not just that, as Cicero famously observed, 'There is nothing so absurd that some philosopher has not already said it.' The uncomfortable truth is that many philosophers have been very poor when reasoning beyond their specialist domains. Bertrand Russell, for instance, was a giant of philosophy, whose work in logic around the start of the twentieth century was one of the most heroic failures in the history of the discipline. But as Russell's biographer Ray Monk says, 'a lot of Russell's work outside philosophy is just rubbish, ill-considered, sloppily written. [...] He gives vent to his prejudices, he doesn't consider relevant aspects of the question he is dealing with.' So at times I will also be pointing out when you should *not* be thinking like a philosopher, or at least like certain philosophers at certain times.

I can't promise that this book will turn you into a great thinker. But, just as you can understand what makes a Messi or Ronaldo so brilliant without becoming the world's greatest footballer, you don't need to be a Confucius or a Kant to appreciate their genius and learn from them. We seek to emulate the best without any illusion that we can equal them, just with the more realistic hope that we can become the best versions of ourselves.

I

PAY ATTENTION

Nature does not ask your permission, she has
nothing to do with your wishes, and whether you
like her laws or dislike them, you are bound to accept
her as she is, and consequently all her conclusions.
A wall, you see, is a wall ... and so on, and so on.

FYODOR DOSTOEVSKY, *Notes from Underground*

As a graduate student, I was given the most gentle and firm
kick up the derrière of my life from my temporary supervisor,
Tim Crane. It was late into the second year of my PhD, and
Crane could see that I needed to up my game if I was to get my
doctorate. The main piece of advice he gave me was to learn to
become a better self-editor. He didn't mean that my work had
too many typos (although I'm sure it did). He meant that I had
to learn to always go over my work with a fine-tooth comb,
looking for anything that wasn't exactly right.

This might sound like curious advice, because it is so unspecific. He wasn't telling me that I was making invalid deductions, inaccurately summarising arguments or getting facts wrong, even though I was probably guilty on all three counts. But he was spot on about the best way of fixing these and other faults. I had to pay much more attention to every word, every inference.

I went on to finish my thesis in just over three years. Crane's advice worked because it put the horse before the cart. All the formal mistakes that are made in reasoning are, in essence, the consequence of cognitive carelessness. That's why the phrase 'sloppy thinking' is accurate. Bad reasoning occurs when we don't take enough care. Attention is the secret sauce of good reasoning that formal manuals of logic and critical thinking miss.

It's also the case that good reasoning fails to cut through when it is not accompanied by attentiveness to what the reasoning is about. For example, why is it that half a century after the height of the civil rights movement, there was still a need to start the Black Lives Matter movement? Why is it that decades after women won the vote there is still systemic misogyny in every democratic society? Why do hospitals and health care trusts need patient advocacy groups when their whole purpose is to help them? It's not for an absence of cogent arguments. That people should have equal rights and opportunities irrespective of their sex, skin colour or ethnic background has not been seriously contested for a long time. Every medic believes that patients' welfare should be their overriding concern. But these principles, which almost everyone signs up to, haven't fully cut through the layers of prejudice and ignorance that centuries of oppression and elite power have wired into the collective psyche. Thinking clearly is one thing, taking something to heart another.

When we have only thought through an issue at an abstract level, we haven't thought it through enough. Thinking is impoverished when it is only about concepts, conducted entirely in our own heads. This kind of detached cognition does not connect enough with our lived experience of the world to change our behaviours, or even what we deep down believe. For thinking to get out of our heads and into our hearts and actions it needs to be rooted in close attention to the world and to other people.

The practice of attention has a strong social dimension. You cannot just attend to how the world seems to you, you have to attend to how it seems to others. So, when thinking about issues such as racism, misogyny and patient agency, we need to pay particular attention to the experiences and testimonies of others, especially those most affected.

In the history of philosophy – especially but not only in the West – this need has not often been fully recognised. It is only recently that many philosophers have come to appreciate it properly, most evidently in the young area of social epistemology. This burgeoning field examines the previously under-appreciated role of communities, networks and other people in the formation of knowledge.

One key concept in social epistemology is testimony. No one can verify the truth of everything for themselves. We have to rely on the testimony of others. But who? When? For what purposes? And whose testimony is unjustly left out? Why are some people's testimonies not heard?

When the perspectives of some are unjustly sidelined or ignored, or those of others are given undue weight, we have testimonial injustice. Contemporary philosophers such as Miranda Fricker and Rae Langton have highlighted how women's voices have been silenced, or at least muffled. Langton has argued that the ways in which sexuality is presented, discussed and portrayed in society, especially in pornography, undermines women's abilities to make sexual choices. Refusals are never taken at face value, in large part because people have been accustomed to thinking that 'no' really means 'she's just playing hard to get', 'she doesn't want to look cheap', or more crudely 'they all want it really'.

Havi Carel has written extensively about how patients in medical contexts are not appreciated as having unique knowledge of their own bodies and states of health. A culture in which doctors are the sole experts also leads to a systematic under-appreciation of the knowledge held by more junior medics, such as nurses, and patients. Carel's work with professional medics has led to changes in clinical practice, proving that these thoughts are not merely theoretical speculations.

Listening to others is not the same as always *deferring* to them. For example, if I argue that wolf-whistling is sexist and someone points to a woman who is perfectly happy about it, that does not show that I am wrong, not least because many other women disagree with her. Nor is the right answer achieved simply by conducting a poll of the people most directly affected. In patriarchal societies where sexist norms are deeply entrenched, a majority of women may say that they are happy with the status quo. Sometimes, doctors do know better than their patients.

To blindly accept what another says is not to listen attentively to them, but to passively hear what they say and accept it. True listening is about engaging as well as hearing, and that may involve disagreement. It shows no respect to someone to believe that they cannot deal with criticism or challenge.

Smart listening also requires paying attention to whom you are attending. For example, many people want to do the best thing for trans people and are rightly keen to listen to their experiences and to what they want. But not all trans people believe the same things, so even the most powerful and vocal advocacy groups are not speaking for everyone.

If all thinking well requires is to pay attention, why go to the effort of trying to improve your skills in logic, or your scientific or statistical literacy? It's well worth doing all these things because they give you the tools to attend more closely and teach you what to look out for. But a remarkable amount can be achieved simply by concentrating hard. Indeed, my contention is that thinking *is* largely about attending. That doesn't mean it is easy. Attending requires tremendous effort, something that is suggested by the origins of the word. It derives from the Latin *ad*, 'towards', and *tendere*, 'stretch', literally meaning 'to stretch towards'. There is an effort required in getting up close to what you are attending to. 'Attend' also means being present, as in attending a wedding. We need to be fully present whenever paying attention. The related French verb *attendre*, meaning to wait, is a reminder that patience and persistence are often required for attention to reap dividends.

To make the case for the primacy of attention, we're going to spend a little time attending to some case studies in the history of Western philosophy. Consider, for example, 'I think, therefore I am.' Even those who know next to nothing about philosophy can usually quote this, and many even know the Latin: *cogito ergo sum*. These three words, written by the seventeenth-century French philosopher René Descartes, seem to embody everything we think we know about philosophy. It's about thinking for ourselves (*cogito*), it's about existence (*sum*), and most importantly, it's about the construction of logical arguments (*ergo*).

It also provides a model of what an argument looks like in its shortest possible form. You start with a premise (in this case 'I think') and infer the conclusion ('I am'), with the real action happening in the movement signalled by 'therefore'. Logical arguments like these draw out the consequences of things we believe to be true, to reveal new and surprising conclusions. They do so formally, by explicitly linking premises to the conclusion. This is generally considered to be the paradigm of reasoning, and philosophers are specialists in deploying it. And so, therefore, it seems logical that it is from philosophy that we can learn how to reason best.

However, I think this risks overstating the importance of formal arguments in philosophy and reasoning more generally. For example, I think the two paragraphs above are an exercise in reasoning: I was making a case for what a philosophical argument requires. But in making this case I was not so much constructing an argument as trying to accurately *describe* philosophy. There is only a very short argument, at the end, in which I say that if reasoning is about drawing out conclusions, and philosophy specialises in it, then philosophy is the best teacher of reasoning skills. But all that argument does is to spell out the implications of what has already been stated. To know if that argument is sound, your main task is not to analyse the progression from premises to conclusion. Rather, you have to check its assumptions: are arguments like these paradigms of good reasoning and are philosophers specialists in them? To answer these questions you have to attend carefully to see what role logical inferences actually play in reasoning and to how often and well philosophers deploy them. What you are doing throughout all this is looking closely and seeing whether the description captures what it intends to describe. There is much more attending required than there is inferring.

When we do attend carefully, we may be surprised by what we find. Consider 'I think, therefore I am.' Is it really an argument? It looks like one: after all, it contains the conjunction 'therefore'. But if it is an argument, it's not a very interesting one. We can generate the conclusion 'therefore I am' from pretty much any statement that asserts 'I'. Why not 'I drink, therefore I am?', or 'I'm pink, therefore I am'? These look equally valid.

From a formal, logical point of view, the argument is circular: the conclusion is only true because it is already contained in the premise. When I say, 'I think', 'I drink' or 'I'm pink', I am already asserting the existence of a subject: I. Descartes' 'argument' simply subtracts the activity or quality attributed to the I, leaving us just with its existence. So in a way the conclusion tells us *less* than the premise on which it is based. If it looks like it is informative, it is only because it is making explicit – 'I am' – what was previously implicit in 'I think'.

Understanding that 'I think' entails 'I exist' needs no more than an understanding of the English language. The same implication occurs whatever the tense: 'I thought, therefore I was', 'She will drink, therefore she will be.' You can even generate the odd mixed-tense version: 'He's dead, therefore he was.' It doesn't take a philosophical training to be able to work this out.

Does this mean that Descartes was a philosophical lightweight rather than the towering genius of reputation? Is philosophy not the pinnacle of human thought but the pedantic art of stating the obvious? Neither, I hope. Descartes was no idiot. When he wrote 'I think, therefore I am', he was aware that it had the same logical structure as 'I drink, therefore I am.' But he also believed there was something that made 'I think' different. In *Principles of Philosophy* he wrote, 'if I say, "I am seeing, or I am walking, therefore I exist", and take this as applying to vision or walking, as bodily activities, then the conclusion is not absolutely certain.'[1]

Why not? Because a conclusion is only as strong as its premises, and in this case the premise isn't certain. When I say, 'I am walking', I could be wrong. I could be dreaming, or I could be in a computer simulation believing that I am pounding the streets when really I'm sitting in a chair in a fully immersive virtual world. So although formally 'I am walking, therefore I exist' is valid, the argument fails if I cannot establish that 'I am walking' is true.

In normal circumstances we would have no reason to doubt that 'I am walking' is true if we seem to be walking. But Descartes was pursuing a particular philosophical project, not advising on what we should think in daily life. He was trying to establish what we could know to be true with absolute certainty in order to establish firm foundations for *all* knowledge. So he needed to know what *must* be true, beyond all doubt.

Descartes' project becomes even clearer when we understand that he was not only trying to establish *if* he existed, but what *kind of thing* he was. Logically, I could say, 'I drink, therefore I'm a drinking thing' or 'I'm pink, therefore I'm a pink thing.' But because we cannot be absolutely certain that we are in fact walking or that we see colours as they really are, these arguments rest on premises that can be doubted. The drink might be a haptic and olfactory illusion; I might be temporarily colour-blind.

'I am thinking' is different, since in the very act of doubting, you are engaged in thinking, which shows that it can't be false. If you think you're not thinking, that only proves you're thinking after all.

We can now see that Descartes was not constructing a logical argument at all. Rather he was attending carefully to his experiences to see what could and could not be doubted. What he found was that almost everything we take for granted could conceivably be false. Other people could be sophisticated robots or puppets; we might be living in a dream or virtual world, not a fleshy, organic one. But the one thing we cannot doubt is that we think, or, more broadly, we are conscious. If I taste a piece of chocolate, the chocolate may not exist but the taste does. If I'm listening to a piece of music, it could be that no one or no thing is playing it, but I'm still hearing it. If you're reading these words now, this book might not exist, but the words are in your mind.

Hence in the *Meditations*, the work that most clearly sets out Descartes' account of the nature of the self, he does not present his conclusion in argument form. There is no 'therefore'. Rather, he reports that his experiments in doubt yield the conclusion that 'this alone is inseparable from me. I am, I exist: this is certain.'

So the most famous lines in Western philosophy are not an argument, but a distillation of an intense series of observations. The philosophers' motto should not be *cogito ergo sum*, but *attendo, ergo sum philosophus*: I attend, therefore I am a philosopher. Paying close attention, not constructing arguments, lies at the heart of the best philosophising.

If Descartes was not making an argument, how do we assess his observation? By attending even closer. Descartes didn't stop with the reassuring conclusion that you do, in fact, exist. He went further, swiftly concluding that he could also know several important characteristics of his self, namely that his mind was indivisible, immaterial and entirely distinct from and separable from his body. And yours is too.

Most philosophers since have judged that Descartes was too hasty. His mistake was to think that because he could conceive of his mind without his body, it must be different from it. But I can imagine that water is not H2O or that goblins are real: that does not mean there can be water that isn't H2O or that goblins are at the end of the garden. You can't leap from mere conceivability (or inconceivability) to conclusions about empirical reality. You don't need to know the problem with such 'conceivability arguments' to spot Descartes' error. If you look carefully, you can see that the path Descartes takes from 'I exist' to 'I am an immaterial mind' is a false one. Pay close attention to how an argument progresses and, more often than not, you'll see the false and fishy moves.

What I'm suggesting is that in a real and important sense, to attend *is* to reason. Consider the most powerful objection to

Descartes' thesis. There can be little doubt who the eighteenth-century Scottish philosopher David Hume had in mind when he wrote, 'There are some philosophers, who imagine we are every moment intimately conscious of what we call our *Self*; that we feel its existence and its continuance in existence; and are certain, beyond the evidence of a demonstration, both of its perfect identity and simplicity.'[2] Hume had quite a lot to say about the problems with this thesis, but his decisive move came when he repeated Descartes' experiment of introspection, only with more care.

For my part, when I enter most intimately into what I call *myself*, I always stumble on some particular perception or other, of heat or cold, light or shade, love or hatred, pain or pleasure. I never can catch *myself* at any time without a perception, and never can observe any thing but the perception.

Try it for yourself. Try to detect the 'I' having your thoughts and experiences. Doing so right now as I am writing this, I observe a gentle gnawing in my stomach, a faint ringing in my ear, a slight ache in the arch of my foot, the sound of a radio in the next room, the recurrence of an annoying ear worm ('Owner of a Lonely Heart' by Yes for some unfathomable reason). I notice that I'm not even aware of the words I'm typing until a fraction of a second before my fingers hit the keys. Once I have described these experiences, I have described everything. There is no additional 'self' which I can observe in addition to them. It would seem my self is simply a 'bundle of perceptions', as Hume put it.[3]

Hume was aware that his observation was not an argument. 'If any one upon serious and unprejudic'd reflection, thinks he has a different notion of himself, I must confess I can reason no longer with him,' he wrote. You cannot argue someone out of a view that is based on a failure to attend properly. All you can do is ask them to pay more attention, in this case to our 'phenomenology': the character of our subjective experience.

Not every philosopher has fully understood Hume's message, as Daniel Dennett once made clear to me. Dennett works as much in cognitive science as he does in philosophy, which for some of his peers means he is not really a philosopher at all. For me it's a strength of his work that he attends so carefully to the facts of experience and findings of psychology and neuroscience, and that he tries to make others do so too. 'I make a point of rubbing my students' noses in surprise phenomenology. They're astonished to discover how poorly resolved the peripheries of their vision are, the fact that they don't have colour vision all the way out to the sides, and so forth. I think that a great deal of the work that's done by philosophers of mind of the non-empirical sort is, shall we say, subliminally guided by a set of shared presumptions about what the phenomenology is, which is just false.'

It is as though we are so attached to how things seem superficially that we are unable to see how they really are, even when it only takes careful attending to reveal the truth. We are like children who draw the sky at the top of the page with no connection to the horizon. How much else about our selves is hiding in plain sight?

Quite a lot, according to those of the dominant schools of philosophy in continental Europe since the early twentieth century, the phenomenology introduced by Edmund Husserl and developed by the likes of Simone de Beauvoir, Jean-Paul Sartre and Martin Heidegger. The emphasis on phenomenology was a response to the philosophy of the eighteenth-century Prussian philosopher Immanuel Kant, who argued that we have no knowledge of things as they are in themselves (*noumena*) but only as they appear to us (*phenomena*).

The phenomenologists take this seriously, concluding that the world as it is given to us in experience *is* our world, the only one we can hope to understand. We have to suspend any belief we might have in a world that exists independently, a 'bracketing off' that Husserl called the phenomenological *epoché*. To go 'back to things themselves',[4] as Husserl instructed, requires looking more closely at the world as we experience it, 'things themselves' without metaphysical preconceptions about 'things *in* themselves'. This approach demands accurate description, which requires close attention. As Husserl said, 'I seek not to instruct but only to lead, to point out and describe what I see.'[5]

The phenomenological approach suggests that we cannot neatly divide between attention to our experiencing self and attention to the world around us. To attend to the world we have to observe how it presents itself to us, for there is nothing else to attend to. Even science, which goes beyond how things immediately seem to us, is only going deeper into the structure of the phenomenal world.

In Japanese philosophy we also see a central emphasis on attention, which is surely why there has been more interest in Japan in phenomenology than in any other modern movement in Western philosophy. When I interviewed the Japanese philosopher Kobayashi Yasuo about what made his tradition distinctive, he pointed to this emphasis on attention over argument. For him, philosophy is not primarily 'a conceptual reconstruction of the world' but is 'based upon a kind of aesthetic reaction' between the human being and the world.

The intellectual habit of paying close attention is one that reaps dividends outside of pure philosophy. One of the things that distinguishes great scientists is their ability to notice things that others have overlooked. Take the discovery of penicillin in 1928. It all started with Alexander Fleming noticing some strange patterns in petri dishes containing bacteria that he had left when he went on holiday. After more careful attending he discovered the 'mould juice' in which he would find penicillin.

When we read about Fleming's discovery, it's tempting to imagine that we would have noticed the patterns in the petri dishes too. But in reality, our attention is easily captured by our prior beliefs and expectations. If we're not actively looking, we can miss obvious things. For instance, you can find many videos online demonstrating 'change blindness', where we fail to notice a change in a scene that is obvious once you become aware of it.[6] Several experiments show that people can even not notice when the person they are talking to is switched mid-conversation.[7] In another, viewers are so focused on following a ball that they don't notice a person in a gorilla costume walking across the screen and beating their chest.[8] Our attention can be misdirected in numerous ways, especially if we're not actively trying to focus it.

Philosophers, however, have not always been good judges of what is worthy of our attention. Ever since Aristophanes mocked philosophers for living in the titular clouds of his satirical play, they have been accused of losing touch with the everyday world. Plato seemed to take this as a kind of compliment, even though his mentor, Socrates, is the butt of much of Aristophanes' jokes. In Plato's dialogue *Theaetetus* Socrates says that philosophers 'do not even know where the court-room is, or the senate-house, or any other public place of assembly'.[9] So Thales of Miletus, 'while he was studying the stars and looking upwards, fell into a pit, and a neat, witty Thracian servant girl jeered at him, they say, because he was so eager to know the things in the sky that he could not see what was before him at his very feet. The same jest applies to all who pass their lives in philosophy.'

I think Plato was wrong about this. The best philosophers do not assume they know the difference between the important and the trivial, the big and the small. Such assumptions blind them to insight. An example of this is the prejudice against smell and taste as inferior, animal senses, which in the West dates back to the writings of Aristotle and Plato. For centuries, when philosophers studied sense perception they focused on sight and hearing, neglecting even touch as too carnal. Eating and drinking were ignored, despite being the only cultural practices that engage all five senses. Now that this prejudice has been overcome, some fascinating work is being done in the philosophy of food.

The French philosopher Roger-Pol Droit issued a call for philosophical attention to the everyday in his witty popular book, *How Are Things?* The title works on two levels: philosophers have always been concerned with the fundamental nature of reality (the field of ontology), but he says they should ask more specifically how are *specific* things like umbrellas, a chest of drawers, a train ticket, a bottle-opener? What do they say about how we live and who we are? Droit's book might look like a playful trifle, but it has serious intent. He's encouraging a philosophical orientation to the world by looking at everything differently. As he put it, 'I try to move the attitude, to change the look and the very way you feel your ordinary life and your ordinary world.'

Droit evokes the childlike nature of philosophy that many have remarked upon, notably Isaiah Berlin, who said, 'Philosophers are adults who persist in asking childish questions.'[10] Droit says, 'I think there is always something childish at the very root of philosophy, in the first astonishment of children, even if this philosophy is highly sophisticated.'

The stress on the everyday is found in many of the world's philosophical traditions. Chinese, Indian and Japanese philosophers instruct on the right ways to eat, to sit, and how to engage with people on a daily level. If you want to understand human life and nature in its fullness and you don't attend to the everyday, vital details might escape your notice.

If you're going to attend carefully, you need to make sure you are in the right state of mind to do so. That's why in many traditions mental preparation has been a core intellectual exercise. For instance, the great Confucian philosopher of the Song Dynasty, Zhu Xi, wrote that 'if you want to read books, you must first settle the mind to make it like still water or a clear mirror.'[11] He advised sitting still in quiet breathing before beginning to read, something that surely would make anyone better able to fully take in what's on the page.

Indian schools of philosophy also stress the need to pay close attention, which is why there is such an emphasis on practices of meditation to still the mind and make it receptive to true perception and insight. Such is the importance of this that many Indian philosophical texts contain precise instructions on how to sit and breathe, something that would seem bizarre in the West.

In such traditions, mental preparation and attention have a moral dimension. The right state of mind is described as 'clear' and 'pure'. A good thinker would be distinguished from a bad one not only by their cleverness but by their sincere intentions. The Indian classic the *Nyāya Sūtras*, for instance, distinguishes *discussion*, which is sincere and based on genuine knowledge, with *wrangling*, which aims simply at winning the argument by any means necessary.

Western philosophy contains only occasional hints of this connection between personal virtue and excellence in reasoning. One rare example is Bernard Williams's identification of *accuracy* and *sincerity* as the two primary 'virtues of truth'. He understood that thinking was not just a technical skill but an expression of character. 'The virtues of accuracy are those connected with finding out the truth, trying to get things right and so forth; and the virtues of sincerity are those of communicating them to other people in an honest way: saying what you believe and so on.' Sincerity guards against self-deception and facilitates accuracy. For Williams, unless enquiry is conducted according to these virtues, we can have no hope of arriving at the truth. That's why 'Nietzsche always said until the end of his life that honesty was the overwhelming intellectual virtue, that it needed courage.' One reason I'm inclined to agree is that Williams was one of the most insightful British moral philosophers of the second half of the twentieth century. His work oozed sincerity because it always seemed to be grappling with what mattered, without being in a rush to come to a premature conclusion.

Intellectual and moral virtue is also found in a comment Wittgenstein once made to Bertrand Russell: 'How can I be a logician before I'm a decent human being?' It sounds odd, but as Ray Monk, the biographer of both Wittgenstein and Russell, explains it, to think clearly about anything you have to 'remove the things getting in the way of clear thought', which includes your personal failings. Both philosophy and honesty about yourself require not just intelligence but the will to be honest. Hence Monk says that when Russell fell into various forms of self-deception, he lacked not intelligence, but 'strength of character'.

Monk is pointing to an intriguing connection between good character and good reasoning. Wittgenstein's remark that 'logic and ethics are one and the same' may sound implausible, but the 'relentless drive for clarity', as Monk put it, requires a clarity of mind and purity of intent that is impossible for the self-deceived or the deceiver of others to attain. To think well you must start by looking at yourself with brutal honesty to ensure that you are reasoning for the right reasons.

That is why the character of the reasoner is not irrelevant to assessing their reasoning. When Russian generals and politicians argued that they began their 'special military operation' in Ukraine to fight fascists and defend themselves against NATO aggression, their lack of integrity gave us good reasons to deny them any benefit of the doubt and to treat even their more plausible pronouncements with scepticism. A clever person with bad motives is dangerous, as they can generate persuasive arguments to serve their interests rather than truth. We need to attend to everything about a piece of reasoning, including the motives and interests of the arguer, even – especially – when the arguer is ourselves.

How to pay attention

- Before thinking anything through, get into the right frame of mind to think. You need a clear mind and the energy to concentrate. If formal exercises like breathing meditations help, use them.
- Attend to what is actually the case, not what you assume is the case. Observe what your experience is really like and how things actually are. Stripping away our preconceptions is harder than it sounds because most of them are deep and implicit.
- Be careful not to jump to conclusions about what follows from your observations. Many mistakes are made by not distinguishing between what something tells us and what we assume it actually means, or what follows from it.
- Look out for attention hijackers. What could be distracting you from seeing clearly, or looking at the right things?
- Beware of confirmation or myside bias. If the facts fit your preconceptions, check that you have not cherry-picked your evidence or ignored other uncomfortable facts.
- Listen to and engage with others, especially those whose experiences are close to what it is you are thinking about. Respect but do not automatically defer to them.
- Do not assume you already know what is important or trivial. Be on the lookout for what might be overlooked on the assumption that it doesn't matter.

2

QUESTION EVERYTHING (INCLUDING YOUR QUESTIONS)

The wisest of all, in my opinion, is he who
can, if only once a month, call himself a
fool – a faculty unheard of nowadays.

FYODOR DOSTOEVSKY, 'Bobok'

'Question everything. Don't assume anything when it comes to what you're told.' These are noble sentiments. The person expressing them also encourages people to check out the facts for themselves and conduct experiments. He sounds like an evangelist for critical thinking. In fact, he is Mark Sargent, one of America's most prominent flat-earthers.[1]

Sargent and other conspiracy theorists highlight the risks of sceptical questioning. Even intelligent people can arrive

25

at crazy conclusions if they don't do it with skill. The simple injunction 'question everything' doesn't tell us how to do it properly. Not everything should be questioned equally or in the same way, and not every failure to find an answer is fatal. To avoid questioning for the sake of questioning we need to understand when it is vital and when it is pointless. Questioning has to be done with care. As Aristotle might have put it, anybody can question, that is easy; but to question the right things, and to the right degree, and at the right time, and for the right purpose, and in the right way, that is not easy.

Questioning is undoubtedly key to critical thinking. The British-Pakistani scholar and public intellectual Ziauddin Sardar says that asking questions became his methodology after he read Ibn Tufail's *Life of Hayy* as a high school student. Sardar describes the twelfth-century book as not just 'the first novel in Islam', but 'probably the first proper philosophical novel'. Living a solitary life on an island, the protagonist 'starts thinking about the stars, the animals around him, and through this thinking he reaches the conclusion that there is a creator'.

Like Hayy, for Sardar a necessary part of enquiry is questioning what makes a good question. 'When is a question a legitimate question? When is a question not a question? When does a question frame an answer in such a way that there's no point in answering?' says Sardar. 'Asking pertinent questions was what I wanted to do.'

Not all questions are worth asking or answering. Consider a tax inspector asking, 'When did you start evading your taxes?' Built into the question is the assumption that you started evading in the first place. This is known as *the fallacy of the complex question*, in which the question assumes what is in dispute. It is a common rhetorical trope, especially in politics. For example, to answer the question 'When will the Prime Minister begin to show leadership?' the PM has to admit that they haven't shown it yet. In everyday life, people often ask such loaded questions. They ask, 'Why did you lie to me?' when it is possible there was no lie, or 'When are you going to stop being so selfish?' when it is they who are being selfish for wanting more of your time and attention.

Too often we ask the wrong questions. 'Most philosophers have this dumb inventory of problems that they've inherited from reading whoever,' says John Searle. 'I want to say there are all these problems out there that "whoever" *didn't* write about.' Searle, an American philosopher active from the 1960s to the present day, saw that the most asked questions, even in philosophy, are often the ones people have got used to asking, not the ones that most need answers.

In everyday life we are always asking the wrong questions. Many people who drink and smoke worry more about the comparatively tiny risk of pesticides on their lettuces. Conservatives question how many people claim more welfare benefits than they are entitled to but ask less about tax-dodging and avoidance, which is a much bigger drain on the economy. Perhaps most of us think too much about how to achieve our life goals without thinking enough about whether those goals are the right ones.

One wrong kind of questioning quickly leads to a paralysing scepticism. Take the question 'How do you know?', so fundamental in philosophy. If you ask it of everything, you soon find that there is no decisive answer.

It's raining. *How do you know?* I can see and feel it. *How do you know that you're not living in a computer simulation, having a particularly vivid dream, or that someone hasn't spiked your coffee with hallucinogens?* Don't be stupid! *That's no answer...*

I love him. *How do you know?* I just do. Everyone knows how they feel inside. *How do you know you're not just in love with the idea you have of him, or that it isn't a kind of shallow infatuation, not true love?* How can anyone know that? *Exactly!*

It is easy to slide from the justified belief that nothing can be known for certain to the deeply sceptical conclusion that nothing is *really* known at all. Some find this thrilling. But it is also toxic since it leaves us with no reason to believe anything and so no basis upon which to act.

Fortunately, there is a fatal flaw in the sceptical challenge: it makes an unreasonable demand and then complains that it can't be met. If knowledge has to be 'beyond *all* doubt', nothing could ever pass the test. However unlikely it is, you can't rule out that the world is a hallucination, a simulation, a dream. Our senses could be systematically misrepresenting our environment. I might be the only conscious creature in the world and everyone else a hologram or automaton. I might not even exist, at least not as a person over time: it could be that I was created two seconds ago with implanted memories that make it seem to me that I've been around for decades. I could be insane. Outlandish though these suggestions are, ruling them out completely is a challenge no one has met for millennia.

Similarly, you cannot prove that the world isn't ruled by the illuminati, since if it is the evidence would be concealed. You can't be 100 per cent sure your partner is being faithful unless you lock them up all day or track their every movement. To demand certainty before you give up a sceptical worry is a fast track to paranoia.

The right way to respond to scepticism is to point out that it demands too high a standard of proof. Setting an impossible challenge and then crying 'fail' when it is not met gives the sceptic an easy but pyrrhic victory. Casting the shadow of doubt in every and any context is just philosophical game-playing. It has nothing to do with a sincere quest for truth.

Take climate change. We have become much clearer about what is happening and what we need to do, but we still have no certainty. It's within the realms of possibility that patterns of solar activity will change and rising greenhouse gases will be countered by decreasing solar radiation. It's possible, but you wouldn't bet on it.

The demand for certainty is foolish and self-defeating because it cuts both ways. Imagine someone standing on the deck of the *Titanic*, refusing to get into the lifeboat, because it is not yet certain the boat will sink. That is true but irrelevant, because it is not certain that it will stay afloat either. However you act, you do so on the basis of uncertainty. All options are uncertain, but they are not all *equally* uncertain.

Full-blown sceptics are rare in philosophy, but problems of scepticism still fill pages of textbooks. This is a pity. John Searle argues that philosophy has been making a 'three-hundred-year mistake' ever since it accepted Descartes' idea that 'the main aim of philosophy is to answer scepticism'. Three hundred years is an underestimate: countering scepticism was a major concern of the Ancient Greeks and has a long history in Indian philosophy. But I'm with Searle when he says, 'I don't take scepticism seriously.' There is merit in trying to address sceptical arguments, but the rest of philosophy can't be put on hold until we have slain the sceptical dragon.

The realisation that nothing can be known with 100 per cent certainty is an important one. Once we've understood that, we can see that the function of further questioning is not to establish certainty but to test the grounds of our beliefs so that we know how firm it is, accepting that it is never ultimately rock-solid.

Perhaps it is because of scepticism that questioning is often assumed to be an inherently negative exercise. To 'call into question' is to doubt, to problematise. This kind of questioning is encouraged by philosophical training. You're on the lookout for bad arguments and you can get so distracted by the many you find that you fail to notice the good ones. The discovery of all that is wrong blinds you to all that is right.

For example, I have always been suspicious of claims for organic food's superiority. When you start asking questions about what 'organic' actually means, the list of the concept's flaws and limitations becomes obvious. The organic/non-organic distinction is not a fundamental one of nature, but one made on the basis of criteria developed by those who control the use of the 'organic' label. So a farmer may work in exactly the same way as an organic neighbour, but her food would not be organic if she did not pay for certification. For the same reason, some foods are made with 100 per cent organic ingredients but cannot legally describe themselves as organic.

Simplistic claims about the purity of organics don't stand up. Organic farmers do not avoid all chemicals, not least because organic manures contain chemicals, as does every living and dead thing. Claims that organic foods are healthier have not been substantiated. Where higher micronutrient contents have been found in, say, organic milk, this is not because it is organic per se but because the cows are pasture-fed. Nor is there good evidence that levels of pesticides in conventional crops pose any serious health risk. Organic foods have their own dangers anyway. In 2011, fifty-three people died after an E. coli outbreak was traced to an organic farm in Germany. Organic standards for animal welfare are comparatively high, but the insistence that alternative medicines be tried before modern ones is a dogma not based in any science. And so on.

All this did not make me anti-organic, but I found myself irritated by the assumption of virtue that the organic label carried and felt not a little superior at my ability to see through the tired platitudes. My scepticism was another victory for the sceptical philosopher over the unquestioning herd.

But in another sense I was not questioning enough: I was not sufficiently questioning my own questioning. I was demolishing a naive, over-zealous view of the virtues of organic food, but that was an easy target. In launching my forensic attack I was sidelining the more nuanced question of whether, on balance, organic foods had sufficient merits to make them preferable to most of the alternatives. The answer to that question, I have come to believe, is, generally, yes. It is certainly true that there are many excellent farms that are not certified organic, some of which are better than the average organic one for sustainability and animal welfare. But perusing shelves, the choice is often a simple one between food that is the product of highly industrialised, intensive agriculture and organics. There are exceptions, but for the most part the industrial farming system treats animals as objects, feeding them grains and soya often grown on deforested land. It also grows crops in huge monocultures reliant on synthetic fertilisers, the production of which is environmentally damaging and creates a hostile habitat for wildlife, threatening biodiversity. The organic alternative may be imperfect, but it is almost always preferable.

I've skimmed over these issues too quickly for a proper case to be made either way, and if you look closely you might come to different conclusions. My point is not to be found in the substance of this particular issue but in the habits and structures of thought it exemplifies. In short, it is very easy for a line of questioning to develop a life of its own, where the negative task of finding fault in something leads you to overlook its merits and the even bigger faults in alternatives.

So as well as questioning arguments, ideas and other people, question your own motives, agendas and goals. Are you becoming too enthusiastic about the chance to show off your ability to think differently from the majority? Are you enjoying the takedown so much that you're not balancing the negative with the positive? And why are you questioning in the first place? What is the ultimate goal? Is it, for example, to put the claims of the organic movement on trial or is it to decide what the best farming methods are? Almost any idea has enthusiasts who overstate its merits. It may not be as great as they claim, but it still might be the best contender in town.

Questioning must not be simply about searching for faults and flaws but also looking for strengths and benefits. It's also about questioning aims, motives, purposes and even your own character.

Relentless questioning can be frustrating. There is a great deal of truth in the old joke the moral philosopher Philippa Foot told me. 'A philosopher is someone of whom you ask a question and, after he's talked for a bit, you don't understand your question.' Foot had a rare honesty about quite how much she didn't understand. In a career that spanned the Second World War to the early twenty-first century, she wrote very little because she rarely felt she had got to the stage where she understood something well enough to make it worth saying. She saw that often the first step towards greater understanding is to recognise how you don't understand what you thought you understood after all. This is especially unsettling when you thought what you understood was obvious.

The 'obvious' is a dangerous category which often confuses received wisdom for certain truth. Some things seem indubitable only because we lack the capacity to doubt them, not because they are literally indubitable. It used to be thought obvious (by many Europeans) that Africans were less intelligent than Europeans, that much work was not suitable for women, that fish didn't feel pain, that homosexuality was disgusting, that the sun rose and set, that objects were made of solid stuff, that popular music was not art.

One of the strengths of philosophers is that they are trained to question apparently obvious truths, such as the existence of an abiding self, that the world is made of matter, that we directly perceive objects, that we have free will, that science describes the world as it is, that aesthetic judgement is just a matter of taste, that words are labels for things. A good recent example of how productive this can be is Simon Critchley's questioning of a principle in ethics that has been axiomatic since Kant wrote 'The action to which the "ought" applies must indeed be possible under natural conditions.'[2] This is usually summarised as *ought* implies *can*. In other words, to say that someone *ought* to do something only makes sense if they *can* in fact do it. It's absurd to say that I ought to visit my sick mother if she is on the other side of the world and I can't afford the plane ticket. Nor can I complain that you should have avoided a crash when it was not your fault. Nothing could seem more obvious.

Yet Critchley maintains *ought* implies *cannot*. Not because he thinks we can do the impossible. Rather, we should aim to do more than is possible in order to avoid the complacency of 'good enough'. Critchley says his flipping of Kant is 'more stringent, and truer to the ethical demands to which we should submit ourselves. I think if ethics is based on a feeling of being able or having the capacity to do something, or being satisfied by one's actions, then one is lost.' It is only by asking this much of ourselves that we can hope to be as good as we can be. To ask more of ourselves than we can give is not to be unrealistic, but to acknowledge that we will always be imperfect.

Critchley's challenge to Kant's axiom is a terrific example of good questioning. He is not trying to pick holes or score points. Indeed, it's the very opposite, since Critchley says that to deny *ought* implies *can* is paradoxical. His questioning leaves much of what he has called into question intact. He is not suggesting we should blame people for not doing what they were never capable of doing in the first place. He is not questioning for its own sake, but questioning for the sake of moving our thinking forwards from a point where we might easily have assumed it had ended. He invites us to consider the thought 'I couldn't have done any better' not as the end of our reflections but the start of them.

Critchley's questioning of Kant could be seen as an example of the virtue of questioning assumptions. Examining assumptions is a core competency of philosophers, who are in the habit of spotting the often false assumptions hidden in apparently strong arguments. For example, cancer screening, health care spending and drug rehabilitation are all obviously good things. So when there are calls to increase them, it is often assumed that this would be a good thing too. Often, it is. But sometimes it isn't. The English, Conservative philosopher Roger Scruton named the assumption that if something is good, more of it is better 'the aggregation fallacy'. More of a good thing isn't always better. It can even be worse. Everything has its ideal level and distribution. A cake is great, but ten cakes is gross. A vaccination is good, but doubling the dose or giving everyone more jabs than is necessary can be dangerous.

In practice we often assume that more of a good thing is better. Supplement makers sell very high-dose vitamin pills that are potentially dangerous; people waste money on more insurance than they need; bands go down creative cul-de-sacs trying to make similar records to the ones that brought them success. Christine Korsgaard argues that the aggregation fallacy also blinds us to the potentially greater benefits of sharing rather than multiplying goods. Governments dish out more benefits to individual citizens when resources would be better spent on public libraries, services and spaces that benefit all.

We tend to fall for the aggregation fallacy when the premise it rests on is not spelled out. As soon as the principle 'if something is good, more of it is better' is made explicit, we can see it is fishy. Such unstated, assumed premises are called 'enthymemes'. If you get into the habit of unearthing them, you often quickly see where thinking has gone wrong.

Take the question of what you should eat if you want to increase your healthy gut bacteria. A lot of evidence points to the health value of a rich diversity of gut microbiota. This has led to increased interest in fermented foods – consumers see them as a way to boost gut health, since they contain a diverse range of 'good' bacteria, known as probiotics. One such product is kefir, a fermented milk drink. Manufacturers use slogans such as 'Boost your gut micro flora' and 'gut-friendly'. If fermented foods contain a lot of good bacteria, it seems common sense that they are a good way to boost your gut biome.

But there is a questionable assumption here: that bacteria which grow outside the body survive and flourish inside the very different environment of the human gut. At the time of writing, we still don't know whether this is true. A survey article for the *British Medical Journal* concluded that although 'probiotic supplementation has several beneficial effects on human health', the jury was out on the benefits of natural probiotics in food. Consider that the human body contains 500 to 1,000 different kinds of gut bacteria, while kefir, an exceptionally bacteria-rich food, contains around forty. We're not getting the majority of our gut bacteria by ingestion. In fact, it is generally agreed that the best way to maximise the diversity of gut biota is to eat a varied diet, rich in dietary fibre.[3]

Another common assumption is that you know whose side someone is on, despite only having very limited information about what they believe. Ray Monk was a victim of this kind of stereotyping when he was critical of Bertrand Russell, whose late-career campaigning and political writing made him a hero of pacifists and many left-liberals. 'If I say that this piece of political work is badly written, it's a shoddy piece of work and it happens to advocate a position, and someone reads that and they too advocate that position, they're not going to separate the position from its shoddy presentation,' says Monk. He says critics assumed that 'I was some kind of right-wing religious fanatic, because I evidently didn't admire Russell as a left-wing secular saint'. The critic of your friend is not always your enemy.

Everyone knows we should question our assumptions. Several years ago I was at a corporate presentation where the speaker wrote the word 'assume' on a whiteboard, struck two vertical lines to make ass|u|me and said, 'If you assume, you make an ass out of you and me.' His expression was an odd combination of self-satisfied and sheepish. It was a neat way to make a point, but perhaps a bit too cute, and one that surely he – and probably many others – had done so many times before that it sounded like a cliché. But such is the natural tendency to make assumptions that we cannot afford to assume that we finally know not to make them.

Questioning assumptions often leads us to throwing them out. However, a key purpose of questioning is not to debunk ideas but to understand better. Hume, for example, questioned our belief in causation, arguing that we never observe one thing *causing* another, only one thing *following* another. You don't see the water extinguishing the fire, you just see the water going on the fire and the fire going out. You *assume* causation, you don't directly *observe* it. Nor can we prove the general principle that everything is the effect of a cause. Reason demands that 'every effect has a cause', but that doesn't tell us if there are any genuine effects in the world.

Hume's theory of causation has generated a huge literature and much debate. But, however you interpret it, it is clear that in practice Hume thought we cannot and should not stop thinking of the world as governed by laws of cause and effect. Hume questioned causation not to throw the concept away but to help us to understand what grounds it. That is to say, it is an idea which we cannot do without, which is central to how we understand the world, but which is not grounded in experience or reason.

Much questioning is more constructive if it is approached in this spirit. For instance, many atheists question religious belief, find that it is not justified by reason or experience, and conclude that it is therefore all nonsense. But if it were that clear, why would so many people believe even though they are not idiots? A more constructive questioning would have the purpose not only of establishing whether religious belief is true, but why people believe, and what it means to have belief.

When we question in that spirit, we are led to consider the extent to which religious belief is based on subjective experience rather than quasi-scientific reasoning, is often mythological in character rather than literally true, and accepts mysteries and paradoxes. Questioning may not so much destroy faith as change how we understand it.

There are times when confidence and conviction are needed. But when we're trying to think as clearly as possible, their absence is a virtue, not a vice. I've found that the best philosophers are the ones who are willing to question not only their own abilities, but the value of philosophy itself. I agree with the musician Mylo, who said, 'Some of my favourite philosophers had a real love/hate relationship with the subject, like Wittgenstein. If you're going to be constantly doubting everything, then you're going to be doubting the validity of your own enterprise.'

Stephen Mulhall, perhaps best known for his philosophical commentary on the *Alien* film series, echoed this when he talked about how philosophers are in the business of muscling in and questioning the assumptions being made. 'If we can do that to scientists and to people who write art and so forth then we ought to, just out of sheer consistency, take seriously the same questions about our own business,' he said. Someone who does this is 'simply a philosopher being consistently philo-sophical, i.e. being philosophical about his own philosophy'.

Simon Glendinning, a philosopher who meticulously pores over the often obscure writings of people like Heidegger, Wittgenstein and Derrida, expresses this self-doubt more forcibly. 'It's always a tricky moment for any philosopher to acknowledge that what you are doing, what you think might be worth doing, might be just a spinning in the wind or just a kind of doing nothing at all, or doing something very badly.'

Similarly, Daniel Dennett says: 'The best philosophers are always walking a tightrope where one misstep either side is just nonsense, just bad stuff. That's why caricatures are too easy to be worth doing. You can make any philosopher – any, Aristotle, Kant, you name it – look like a complete flaming idiot with just a slightest little tweak.'

Not every philosopher shares this self-doubt, or even a willingness to question everything they believe. Timothy Williamson has the prestigious position of Wykeham Professor of Logic at Oxford, indicating that he is both highly esteemed and mainstream. When I asked him if he ever felt any anxiety that his philosophising might be empty, he answered with a swift and emphatic 'no', saying, 'It's really neurotic in many cases to worry about whether what people are saying is just completely empty.' He agreed that 'descending into bullshit' is 'an occupational hazard', but said 'It's hopelessly exaggerated to think that means that it might turn out that philosophy is by its nature always empty.'

For me, the worry is not that 'philosophy is by its nature always empty', but that the *kind* or *instance* of philosophy (or thinking) we might be doing is empty. Williamson did not have that concern about the dominant style of Anglophone academic philosophy he practices, since he believes that despite its technicality, philosophy is continuous with various other areas of human thought such as natural science. If that's right, then if philosophy is empty, all human reasoning is empty.

I'm not convinced by Williamson's confidence. It rings of unphilosophical complacency. The doubt he, and others like him, should entertain is that philosophy is not as continuous with science and rational enquiry in general as it seems. It's possible that philosophy is applying methods of enquiry which work well for some problems to other questions that are not suited to them at all. I don't think this is (usually) true, but I think it's important to test whether it is true and not just assume that it is.

Another philosopher who was not as self-doubting as he should have been was Michael Dummett, a giant in the philosophy of language and also a practising Roman Catholic, unusual among his peers. Philippa Foot once asked him, 'What happens when your argument goes one way and your religious belief goes the other?' He replied, 'How would it be if you knew that something was true? Other things would have to fit with it.' As Foot explains this, 'They [religious believers] think they know that and could as little deny it as that I am talking to someone now.' For Dummett, his religious faith was beyond question. Philosophical doubt stopped at the church door.

Many consider it rude and disrespectful to challenge a person's religious convictions, but I can't see why faith should be immune to the deep scrutiny we apply to our other beliefs. Many religious thinkers agree. Ziauddin Sardar argues that Islam has historically been very open to the idea that we should use our rational faculties, even to question religion. This clashes with the received opinion that Islam – which means 'submission' – requires a suspension of critical thought. 'The Qur'an constantly asks the reader to think. The most common phrases in the Qur'an are "Have you not thought?", "Did you not think?", "Look at the signs." The interesting thing for me is that the Qur'an itself, although it's clearly a religious text, continuously asks questions.'

Although it is, as Williamson put it, neurotic to *always* be questioning yourself and what you do, to do so *regularly* is simply good philosophical hygiene. At the very least it helps to puncture complacency and arrogance. Philosophers pride themselves on their ability to question everything. If they exclude themselves from that, or the beliefs that they hold most dear, they are inconsistent: the polite term for hypocritical.

Like many important facets of critical thinking, the importance of questioning is easy to see but the habit of doing it well is difficult to instil, particularly within the growing cult of positivity that seems to be taking over Western society, in the Anglophone world at least. We are encouraged to be super-supportive, super-excited and relentlessly positive about other people's ideas and projects. If someone has a business idea that you think sounds terrible, it is bad form to express any doubts and so 'trample on their dreams'. The possibility that raising doubts might save them from losing large amounts of money on an ill-conceived venture is too negative to countenance. At a time when challenging is often confused with undermining, the value of examining our assumptions needs to be championed more than ever.

How to question

- Check you are asking the questions that need to be asked, not just the ones that everyone else is asking.
- Check the question is well formed. Some questions force you to choose from a limited number of answers, none of which gets at what matters.
- Don't question for the sake of questioning. Ask yourself what the purpose of the questioning is.
- Don't take the lack of certain answers as a reason to embrace scepticism. Do not demand certainty when it is not possible.
- Question your motives. Are you questioning in order to better understand or with the aim of taking something down or defending your prior beliefs?
- Don't become too focused on the bad answers your questions get. Sometimes a single good one is enough.
- If something seems obvious or is taken for granted, it's always worth taking a closer look.
- Be prepared to question whether you're not just barking up the wrong tree but exploring the wrong forest. Be open to the possibility what you are doing is fundamentally misguided.

3

WATCH YOUR STEPS

A hundred suspicions don't make a proof.

FYODOR DOSTOEVSKY, *Crime and Punishment*

During the Covid-19 pandemic when meeting with people outside your household was banned, the home and office of the British Prime Minister, Boris Johnson, was the scene of several social gatherings involving wine, cheese and even music. Johnson denied that any parties had taken place, but subsequent police investigations resulted in 126 fines being issued for breaches of the rules, including one for Johnson. This showed that Johnson had not told the truth when he insisted 'I certainly broke no rules.' So as his predecessor pointed out in the House of Commons, 'Either my Right Honourable friend had not read the rules or didn't understand what they meant and others around him, or they didn't think the rules applied to Number 10.' He either broke the rules knowingly, and so lied; or he did so unknowingly, meaning he did not understand the laws that he himself had introduced, which makes him incompetent or inattentive.

The fact that somehow Johnson kept his job shows that having a solid argument isn't always enough to persuade people to act on its conclusions. The argument itself nonetheless remains an example of the power of asking what follows from known facts. I contend that 'What follows?' is the key question of logical reasoning. To test whether an argument is a good one, all you need to do is ask: *does it follow*? Does it follow from the fact that all pigs are mortal, and Percy is a pig, that Percy is mortal? (Yes.) Does it follow from the fact that a food contains carcinogens that, if you want to avoid cancer, you should avoid eating it? (No.) Does it follow from the fact that Otto in *A Fish Called Wanda* reads philosophy that Otto can't be stupid? (No, because as Wanda says, stupid people do read philosophy, 'They just don't understand it.') Does it follow from the fact that no true miracles have ever been reliably recorded that you should disbelieve any claim that one has occurred? (Sort of.)

One of the most important habits of reasoning is to ask, 'Does that follow?' You can almost always answer that question correctly, even if you know nothing about logic – just as long as you are paying close attention. Take an example I used above, which might have made you do a double-take. I said that it did *not* follow from the fact that a food contains carcinogens that you should avoid eating it, if you want to avoid cancer. Why doesn't it follow? Surely the logic is the same as saying that if you want to avoid being poisoned, you should avoid eating things containing poison. But if you think more carefully, you'll notice that in both examples, although the verb 'contain' is used, there is no indication of *how much* poison or carcinogens the food contains. In both cases, dosage is all. Any hot drink, slice of processed meat or charred pizza base contains carcinogens. Almonds contain cyanide. But the levels are so low that, when consumed in normal quantities, they pose no risk to human health. (It should be noted that today many people do eat processed meat in quantities that should never have become normal.) If you avoided all food and drink that had even a trace of toxins, you'd very quickly die from the more certain cause of starvation.

The question 'Does it follow?' is simple enough. But to understand more deeply how to ask and answer it, we need to distinguish between several ways in which one thing can follow from another. The gold standard of reasoning about what follows is generally thought to be *deduction*. We use the verb 'deduce' quite loosely in everyday English, but in logic it has a very specific meaning. In a deduction, if the premises – the statements you are basing your reasoning on – are true, then the conclusion *must* follow. When a conclusion follows by necessity, the argument is *valid*.

To go back to an example above, if your premises are that all pigs are mortal and Percy is a pig, it *must* be true that Percy is mortal. What's powerful about this hardly revelatory argument is that what makes it valid is its structure: we know *any* argument with the same structure is valid. That structure is:

Every x is a y
This is an x
Therefore this is a y

So, for example, it is also valid to deduce, 'Every citizen has rights of residency, I am a citizen, therefore I have rights of residency.' However, being valid is not much use if your premises are false. If not every citizen has rights of residency, your deduction is useless. We want our arguments also to be *sound*, which requires both that the premises are in fact true and the argument is valid.

That's it. That's how deduction works. Everything else there is to say about it only spells out what you might have missed if you weren't paying enough attention. This could be quite a lot, because the sad truth is that experimental psychology has shown that most human beings have little natural aptitude for abstract, formal reasoning. This shouldn't depress us too much. Our problem is that we're actually pretty good at using reasoning to solve real-world problems, especially when thinking with others. It is only when we are asked to forget about that and just focus on the structure of arguments, reasoning with xs, ys or abstract nouns, that we find it hard. If we're forced to set aside all the common sense and practical thinking skills that we need for our survival, it's little wonder we flounder.

When most people are introduced to deduction, it usually takes a bit of time for them to understand the difference between *valid* and *sound* arguments. I have already said everything that has to be said about this difference, but if you're new to the distinction, you may have missed its full import. So here's a test. Is this a valid argument?

All rugby players are Neanderthals.
Emily Scarratt is a rugby player.
Therefore Emily Scarratt is a Neanderthal.

The answer is yes, it's valid. Remember that validity is defined as: if the premises are true, then the conclusion must by necessity follow. The key word here is 'if'. *If* it were true that all rugby players were Neanderthals and Emily Scarratt was a rugby player, it would by necessity follow that Emily is indeed a Neanderthal, just as surely as Percy's mortality would follow from the fact that all pigs are mortal and he is a pig. But in this case the premises are not true. So although the argument is still *valid*, it is not *sound*. Scarratt need not call in the libel lawyers.

The distinction is simple enough, but it requires us to over-throw a lifetime of linguistic habit. Most people use 'valid' in a much looser sense, simply meaning 'fair', 'reasonable' or 'true', as in 'That's a valid point.' But in logic there are no valid *points*, only *arguments*.

Even when we have got a grip on the difference between validity and soundness, we're not always good at spotting which arguments are in fact valid and/or sound. Take this one:

If a food is natural, it is good for most human beings.
Blueberries are a natural food.
Therefore blueberries are good for most human beings.

Hopefully you've seen that this argument is valid but not sound. If the premises were true, the conclusion would follow. But the first premise is not true, as anyone who mistook hem-lock for wild parsley would soon find out. If you got this wrong it is probably because you were misled by the fact that the con-clusion is true. But sometimes a bad argument generates a true conclusion by chance. That doesn't make it a good argument. Consider this:

The Nazis warned that smoking was bad for health.
All governments ought to do what the Nazis did.
Therefore governments ought to warn that smoking is
    bad for your health.

Here the right conclusion has been reached by a valid argu-ment, but one which contains a premise which is outrageously, horribly wrong. When assessing arguments we're not assess-ing each claim one by one. We're looking at the *connections* between the claims and whether the claims hold up. Take this argument:

If anthropogenic climate change is real, the rate of
    global warming over the past forty years would be
    around 0.32° F (0.18° C) per decade.
The rate of global warming over the past forty years is
    around 0.32° F (0.18° C) per decade.
Therefore anthropogenic climate change is real.

This argument again has a true conclusion, and it also has true premises. Nonetheless, it is invalid, and therefore also automatically unsound. Once more, the key word is 'if'. The problem is that 'if x, then y' does not entail 'if y, then x'. For example, 'If it rained last night, the ground will be wet' does not entail 'If the ground is wet, it rained last night.' The ground could still be wet even if it hasn't rained. It might have been watered, washed or flooded. Similarly, although it is true that if anthropogenic climate change is real, the earth's temperature would have risen, it is also possible that the temperature could have risen for other reasons. That possibility is what has allowed climate change denial to remain plausible to many for so long. In principle, global warming could be the result of solar activity or other natural cycles. It's just that the evidence says it isn't.

This logical mistake is known as *affirming the consequent*. If we start with the premise 'If x, then y' and we then affirm the truth of the consequent, y, it is invalid to conclude that x is also true. An obvious illustration of why this is invalid is 'If this car is a Lotus, it is very expensive; it is very expensive; therefore it's a Lotus.'

Compare this to *affirming the antecedent*, which is a valid form of argument. If we start with the premise 'If x, then y' and we then affirm the truth of the antecedent, x, it is valid to conclude that y is also true. 'If this car is a Lotus, it is very expensive; it is a Lotus; therefore it's very expensive.' This shares the same form as the Percy the pig argument.

47

Simple enough, you might think. So is this a valid argument?

If today is 1 May, then it's International Labour Day.
Today is International Labour Day.
Therefore it's 1 May.

This surely does look valid to everyone other than a logician trained to spot that it is actually a clear example of the fallacy of affirming the consequent. So what's going on?

Once again, the terms used in logic have a precise meaning that differs from their normal usage. In ordinary English the conditional 'if' sometimes means just 'if', but sometimes 'if and only if'. For example, when a parent says, 'If you tidy your room, you can play your computer game,' they do not mean to suggest that there might be other conditions under which the playing of computer games will be allowed. They mean 'If *and only if* you tidy your room, you can play your computer game.' In context, this implication is obvious and no parent would actually spell it out. On the other hand, when I say, 'If I win the lottery, I'll go on holiday to Venice,' I don't mean to suggest that I'm definitely never going to Venice unless I win the lottery. In context, it's clear that this 'if' is just 'if', not 'if and only if'.

In logic, 'if and only if' is called the biconditional and is usually written 'iff'. In the Labour Day example, in ordinary speech 'if' is naturally, in context, assumed to mean 'iff'. Read like that, the argument is indeed valid and sound. 'Iff x, then y' does imply 'Iff y, then x.' So when people routinely fail logic puzzles that use 'if', they are not necessarily being stupid. It is often because they are assuming that an 'if' is actually an 'iff', or vice versa, when in philosophy, 'if' is always just 'if' and 'if and only if' is always 'iff'. This illustrates how, whenever we are trying to assess an argument that rests on a conditional, we have to ask whether it's employing an *if* or an *iff*.

The essence of how to make valid deductions can be summed up in a couple of pages, as I have done. But don't be too pleased by this. The strange thing about deductive arguments is that, considering they are the supposed gold standard of philosophy and of reasoning at large, they're not often very useful. Their strength turns out to be their weakness. For a deduction to be valid, the conclusion must strictly follow from the premises. But that means that, in effect, everything that you find in the conclusion *is already in the premises*. All the conclusion does is spell it out. If you know all pigs are mortal and that Percy is a pig, you should already know that Percy is mortal. So, in a sense, all deductive arguments assume what they prove.

This is why deductive arguments are hopeless at settling arguments when what is assumed is precisely what is in dispute. For example, a popular argument against same-sex marriage is that since marriage is a union between a man and woman, and same-sex couples are not a man and a woman, therefore there can be no same-sex marriage. The argument is valid, but the whole point of campaigning to extend marriage to same-sex couples is the belief that the institution should not continue to be reserved for heterosexuals. To state in your premise that marriage *must* mean a man/woman union is to assume what you are supposed to be arguing for. Assertion is not argument, just as denying isn't refuting. So the argument cannot be deemed sound because one of its premises is contentious.

For an argument to be valid and sound, its conclusion has to be already contained in its premises, which in turn must be beyond reasonable dispute. In other words, no substantively new truth can be generated by it. So why use deduction at all? One reason is that it is not always obvious that the conclusion is already contained in the premises, and so showing that it is can be illuminating. For example, there is a sense in which the answer to the sum $6{,}324 \div 37.2$ is already contained within it, but until you've worked it out, you have no idea what it is. All the information can be in the premises of an argument, but working out the conclusion can still be informative.

Sometimes we haven't thought through the logical consequences of our beliefs. At the very least, spelling them out forces people to be precise. If you believe that it is always wrong to kill a living thing for our own purposes and that therefore eating meat is wrong, it might help to have someone point out that by the same logic you shouldn't kill flies, plants or even bacteria. This suggests the principle expressed in the first premise isn't precise enough and should be refined to something like 'It is always wrong to kill another animal for our own purposes, unless it is necessary to do so in order to survive.' That sorts out the bacteria and plant problem. But it still leaves question marks over flies, insects and all kinds of pests. Maybe the principle needs further refining. Working out what precisely follows from our beliefs can be a useful way of checking whether our beliefs are correct after all.

For example, Mary Warnock argued that if somebody has a right, then it often follows that someone else has a corresponding duty. Warnock has had to think long and hard about such issues as chair of two major UK government inquiries in which rights loomed large, one on special education and another on human fertilisation and embryology. She offered as an uncontroversial example of the rights/duties link, 'If you have a right of way over my property then it's my duty to ensure that you've got a free passage.' Warnock then applied the same logic to the claim that people have a right to a child. Given that it is not possible to place on anyone else the duty to make sure this happens, she was 'not sure it makes sense to talk about the right to have a child'. The only right a would-be parent uncontroversially has is not to be prevented from having a child. This has implications for the public provision of fertility treatment, because if having a child were a right, the government would have a duty to make it possible.

It also needs to be remembered that deductions can involve several steps, and that the two premises plus conclusion examples standardly used to explain how deduction works are the most simple. The more steps there are, the easier it is to slip up, which is why being highly sensitive to what necessarily follows is a core thinking skill.

One of the clearest giveaways that we have failed to identify what follows is that we contradict ourselves. If you find, for example, that your conspiracy theory requires postulating *both* that the government is incompetent *and* also capable of the most remarkable cover-up in history, something has gone wrong because they both can't be right. On other occasions, there may not be a glaring contradiction but there can be deep tensions. Say you maintain that big business does not care about the environment because it cares only about profit, and that green business is good business, because it is much more efficient. If the latter were true, why doesn't greed turn businesses green? You'd have to conclude that businesspeople are not only greedy but very bad at doing the one thing they are supposed to excel at: getting rich.

Philosophers are specialists in sniffing out inconsistencies and removing them. The late Jeff Mason, a philosopher friend of mine, called it an 'inability to let sleeping contradictions lie'. Nicholas Rescher, who has written extensively about the nature of philosophy, has argued that this is what philosophy is largely about. Philosophical problems emerge when we discover an aporia or an apory: 'a group of contentions that are individually plausible but collectively inconsistent'. For instance, many philosophers have argued that although we seem to have knowledge, we also seem to lack the justifications that would allow us to claim our beliefs as true knowledge. Others have pointed out that we seem to have free will, but if the world is governed by physical cause and effect, that would seem to make free will impossible. Both these aporias are comprised of two claims, both of which seem plausible, but both of which can't be right, and it isn't easy to give up either. The philosopher's job is to find a way out of this conundrum, to eliminate the contradiction by either reconciling the two clashing beliefs or showing how we can give up one after all. At the end of the process the contradiction has been banished and we return to consistency.

Philosophers aren't just good at removing inconsistencies, they are also skilled at spotting ones that others have missed. Onora O'Neill provides a good example of this. O'Neill has made major contributions to public life, most notably as chair of the Equality and Human Rights Commission. When writing about the issue of trust in public life, she found that survey data consistently showed that people reported low levels of trust. But O'Neill spotted something inconsistent in this narrative, illustrated by a questioner at one of her Reith Lectures who said that she didn't trust surgeons because her operation had been postponed. As O'Neill pointed out, 'If she really didn't trust surgeons she would have been delighted that the operation was postponed.'

O'Neill had spotted an inconsistency between what we say and what we do. People say they don't trust others, but they act in ways that require trust all the time. They take the medicines doctors prescribe, allow financial advisors to invest their money, pay electricians to fiddle with potentially dangerous cables. People may say they don't believe the news, but if they were sincere they wouldn't even read it.

O'Neill's trust example is a good one because it illustrates how most contradictions are not blatant. People rarely assert one thing explicitly and then do the opposite. Most of the time, the contradictions only come to the surface if you examine what people say and do more carefully. The question 'What follows?' is a key one here. What would follow if you really didn't trust people, and does reality match this expectation?

Sometimes the need to see what follows requires taking a number of steps: *a* follows from *b*, *c* follows from *b*, *d* follows from *c*, and so on. The philosopher Tony McWalter made use of these skills when he became a member of the UK Parliament. He was worried about what would follow from allowing detention without trial for up to ninety days, as was proposed in the more feverish days of the 'war against terror'. 'The incredible rush always with all of these things is completely anti-philosophical,' he said. 'One of the things that you expect a philosopher to do is not only to see the consequences of a proposal, but the consequences of the consequences; and even the consequences of the consequences of the consequences. I think that's why we do philosophy, because policy has unobvious repercussions.' Aware of what these might be, he opposed detention without trial.

However, you have to be careful to check that what you *think* follows really *does* follow. The longer the chain of reasoning, the higher the chances of making a mistake which gets amplified the further you go, like Chinese whispers. In the discussion where McWalter made his comment, his colleague Jonathan Rée warned about the dangers of being too confident that you can work out the actual implications of a position. 'Talking about consequences of consequences of consequences is something that may make you feel very pleased with yourself,' said Rée, 'but remember that philosophers talked about consequences of consequences of consequences and found themselves solidly backing the Soviet Union, China, Nazi Germany.'

Even thinking about what directly follows from a claim can be tricky. Take accusations of eco-hypocrisy. Many assume that if someone believes the failure to tackle climate change is a moral one, they would be hypocritical to take long-haul flights. But it is possible that they believe climate change can't be solved by individual choices and can only be halted by intergovernmental actions, so a refusal to fly would be an empty gesture with no impact. You may disagree, but there is no obvious inconsistency between their climate-heating actions and their climate-cooling aspirations. If, on the other hand, they criticise others for using disposable coffee cups and plastic shopping bags, then they are being inconsistent when they jet off.

Although consistency is one of the key aspirations of good thinking, and a test of whether it is present, it is not to be achieved at all costs. As Ralph Waldo Emerson memorably put it, 'A foolish consistency is the hobgoblin of little minds, adored by little statesmen and philosophers and divines.' A 'foolish consistency' is where one achieves consistency only by embracing absurdity, or at least implausibility.

To stick my neck out here, I think one example of this is an attempt to solve the ancient Sorites paradox. This puzzle concerns the seeming impossibility of determining when certain concepts apply and when they don't. Take 'tall'. At 201cm high, the writer, director and actor Stephen Merchant is certainly tall. Would he stop being tall if he shrank slightly to 200.99cm? Of course not. Now imagine asking this question again and again as we take off a tenth of a millimetre at a time. Such a tiny amount could never make a difference between a person being tall or not. And yet, of course, if we kept up this process long enough, we'd end up at the height of Merchant's collaborator Ricky Gervais, who at 173cm is certainly not tall. Keep going yet more and you'd get down to 107cm, the height of the star of one of Gervais's comedy shows, *Life's Too Short*, Warwick Davis.

The aporia here is that it seems that there must be a difference between tall, medium and short, but when you try to find where that difference lies, you can't. The most plausible resolution of this, I think, is simply to accept that words like 'tall' and 'short' are inherently vague. Some people clearly are tall, others clearly aren't, and in between we might be unsure. The paradox arises because we are being asked to treat the concept as though it had mathematical precision. But why should language, which evolved organically, have such a character?

For some philosophers, the prospect of accepting that concepts are inherently vague is terrifying. They think that if we can't use language precisely, rigour in philosophy is impossible. So, to save precision, they argue that the apparent vagueness of such terms is due to our limitations, not those of the concepts themselves. There really *is* a sharp divide between tall and not-tall people, and we should not confuse our inability to specify where that line is with its non-existence. The vagueness is in our heads, not in the world.

This seems utterly bonkers to me, the epitome of a foolish consistency. But serious philosophers much cleverer than I have argued for it. The most prominent is Timothy Williamson, who said to me, 'One has to ask why [some people] think that a hypothesis that sounds odd can't be true. Lots of odd-sounding hypotheses in science have turned out to be true.' This only goes to show, again, how philosophy is often, once all the arguments have been made, a matter of judgement and also temperament. People's tolerance for vagueness and imprecision varies, and not just because some are more rational than others. For my part, although 'Follow the argument wherever it leads' sounds like a noble principle, I'm not going to follow any argument that leads me off the edge of a cliff.

Some forms of reasoning invite us over such cliffs, but for constructive reasons. For example, people often say, *You can't put a price on a life*. If that means that the value of life is not a monetary one, I hope we'd all agree. But for some people it means that no expense should be spared to save lives. The principle then becomes, *If we have the resources to save a life, it should be saved, whatever the cost.* Is that a good principle?

Imagine a life could be saved, but only by diverting a country's entire cultural and education budget. If we believed that *If we have the resources to save a life, it should be saved, whatever the cost,* the logical conclusion would be that *We should save the life by diverting our entire cultural and education budget.* Most would think this conclusion is absurd and so there must be something wrong with the principle that generated it.

This is a vivid illustration of the value of following an argument to its logical conclusion. When you do that, you will sometimes discover that there is something very wrong with where you started from. This is how a *reductio ad absurdum* argument – a reduction to absurdity – works. If you can show that a certain belief leads logically to another belief which is clearly absurd, there must be something wrong with the original belief.

A *reductio* works on the basic principle of deduction: in a valid deductive argument, if the premises are true the conclusion must also be true. So if the conclusion is demonstrably false, or absurd, but the argument is valid, something must be wrong with the premises. This leaves you with three options: reject the premise, refine the premise, or bite the bullet and accept the apparently absurd conclusion.

Before completely rejecting the premise it is worth trying to refine it. After all, if it seemed credible in the first place it probably contained a germ of truth. In this case, maybe the problem is that if we diverted the entire culture and education budget to save just one life, more deaths would occur in the long run, as a healthy nation needs to be educated and stimulated. Our mistake was to make the principle about resources to save *a* life, not *life in general.* Perhaps we should have said simply: *Resources should be used to save lives above all else.*

That avoids the absurdity of throwing everything we have at saving one life, but it would still mean spending almost all public money on health and defence. It would not matter that our lives became more impoverished, as long as they became on average longer. We might, for example, educate only those whom we need to save lives and have the majority of kids leave school at age eleven to help to earn the money to pay for it all.

You can go away and keep trying to better define what 'no price on human life' means, but in the end I think most people would accept that, in this case, the *reductio* argument leads us to reject the idea that saving lives should be the only priority for public spending. Any government or health care provider has to set a limit on how much can be spent trying to keep people alive. This may sound distasteful, but it's a harsh reality.

However, it's important to note that a *reductio* argument does not usually compel anyone to give up their premises. There is always the alternative of 'biting the bullet' and accepting the conclusion, absurd though it might seem. In the 'price on a life' case, you could argue that although it seems absurd to say we should spend no money at all on anything that doesn't save lives, all that shows is that we are unwilling to make the moral sacrifices we should be making. In an ideal world, there would need to be economic activity to generate the money needed for health care, but things like education or art for their own sake would be rejected as luxuries.

Something very close to this is in fact the position of the moral philosopher Peter Singer. Singer asks, if you're passing a pond and a child is drowning in it, and you could wade in and pull the child out, should you do it? Of course you should. Even if it would make you late for a meeting and would ruin your new suit? Still, of course. The sacrifices you need to make are trivial compared to the loss of the child's life. So it seems we agree with the principle that 'If it is in our power to prevent

something very bad from happening, without thereby sacrificing anything morally significant, we ought, morally, to do it.'

Now Singer's got you. Say, like me, you're about to head
out for a fancy coffee and a croissant, which will set me back
over £5. If I gave up this indulgent habit and instead sent the
money to the right charity, I could give someone their sight
back, stop them contracting malaria, maybe even save their
life. Compared to that, the pleasure of my elevenses is trivial.
So according to the principle you may well have just endorsed,
there is a moral imperative for all my – and your – little treats
to stop. In fact, Singer says, we 'ought to give as much as possible, that is, at least up to the point at which by giving more
one would begin to cause serious suffering for oneself and one's
dependants'. It's not just the croissants that have to go. It's only
cheap clothes from now on, no fancy consumer goods like tele-
visions, and no holidays away or meals out.

For many this is a *reductio ad absurdum*. Any moral principle
that requires us to give up so much is surely too demanding. But
Singer bites the bullet. His morality *is* extremely demanding,
but that doesn't make it wrong. 'Most people can give 50 per
cent of their income away,' he told me, even though 'it's predict-
able that most of them won't.' Far from backing off, he doubles
down. 'For us who are sitting here comfortably enjoying our
lives, secure in terms of meeting our basic needs, to say, "Don't
you think that what really makes life rich is to be able to go to
the opera and look at great masterpieces at the national gallery,"
while there are other people who are going to bed hungry or
who can't afford to treat their child who has diarrhoea, or who
have to walk two hours a day to get safe drinking water, or just
to get water that isn't even safe – no, I think that that's self-
indulgent really.'

That's the problem with *reductio ad absurdum* arguments: one person's absurdity is another's uncomfortable or

counter-intuitive truth. Nor is anything so absurd that some intelligent person has not believed it.

There's another kind of argument based on following through the implications of a position, but in the opposite direction: following back. In a *transcendental argument* you start with something that is evidently true and you ask what else *must* be true for that to be the case. John Searle tried using a transcendental argument to establish 'external realism': belief in the real existence of the external world. Searle takes as his starting fact that there is such a thing as normal discourse and it works. People agree to meet at certain places at certain times and, lo, they generally succeed. Searle argues that 'We couldn't have our normal understanding of that unless we assume there is a place, in space, in time, that is independent of us and we can meet at that particular place. That is external realism.'

This might strike you as a little simplistic, but remember it is just a summary. Note also that it is not the same as *naive realism*: the belief that the external world is more or less as it appears. It is actually an argument for *structural realism*: the belief that the external world may appear very differently from how it essentially is, but that it must have certain structures that its appearance systematically maps on to. Time and space are two such structural features. Unless our experience of time and space bore a close and systematic relationship to whatever the underlying structure of the world is, we couldn't ever go on dates or arrive at meetings.

Transcendental arguments sound rather hifalutin, but the basic principle can be used for more mundane matters. The basic question we ask is 'If *this* is true, what else *must* be true?', or in a weaker version, 'If *this* is true, what else is *most likely to be* true?' Here is a trivial but useful example. If you can't find your keys anywhere you'd expect to find them, they must be somewhere where you *don't* expect to find them. And if you used them to get in, that somewhere must be in your home. That might sound obvious, but I'm sure I'm not the only one who has asked 'Have you looked *there*?', only to be told that there's no reason to think that they are *there*. Yet the whole point of keys being lost is that wherever they are, it's somewhere you have no reason to expect to find them.

In what we might call such 'practical transcendental arguments', we must avoid the trap of assuming that something *must* be true when there is more than one possibility. If you find your partner has been calling an unknown number a lot recently, that doesn't mean they *must* be having an affair. Maybe they're arranging a surprise for you, or perhaps they do have a secret, but it's not that. It's a common failure of imagination to assume that 'I can't think of any other explanation' means 'There is no other explanation.'

Both *reductio*s and transcendental arguments trace the necessary connections between certain facts. Sometimes, however, the move from one apparently true claim to another occurs not by discrete steps but by a more gradual slide. In a 'slippery slope' argument, an unwanted conclusion may logically follow from a premise, but more often the conclusion is inevitable for other, generally psychological reasons.

Take a popular argument against legalising assisted suicide for the terminally ill. Many who oppose assisted suicide argue that the problem is not that the people the law intends to help should be denied the 'right to die', but that if that right is granted, it won't stop there. The old, the disabled and those who want to keep living as long as possible will increasingly be seen as a burden and feel under pressure to end their own lives early. As Jamie Hale, disabled poet and activist said, 'I can envisage no safeguards that would prevent people being pressured into ending their lives, by interpersonal, financial or social means.'[1] Research by the disability equality charity Scope found that 'the majority of disabled people believe the current ban on assisted suicide protects people from pressure to end their lives' and that two-thirds said they would be concerned by a change in the law.[2]

As Mary Warnock said, often 'When people employ a slippery slope argument they speak as though there's a logical inevitability between one step and then sliding all the way down the slope to the next awful outcome.' But usually there is nothing logically inevitable at all. As Warnock says, these arguments turn on human nature. 'Slippery slope arguments really amount to saying, "If you once let them start, human nature being what it is, they'll go all the way."'

So when assessing a slippery slope argument, you have to question what the risks of the unintended consequences really are and whether anything can be put in place to make the slope less greasy. In the case of assisted suicide, advocates claim that laws can be framed so that abuse is almost impossible. Opponents argue that you can't legislate against the changes in public attitudes that will follow and that in any case, the risks are so high, why take them? (As with all arguments based on risk, you also have to consider the risks of *not* changing the law, which include many people having to suffer longer and more distressing deaths than they would have wanted.)

Slippery slopes are often presented as though sliding down them is inevitable. But, more often than not, there are ways of giving ourselves more grip.

The importance of statistical literacy has become increasingly obvious in recent years, as citizens have struggled to make sense of the meaning of R-numbers, death rates, exponential growth, vaccine efficacy and so on. This is an area of critical thinking in which philosophers aren't the experts. Nonetheless, philosophical habits of thought can help us to get a better handle on numbers, even if we don't have any specific statistical training.

A philosopher is used to asking of any purported fact: what does it mean? Where does it come from? What follows from it? Ask these questions of numbers and they quickly begin to make more sense.

Facts do not speak for themselves, and numbers are especially ineloquent, rarely wearing their meaning on their sleeves. For example, a lot of headlines were generated in March 2021 when the United Nations Environment Programme (UNEP) published its Food Waste Index Report, with the eye-catching statistic that 'around 931 million tonnes of food waste was generated in 2019'.[3] It sounds like a lot, but is it a big number?[4] You have to search the report quite carefully to find that this represents 17 per cent of food available. Given that some waste is inevitable, that may not be as dreadful as you feared. You'd have to do your own maths to work out that, given the world's population in 2019 was 7,673 billion, all this food waste divides up on average to 109 kg (240lbs) per person, around two kilograms per week.

However, this isn't the full story. Philosophers have an almost knee-jerk reaction to any claim, which is to ask for a definition of the terms used. What exactly is 'food waste' in this report? The answer might surprise you: 'For the purposes of the Food Waste Index, "food waste" is defined as food and the associated inedible parts removed from the human food supply chain.' So husks, shells, bones and so on all get counted as food waste, even though none were ever edible.

This or very similar definitions of food waste are widely used. The EU defines food waste as 'any food, and inedible parts of food, removed from the food supply chain to be recovered or disposed'.[5] The UK government gets most of its food waste data from WRAP (Waste & Resources Action Programme), a charity it helped to set up. Its measures include unavoidable waste 'arising from food and drink preparation that is not, and has not been, edible under normal circumstances'.[6]

Most of us are more interested in statistics that deal specifically with avoidable food waste. If you go looking for them, you find that now WRAP does make more efforts to provide statistics that exclude inedible parts alongside those that include them, although it isn't always immediately obvious which kind is being reported, especially when you're reading about it secondhand through the media. The headline figure of its 2021 report was that in the UK there was 9.5 million tonnes of total food waste per year, of which 6.4 million was edible food. That's a staggering 96 tonnes per person.[7] The US Department of Agriculture's Economic Research Service (ERS) also records a figure for food *loss*, which is 'the edible amount of food, postharvest, that is available for human consumption but is not consumed for any reason'. On this definition, food loss in the USA adds up to 30–40 per cent of the food supply, which at 133 billion lbs averages out at an astonishing 400 tons per person.[8]

Having got a better idea of what these numbers mean, we next need to ask where the data comes from. Here the answer is: diverse sources, some more reliable than others. This is one of the big take-home messages of the aforementioned UNEP report, which concluded: 'Global food waste data availability is currently low, and measurement approaches have been highly variable.' Only seventeen countries are judged to have high-quality data, with a further forty-two assigned a medium confidence. In practice this almost certainly means food waste is higher than is currently estimated.

Our final question is: what follows from these facts? The short answer is nothing, unless you know more information. We can assume that zero waste is not in practice attainable. It would require a perfect alignment of supply and demand, zero transport or storage failures, precise portion control and no cooking mishaps. So there must be a proportion of food waste significantly above zero that is optimal. What is it? We don't know. But we do know from numerous reports into avoidable food waste that it is much lower than it is currently.

There's been nothing in this discussion of food waste statistics that obviously looks like philosophical reasoning. But it has been powered entirely by philosophical habits of thought, without any special knowledge of statistics or the food system. The result is a clearer picture than the one we would have had simply from reading the headline reports.

Interestingly, it is also a picture in which the actual, precise numbers turn out to be not especially important. The key conclusions we should draw are that there is a heck of a lot of food waste globally, that rich countries waste much than poor ones, that we need to be aware that sometimes reporting of food waste includes inedible parts and is highly variable in accuracy, and that there is a lot of scope to reduce food waste. We set out to interrogate the quantitative data and ended up finding quite a lot of qualitative information. It is probably no coincidence that a philosophical approach resulted in this, because in philosophy you often find that the question you start out with is not the most important one after all, and so is not the one you end up answering.

Asking the questions 'What do they mean?', 'Where do they come from?' and 'What follows from them?' reveals a lot about so many statistics. For instance, we are often told that a study's results are 'statistically significant'. The philosopher instinctively asks: define your terms. All 'statistically significant' means is that the results suggest that it is unlikely that you would get the same result by chance. And what does 'unlikely' mean here? Something like a one in twenty, which means one out of every twenty statistically significant results would actually mean nothing at all.[9]

However, the key thing is that a number being *statistically* significant doesn't necessarily make it 'significant' in any other important sense. Doubling a risk of death sounds scary, for example, but if that risk is extremely low – say, one in 10 million – it almost certainly doesn't matter if something with clear benefits doubles it.

Compare this with *clinical* significance. A result is clinically significant if it points to a change which results in a difference worth making to life expectancy, symptom relief, cost-effectiveness, ease of medical interventions and so on. However, just because a result is statistically significant, that doesn't automatically mean it is clinically significant, or vice versa. Take one study which showed that a particular drug treatment 'significantly' extended the life of cancer patients, in the statistical sense. But this significant increase was from 5.91 to 6.24 months, or just ten days. Even if you think that is significant (most clinicians do not), when we factor in the negative effects of the treatment on the patient and the costs, no expert would think the drug was worth giving.

Understanding what the statistics mean here also answers the 'What follows from them?' question: namely, nothing practical. In other cases, what follows is less obvious but clear enough if you pay attention. Recurring examples of this are studies showing a link between something – foods, drinks, pesticides, cleaning materials, cosmetics – and an increased risk of one or more serious diseases. It's easy to assume that it follows that these things are bad for your health. But almost everything has a range of effects, some good and some bad. Whether something is healthy or not depends on how it affects us on balance. That's why it is often very good indeed for your health to take a medicine that has some side effects or increases your chances of getting some other illness. Unless you know *all* the effects of something, good and bad, you can't know whether its bad effects are reason enough to avoid it.

It's also worth asking where the stats come from. In the cancer drug study I mentioned, the data is bona fide. But remarkably often the source of a statistic has a vested interest in it. If a claim about the health benefits of chocolate comes from a study funded by confectioners, be wary. Even genuine research is vulnerable to vested interests. Many studies are promoted in press releases by a university's marketing department. They often make more of the statistical significance of findings than the researchers themselves do in the actual paper. Time-poor journalists often simply work from the press release without reading the source research, a practice the investigative journalist Nick Davies calls 'churnalism'.

Numbers are potent weapons of propaganda, and improving your statistical numeracy is certainly worthwhile. But a great deal of clear thinking about data can be achieved simply by applying general philosophical principles to them. Despite what anyone says, the numbers do not just speak for themselves. Until we make sense of them, they are just digits.

Being alert to what does or does not strictly, logically follow from beliefs, facts and numbers is a core critical-thinking competency. It is widely thought in philosophy that to excel at this you need a knowledge of formal logic. This can be a daunting prospect. Just seeing $\forall x. \exists y. Q(x, y) \land \neg \forall u. \exists v. Q(v, u)$ is enough to make me break out in a cold sweat. I never mastered it, taking comfort in the fact that I am far from alone and the vast majority of the most important works of philosophy don't use it – except those that are about formal logic.

I was also reassured when Hilary Putnam argued that too much significance was placed on mathematical logic in twentieth-century Anglophone philosophy. Putnam lamented that logic became the default way to pursue the laudable goal of 'tightening up' our thinking. 'That should not be what tightening up something in philosophy means,' he said. 'I think we still suffer from the idea that formalising a sentence tells you what it "really" says.' He thought that the 'dream that we can take over formalisms from some exact science and then we will really be making progress' has affected other disciplines such as sociology, economics and social sciences. 'Part of the appeal of mathematical logic is that the formulas look mysterious – You write backward Es!'

Still, it's worth understanding why many philosophers find logic invaluable. Timothy Williamson says that 'For me, translating what somebody says in English into symbols, when it's some kind of complex statement, tends to make what they're saying clearer. Formulas are a bit like logical maps, they just make it very clear what the logical relations are.' His preference is partly a matter of temperament. 'Many other people go the other way: they like to translate from symbols into English to understand what the symbols are saying.'

However, even Williamson says that 'I don't think all philosophers have to be well versed in formal methods. [. . .] There's plenty of good philosophy that's written in ordinary prose and in many cases it would not benefit from being formalised.' There are few, if any, substantive issues outside of logic itself that depend on a formal logical proof.

You may be relieved that to learn how to reason well you don't need to know your ∀s from your ∃s. (If you're curious, '∀' is the universal quantifier, meaning 'for all' or 'for every', while ∃ is the existential quantifier, meaning 'there exists'.) The fundamental question of deductive logic is 'What follows?' and we have seen how that can be answered without the use of symbols. Indeed, most of our reasoning does not take the form of deduction at all, formal or otherwise.

Perhaps surprisingly, this is something even the hardest-nosed philosophers have acknowledged. Michael Martin is the epitome of an analytic, technical philosopher who doesn't mind that his work is not intelligible to laypeople. In seminars, I've seen him take people's arguments apart with forensic precision. Still, even he said, 'Very few philosophers, certainly almost none of the ones who are interesting to read, give you explicitly valid arguments.' Ray Monk says that we have to remember 'what a limited weapon a valid argument is and how rare it is that we're persuaded to believe something or adopt something on the basis of a valid argument'. Patricia Churchland, a 'neurophilosopher' who pays more attention to scientific fact that speculative theories, puts it even more forcefully: 'Who thinks deduction gets you around the planet? Really? I mean like maybe I do a deduction about twice a week.' Aware that she may sound a little flippant, she quickly adds: 'I'm being ironic. I don't know how many times I do a deduction but it's not very often.'

It's well worth internalising the basic rules of deduction, as it instils habits of checking for consistency and coherence. But for most practical purposes, we need to turn to a different form of reasoning, one which is both less logically watertight than deduction but also, thankfully, much more useful ...

How to watch your steps

- In any argument, a key question to ask is: does it follow?
- Be alert to the fact that bad arguments can sometimes contain true conclusions, and even contain only true statements.
- Whenever you come across an 'if', check if it is the conditional 'if' or the biconditional 'if and only if' (iff).
- It can be useful to learn formal fallacies, such as affirming the consequent. This will alert you to the fact that 'if x then y' does not entail 'if y then x'. If I'm a human, I'm a primate, but if I'm a primate I'm not necessarily a human.
- Aspire to consistency, but it's better to leave a contradiction unresolved than to resolve it with an absurdity.
- A *reductio ad absurdum* argument works on the principle that if a belief logically entails something absurd, there's something wrong with the belief. Either that, or you have to bite the bullet and claim that what seems absurd isn't really crazy at all.
- Beware not to head down a slippery slope, when accepting something that appears reasonable forces you to accept something else that isn't. But also be wary of warnings that a slope is slippery. Slippery slopes are rarely logical and most are psychological or social. They can often be de-iced.
- When presented with statistics, or any other fact, ask: what does it mean? Where does it come from? What follows from it?
- Don't be too impressed by claims of statistical significance. It's often not significant in any reasonably significant sense.

4

FOLLOW THE FACTS

It is better to be unhappy and know the worst,
than to be happy in a fool's paradise!

FYODOR DOSTOEVSKY, *The Idiot*

If the human race is to combat climate change, eradicate poverty, and feed the growing population, it will not be because people were moved by the power of deductive arguments. It will be because enough of us accept the evidence about what is happening, why it is happening, and what can be done to change it. Deduction only plays a supporting role in this. Data needs to be crunched, hypotheses judged consistent or not with the evidence, and so on. But the fundamental basis of reasoning about matters of fact is *empirical*: based on observation and experience. We observe and measure what is happening to the climate and we interpret that on the basis of theories that are themselves based on previous observations. This reasoning from particular observations to general theories is *inductive*, not *deductive*. So how does induction work?

Our dependence on past observations raises a deep philosophical question. If all our knowledge of the world is based on a limited number of past experiences, how can we be sure that this knowledge is correct, and will continue to be so in the future? There is a logical gap between saying, 'Such-and-such has always been observed to happen' and 'Such-and-such always happens, and will continue to happen.' Who is to say that the force of gravity won't change tomorrow, or that water might undergo a molecular transformation and become something subtly, or totally, different from H_2O? For centuries this 'problem of induction' has kept philosophers awake at night.

You might wonder why they can't just sleep it off. Surely the problem of induction is nit-picking at best, crazy at worst. No one, not even a philosopher, seriously doubts that the sun will rise in the morning or that the next coffee will perk you up as much as the previous thousands have. Induction only makes insomniacs of philosophers who are struggling to solve the deep philosophical problem. They're not scared the dawn won't come.

For practical purposes, the only take-home message from the problem of induction is that any belief that is based on observation, on evidence, is always less than 100 per cent certain. And since most of the beliefs that make a difference to how we live are based on past observations, we have to accept that there is no certainty in matters of fact. Our data is always limited. It's not just that our observations are in the past: there is always more we haven't observed than we have. So although there may be some facts about basic physics and chemistry that are so well tested that they can be taken as settled, in the messy world of complex entities that we deal with, little to nothing is so clear-cut.

It is tempting to accept all of this and conclude that although we lack certainty in empirical matters, the laws of nature are *very probably* constant and so many of our beliefs are *probably* true. Colloquially, I think this is fine, and you could skip this paragraph if you're not curious as to why it's not strictly accurate. In a technical sense, 'probably' isn't the right word. To say something is probably true you need to have some sense of what the probabilities are. We know a coin has a 50/50 chance of landing heads because a coin is symmetrical and has two faces. We know that a person in a developed country has around a 50 per cent chance of contracting a cancer at some point in their life and around a 25 per cent chance of dying from one because we know what proportion of the population are affected by the disease. However, the general belief that the laws of nature are constant is not based on any statistical data. Indeed, in ordinary probabilistic terms, the chances that they are constant would be judged to be 100 per cent, because all observations confirm it. The philosophical problem concerns the rationality of making *any* probabilistic calculation on the basis of past experience alone. In other words, probabilistic reasoning *assumes* that induction works, it does not justify or explain *why* it works.

Although the shadow of doubt inevitably falls on every belief we have about the world, we cannot allow it to obscure the light of experience. Once you accept that uncertainty is inevitable, you can see that whenever we are assessing an empirical claim, 'It *could* be wrong' is not a good enough reason to act as though it *were* wrong.

For example, there is a lot of evidence that refined sugars are bad for our health. But there's still not enough to be *absolutely certain* that they are in and of themselves problematic. It *could* be that the real problem is with something else so commonly consumed with them that we think sugar is the culprit. However, this *could* is so implausible that you'd be a fool to act on any assumption other than that your refined sugar consumption should be limited. The past is an imperfect guide, but ultimately it is the only one we've got.

This leads us to the really difficult question: when should we take seriously the possibility that past experience has misled us? Bertrand Russell famously described the chicken who learns from experience that every day the farmer will come to feed it and rashly assumes this is how it will be forever – until the day the farmer comes to wring its neck. Human beings get their metaphorical necks wrung all the time. War, illness, financial disaster, pandemics – all have the capacity to shake us out of our complacent belief that the future will be just like the past. Our worry is not that the laws of nature might suddenly change but that, like the chicken, we have mistaken a temporary pattern for an enduring one.

This worry is not a neurotic, academic one. The problem is that, when thinking about the future, it is always possible to draw one of two completely different wrong conclusions from experience. One is to falsely believe that past experience doesn't apply because the situation you are thinking about is importantly different. The other is to falsely believe that the situation you are thinking about is yet another example of a familiar kind when it *really is* importantly different. Some things really are unprecedented.

The evidence of experience is that it is hard to make good predictions on the evidence of experience. Every year experts predict house prices, stock markets, election results, wars and so on and every year most experts get it wrong. This should not surprise us. Pretty much everything is the result of so many different, interacting and changing causes that the past is inevitably an imprecise guide to the future. That's why when many technologies are new, even well-informed people can't imagine why large numbers of people would use them. In 1977 the computer engineer and manufacturer Ken Olsen said, 'There is no reason anyone would want a computer in their home.' In 2007, former Microsoft CEO Steve Ballmer proclaimed: 'There's no chance that the iPhone is going to get any significant market share.' And in 2013, BlackBerry CEO Thorsten Heins said that tablet computers 'are not a good business model' and that 'In five years, I don't think there will be a reason to have a tablet anymore.' Until recently, humanity had no experience of life with these technologies, so we had little idea what effect they would have on us.

We may be poor predictors, but we don't have the option of sitting back and waiting to see what the future brings. Those who say the best plan is not to plan and that we should live wholly in the present face the problem that the future has a habit of coming around after all. It may be hubris to plan a retirement on the assumption that your investments are totally safe and you will be there to enjoy it. But it is also rash to not plan at all and to spend your autumn years struggling when a little foresight would have made you comfortable. The future is uncertain, which is why retirement plans should be seen as contingency plans, just in case life ends up treating you well enough for you to enjoy it.

To increase our chances of avoiding misjudgements when thinking about the future we should always question our assumptions about what we think is fixed and constant and what is subject to change. We need to ask whether the most important feature of a future event will be its similarity to or difference from past precedents. It's not easy to answer and there's no algorithm that can tell you. But at least if we ask the question we can avoid making rash assumptions. There is also a useful heuristic – a rule of thumb – to guide us: the more that fixed and stable laws of nature guide what we are anticipating, the more confident we can be that the outcome will not surprise us, as long as we correctly understand those rules of nature.

It sounds obvious, but people often misjudge how far certain domains of human life are ruled by laws, or not. Some treat economic theories as though they were scientific laws and trust their models too much. Others are unwilling to accept that human beings don't easily change and so make optimistic or pessimistic assumptions about how future generations will be different. Still others mistake culturally determined features of human behaviour for fundamental human nature, and so believe, for example, that the roles of men and women are more fixed than they are.

The most useful general principle that can help us to increase our ratio of anticipated to unanticipated events and situations is David Hume's unnecessarily gendered general maxim, 'A wise man . . . proportions his belief to the evidence.'[1] This sounds so obvious as to be platitudinous, but it is a principle that is easier to assent to than to actually follow.

Hume gives a great example of this in his discussion of the argument that the order of the world is evidence that it had a creator. This argument was made famous by William Paley, who argued that if he came across a watch, he would never say, 'For anything I knew, the watch might have always been there.' Rather, he would have concluded: 'There must have existed, at some time, and at some place or other, an artificer or artificers, who formed [the watch].' If that is so for the watch, he argued, it must be even more true of the universe as a whole, since 'Every indication of contrivance, every manifestation of design, which existed in the watch, exists in the works of nature; with the difference, on the side of nature, of being greater or more, and that in a degree which exceeds all computation.'[2]

Hume clearly saw Paley's mistake. When we infer a watch-maker from a watch, we are basing that inference on experience because everything we know about watches tells us they are human artefacts. But our experience of universe creation and creators is non-existent. There simply is no past precedent we can use to say, 'Every other universe was created by a God, so ours must have been too.'[3]

The argument from design is a very particular one, which you might not think has much to tell us about more mundane reasoning. But in fact it tells us a lot. Many people find Paley's argument, or some version of it, persuasive, even when its errors are pointed out to them. I think this is because we are natural pattern seekers, too quick to make analogies and comparisons when a more careful look would show us that they don't work. Hence we are too quick to over-generalise from experience, to use too narrow a set of data to draw too many conclusions.

One of the key drivers of this rash haste to mis-generalise is the availability heuristic, or availability bias. Quite naturally, we tend to reason on the basis of the evidence that is most available to us, rather than on the full evidence base. This can lead us to make big mistakes, particularly when calculating risks and probabilities. For instance, after 9/11 people were much more aware of the dangers of flying than they were of driving and so many people chose to drive instead of taking a flight. Gerd Gigerenzer calculated that as a result, 1,500 extra people died on America's roads in the twelve months after the terrorist attacks, half the number who actually died directly because of the destruction of the World Trade Center all because their minds were focused on a lesser risk than the one they took.[4]

Paley was the victim of the availability heuristic in a different way. When the evidence we need is lacking we often look for the closest thing we have to it, even when it is not good evidence at all. For instance, in the absence of good information, people often buy something on the basis of a single review or recommendation, without having any reason to trust it. In Paley's case, the only evidence about creators available to him concerned artefacts. There was no evidence about Gods. But

Paley still argued on the evidence of those 'artificers', rather than admit he had nothing to go on.

I remembered an example of this use of proximate but erroneous evidence when I was listening to someone talking about whether we should believe Elon Musk when he said he'd send a crewed mission to Mars in 2026. The pundit thought Musk was probably being a bit optimistic, but he pointed out that many people said Musk could never develop electric cars as quickly as he has done, or that his space programme would not be a success, and they were wrong. The lesson he was drawing is that experience shows us that Musk's promises have a habit of sounding unrealistic but he has repeatedly delivered on them.

Set aside the fact that Musk's critics have often been right too. ('Next year, for sure, we'll have over 1 million robotaxis on the road,' said Musk in 2019.) Even if Musk had been right time and again on electric cars, developing an existing technology is very different from launching an unprecedented mission into deep space. The technical challenges of sending people to Mars or putting people and satellites into the Earth's orbit make the problems of self-driving cars and battery life look simple in comparison. This is another example of the importance of asking whether the most important feature of a future event is its similarity to or difference from past precedents. Evidence of Musk's ability to deliver on cars and satellites might look like it is evidence of his ability to deliver on a Mars mission, but when you think about it, it's like believing that because someone has been a great soccer manager, that shows they could be a brilliant orchestra conductor.

Empirical theories are only as good as the evidence they are based on, and in many cases that is not as strong as we often believe. Several years ago I came across an example of checking the robustness of the evidence. I was shocked to see that a local health food store had put up a copy of a news report in its window that claimed: 'Pregnant women living in areas where tap water is heavily disinfected with chlorine nearly double their risk of having children with heart problems', and that 'Scientists say expectant mothers can expose themselves to the higher risk by drinking the water, taking a bath or shower, or even by standing close to a boiling kettle.' All this sounded implausible, but the article cited a scientific research paper in the journal *Environmental Health*.[5]

Furious at what surely had to be scaremongering misinformation, I set about checking it. It soon became clear that the text in the shop window came not from the scientific paper, but from a report on it in the *Daily Mail*, the UK's leading purveyor of fear.[6] The source scientific paper said nothing at all about the implausible idea that taking a bath or standing close to a boiling kettle presented a risk. As for the 'doubled', you only have to look at how low the risk is in the first place to see that doubling is not especially alarming. The risk of anencephalus rose from 0.01 to 0.17 per cent, hole-in-the-heart defects from 0.015 to 0.024 per cent, and cleft palates from 0.029 to 0.045 per cent.

You might think that, although the increased risks in each case are still tiny, any increase at all is still cause for concern. But what the newspaper report didn't say was that the overall risk of *all* birth defects was more or less the same whatever the level of chlorination. (In fact, cases were highest in the group living in the area with the most chlorine, but by such a small margin as to make this statistically insignificant.) The report could equally have said that chlorination *reduces* the risk of hydrocephalus, tetralogy of Fallot, chromosome anomalies and Down's syndrome. That makes the headline profoundly misleading: 'Chlorine in tap water "nearly doubles the risk of birth defects"' is very different from 'Chlorine in tap water "nearly doubles the risk of *some* birth defects *and halves that of others*".'

Anyone who was critical and careful enough could have reached the same conclusions as I did, even without a training in epidemiological research, infant health or statistics. All they needed to do was to check the source with due care and – you guessed it – attention.

Although getting into the nitty-gritty of arguments, examining all the facts in great detail, is usually exactly the right thing to do, sometimes it is better to ignore the details of a particular case and base our judgements on general truths and trends. This is a good strategy when we don't know enough about the specific case but we do know a lot about 'this kind of thing'.

An obvious example is email and phone scams. If someone is asking you for personal or bank details, you can't afford to always work out whether or not they have a bona fide reason to do so. It's far better to adopt the broad principle that when people ask for this kind of thing they're probably fraudsters. This is a fallible principle, of course, but failure is inexpensive: if a bank has genuine business with you, they won't give up on it because you refuse to do exactly what their own fraud teams tell you not to do and hand over your bank details to a caller.

This kind of argument is a *meta-induction*: arguing from the experience of a broad category of precedents rather than focusing on the specifics of the case. Meta-induction is what legitimately allows you to disbelieve reports of miracle cures, sightings of ghosts, get-rich schemes, wild conspiracy theories, all without having to test the exact claims of each.

Meta-induction is also a useful tool for hypochondriacs. What's worrying about getting any kind of medical symptom is that you don't know what is causing it, and there are always scary possibilities. But if you're not a doctor it is rash to read too much into your knowledge of the symptoms. The most significant fact we know is that most illnesses are not serious.

So until we have good reason to think that any particular one is, we should assume that it is another one of these things that will pass. That does not mean that you shouldn't see a doctor and get it checked out, nor that you should discount the possibility of something serious. It just means that the working hypothesis is 'probably not terminal' until proven otherwise.

Meta-induction is the best way of thinking when our knowledge of and confidence in general truths is much greater than that of the case in question. We don't use it enough because, when we are confronted with a particular situation or problem, its specific details tend to strike us as more significant and important than they are. Details *are* important, but unless you know which ones matter, and what they mean, focusing on them means you're trying to think above your pay grade. The more you get bogged down in detail, the more likely you are to go wrong. Better to focus on what you do know: you'd have to be very unlucky if this was the thing that killed you.

When it comes to predicting the future, the meta-inductive approach reminds us that the most secure predictions are very general and based on perennial features of the world that we have no reason to think will change. People will continue to be greedy, cruel and prejudiced, but the forms that these will take will forever shift. But we will also continue to see kindness, generosity and love, so fears about a descent into barbarity are as far-fetched as hopes of a coming utopia. You don't have to be a Nostradamus to see this. In fact, it might help that you are not. Nostradamus was looking out for big dramatic events that no one could accurately predict. Had he been more modest he would have been right more often, but also less famous. Bold prediction is attention-grabbing, but whenever I hear someone confidently map out the unknown future, I see an arrogant self-promoter who is best avoided.

*

We've seen how deduction and induction together cover all the legitimate, rational ways we have in which to make inferences. Either we're working out the logical implications of something or we're drawing conclusions from experience and observation. However, the inductive side of this division contains a method of reasoning that deserves to be treated separately: abduction, or inference to the best explanation.

For example, let's say you wake up in the morning and find a vase broken on the floor. The doors and windows are all closed and there was no one else in the house. Many things could conceivably have caused it to fall: a minor earthquake, a gust of wind, an intruder who otherwise left no trace, an exceptionally large fly, the cat, or the vase suddenly attaining consciousness and leaping off the shelf when it realised the futility of existence. Unless your home is wired up with CCTV cameras and seismometers, you probably won't be able to gather all the evidence needed to fully assess these possibilities. Real life is rarely like a whodunnit, in which all the evidence ends up pointing to only one possible explanation. But you still have good reasons to conclude that it was the cat who most likely did it. You can never prove it, but it is the best explanation by a long shot.

Abduction is simply the fancy word for arguing to the best explanation. It is now generally agreed that there are four key criteria you can apply to test if an explanation really is the best one. The first is *simplicity*. All other things being equal, simpler explanations are preferable to more complicated ones. If your doorbell rings, for example, assume it is because someone rang it, unless you have a very good reason to suspect it was a fault or some other kind of freak occurrence. In the case of the broken vase, your cat jumping on the furniture, as is its wont, explains simply why the vase was knocked over, while all the other explanations are fancifully complicated in comparison.

This relates to the second criterion: *coherence*. Does the explanation fit all the other relevant, known facts? The cat jumping on the furniture does, the other competing explanations certainly do not. There were no reports of an earthquake and, anyway, why would it only disturb one object when all the others were exactly as they were when you last saw them? How could a strong gust of wind have blown through a closed room? Surely you would have noticed a fly big enough to knock down a vase if it had been buzzing around your house. As for the suicide explanation, the less said about that the better. If the cat did it, however, everything else is as you would expect it.

This feeds into the criterion of *comprehensiveness*. The best explanation explains as much as possible and leaves as few loose ends as possible. All the other explanations for the broken vase solve one mystery but create even bigger ones.

The final criterion is not always possible to apply: *testability*. Generally speaking, we should prefer explanations that can be tested, either directly or because they generate predictions that can themselves be verified. For example, if you're trying to understand why your radio signal is poor, the hypothesis that it is in a reception blind spot is easily tested by moving it around the house, because it predicts the signal won't be equally bad everywhere. In contrast, it's hard to imagine how you'd test the theory that the FBI are blocking the signal. With our vase, the only tests would be to ask what else we would expect to find if the theory were true. If the cat did it, for example, then you'd expect other objects in its path to at least have been moved.

So the best explanation is the one that scores highest for *simplicity*, *coherence*, *comprehensiveness* and *testability*. (It's a shame that SCCT isn't a particularly good mnemonic to remember these four criteria. You could go for TICS: testable, inclusive, coherent, simple. Tick.) When applying them, two Latin words can come in helpful: *ceteris paribus*, all other things being equal.

A comprehensive theory is preferable to a more partial one, *ceteris paribus*, but not if the price of its comprehensiveness is wild implausibility. That everything is made of cheese is a very comprehensive theory, but I don't think physicists should down tools right now and embrace it.

In applying these criteria, we are ultimately drawing on the lessons of experience, which makes abduction a form of induction. But it has enough distinctive features for us to think of it as a method of reasoning in its own right.

Sometimes, the best explanation we can come up with is still not a very good one. When we can't find something and we jokingly say, 'It must have just vanished,' we are nodding to the attraction and the irrationality of preferring a bad explanation to none at all. In such circumstances, it can be better to accept that we don't know than to take the best explanation available.

Too often, however, we do prefer widely implausible explanations to none at all. That is in part the appeal of some conspiracy theories and solutions to unexplained mysteries. If we can't think why else the Nazca people of Peru drew their long lines in the desert, we might be tempted by the theory that they were designed to be seen by aliens. Before there was a theory of evolution, the idea that the universe was designed by an intelligent God looked to many as the best explanation for its existence even though some, like David Hume, could see it was a very bad one. That is why the rhetorical question 'How else do you explain it?' should be treated with caution.

A better grasp of abductive reasoning would save a lot of people from spurious conspiracy theories and other fantastical ideas. However, it also explains why they can be so seductive.

Abduction makes a virtue of simplicity, as did a famous fourteenth-century Franciscan friar. William of Ockham was a philosopher, monk and theologian and one of the intellectual stars of his day. Now, however, he is remembered almost entirely for one thing: his razor. Often summed up as the principle that we should always prefer a simpler explanation over a more complicated one, the original Ockham's Razor – a principle, not a blade – specifically concerned the number of things we ought to assume to exist. 'For nothing ought to be posited without a reason given, unless it is self-evident or known by experience or proved by the authority of Sacred Scripture.' As with so many principles, the original words were made snappier by successors and the razor is most commonly defined as the principle *Entia non sunt multiplicanda sine necessitate* – one should not multiply entities beyond necessity. Use the razor to cut out what is not necessary.

It's not difficult to find examples where Ockham's Razor clearly favours the most rational explanation. It's more reasonable to assume your cat knocked over the vase than it is to postulate that the cat and a minor earthquake worked in tandem. The latter is of course a possibility, but in the absence of any particular reason to think this freak combination of events occurred, prefer the simpler one.

However, the desideratum of simplicity in reasoning turns out not to be very simple to apply. As Jerry Fodor points out, the logical consequence of saying, 'I've got a really simple theory, so you should prefer mine to yours' is 'I've got a really simple theory: there isn't anything. You couldn't get simpler than that.' As Fodor argues, the price of this simplicity is a lack of explanatory and predictive power. It's *ceteris paribus* again: the simpler theory is only preferable all other things being equal. Don't multiply entities behind necessity, for sure, but sometimes it is necessary to postulate more rather than fewer.

Often, what looks simple is merely simplistic. Take the explanation for why the Twin Towers collapsed after they were hit by planes on 11 September 2001. You need to be a structural engineer to understand this and I won't attempt a summary.[7] To the layperson, the collapse looks – literally – like a controlled explosion, which is what many conspiracy theories insist it was. The chain of cause and effect for an explosion would be simple and easy to understand: explosives undermine the support structures of the building at strategic places, as they do in a demolition, and the whole thing comes toppling down. In contrast, the official theory, that the collapse was due to the aircraft crashes, has several stages of cause and effect, including aircraft fuel spreading, thermal expansion of the concrete floors, buckling of rigid steel columns, build-up of strain on the floors and eventual collapse. If you're after simplicity, the controlled explosion theory is very appealing.

It takes more care to spot that, all things considered, a controlled explosion is actually a less simple explanation. For one thing, remember that Ockham warned against multiplying entities beyond necessity. The official explanation requires only those entities that are known with certainty to have been present: the towers, the plane and the fuel. The controlled explosion theory requires the presence of additional entities, not only the bombs but the agents who planted them and the people who plotted to put them there.

It's also clear that if we compare the two postulated plots – one by al-Qaeda and one by the US government – the latter is far, far more complicated. For the FBI to have stage-managed a hijacking of four planes, got al-Qaeda to take credit for it, wired up two huge buildings to bring them down, all the while persuading everyone in the FBI to go along with this heinous act and keeping others in the dark, is beyond credulity. Everything we believe about how al-Qaeda did it, in contrast, is all too plausible.

If you allow yourself to have a simplistic notion of simplicity, it quickly becomes a vice. *Ceteris paribus* demands that Ockham's Razor has to be used in combination with the other criteria for abduction: coherence, comprehensiveness and testability. But even when you do that, careless use can lead to the wrong conclusions. For example, abduction says that explanations should be coherent and comprehensive. But that is precisely the appeal of many conspiracy theories: they explain everything, in ways that make it all fit together. When it comes to creating a unified, single story, conspiracy is more persuasive than cock-up. 'The government controls everything' is a tidier idea than 'Stuff just happens.' But again, if we think harder, this apparent coherence and comprehensiveness comes at a cost. It requires us to attribute a degree of power and control to hidden actors that is a million miles from what experience tells us is possible. If it were that easy to fool an entire nation, dictatorships wouldn't need to resort to overt tools of repression.

The fourth criterion of testability can also play into conspiracy theorists' hands. The whole point of a conspiracy is that it is secret and so the evidence is hidden. The lack of evidence can therefore in a perverse way be counted as positive evidence that what is happening is surreptitious. The right rejoinder to this is to insist that even if extraordinary claims do not require extraordinary evidence, they still require evidence. To say, 'Of course there's no evidence – it's all being covered up' is a justification to believe any conspiracy theory whatsoever.

Some believe that elegance, not simplicity, is the hallmark of truth, quoting Keats's line 'Beauty is truth, truth beauty' as though it were a fact. Pleasing explanations often have an almost aesthetic quality. Mathematicians talk of elegant proofs, scientists of beautiful theories. The Argentinian novelist, mathematician and logician Guillermo Martínez worries that we could be seduced by this. Mathematicians may say a proof is more elegant, but 'There's no way of really explaining that aesthetic judgement.' Sometimes an explanation is 'not as elegant, not as accurate perhaps, but it suits better'. The use of computers is also changing the mathematical landscape. 'Before, a proof was something that a normal person in a normal life could check from beginning to end. Now a proof can be something run by a program, so the complexity, the kind of calculation, is totally different. Now a person in his whole life is not able to reach the end of the proof. What is elegant for a computer is no longer elegant for a person.'

Martínez is right to be cautious. The world is sometimes messy, and therefore some explanations of how it works will be messy. Explanations often achieve elegance only by ignoring the rough edges of reality. Very few things in the world lack imperfections and redundant features. Most organisms are 'kluges', a ragbag of parts that have evolved *ad hoc* to fulfil a particular purpose on the basis of their availability rather than their optimality. No one designing a bipedal ape would have given humans the spines we have, for example. Any explanation which would make the thing being explained simpler or more elegant than it is should be treated with suspicion. Ockham's Razor needs a second part: *Only expect as much simplicity in an explanation as the* explanandum – *the thing being explained – allows.*

One problem with formalising critical thinking is that is divides arguments into different kinds (deductive, inductive, abductive) when in practice our reasoning often employs elements of more than one. So people trying to follow the thinking rules can be distracted by the question of what kind of argument they are dealing with. If they simply asked 'Does it follow?' and paid close attention, they would see the strengths and weaknesses of an argument easily enough.

Take the common argument that drug prohibition doesn't work, because drug use remains high when it is prohibited. This is the basis of a reasonable argument, for some drugs at least.

But in its simple form, the conclusion just doesn't follow. First of all, you have to ask what it means to say prohibition 'doesn't work'. In the enthymematic form of the argument above, the conclusion 'It doesn't work' follows from the one premise 'Drug prohibition doesn't stop drug use.' To make this follow deductively you'd need to add another premise: 'If prohibition worked, there would be no drug use.' But that is highly questionable. Many policies don't eliminate the undesired effect, they simply control it. Dangerous driving laws don't stop dangerous driving, but you can be sure the roads would be even less safe without them.

If we want to assess the efficacy of prohibition we need to understand what the effect is supposed to be. Is it less drug use? Or is it rather less harmful drug use? Would we be happy if legalisation significantly increased the use of certain drugs but also significantly reduced the amount of harm caused by that use? Or is the main aim of legislation simply to make a statement that our society does not want to tolerate this kind of behaviour? All of this takes us to a more nuanced discussion about prohibition than whether it stops people taking drugs.

Once we have decided on the desired outcome, the argument becomes inductive in character. What is the evidence concerning the effects of drug laws on drug use and drug-related harms? I don't know, but anyone who cares to look will find there is a lot, since we can not only compare different territories with different laws, but what has happened within territories that have changed their laws, such as Portugal. (To judge how successful it has been, the need to follow the numbers is exceptionally important.) In making these assessments you'll have to employ a lot of argument to the best explanation, because there are competing possible reasons for almost all the changes in usage, death and crime rates since all personal drug use was decriminalised there in 2001. But the overall picture is clear: at worst, decriminalisation has not made Portugal's drug-related problems worse relative to other European countries and at best it has reduced them.

Thinking through the merits and problems of drug decriminalisation requires applying all the major principles we have covered so far: check your facts, pay attention and ask what follows. (Maybe there is another acronym here: faf. Faffing about is not such a waste of time after all.) There is no algorithm for reasoning soundly, but when these key thinking skills become habits, it is usually clear which way rationality pushes us, even if you can't remember the differences between deductive, inductive and abductive arguments, universal and existential quantifiers, sound and valid arguments.

How to follow the facts

- Remember that reasoning from evidence always yields less than certainty because data is limited and there is a logical gap between all we have observed and all that is and will be.
- Ask yourself of present or future situations: is its most important feature its similarity to or difference from past precedents?
- The more something is guided by fixed and stable laws of nature, the more confident we can be that it will not surprise us, as long as we correctly understand those rules of nature.
- Do not be too quick to over-generalise from experience, to use too narrow a set of data to draw too many conclusions.
- Proportion your beliefs to the evidence. Empirical theories are only as good as the evidence they are based on, and in many cases that is not as strong as we often suppose.
- Avoid the availability heuristic: reasoning on the basis of the evidence that is most available to us, rather than on the full evidence base.
- When you read or hear about any striking claim, check out its source.
- When you don't know or understand enough about an issue and there is no reliable expert opinion, don't try to think above your pay grade. Employ a meta-induction and think about what tends to be true of this kind of thing.
- Look for the best explanation, the one which is, *ceteris paribus* (all other things being equal), the simplest, most coherent, most comprehensive and most testable. (Remember TICS: testable, inclusive, coherent, simple.)
- Use Ockham's Razor – *do not multiply entities beyond necessity* – with the addendum *only expect as much simplicity*

in an explanation as the explanandum – the thing being explained – allows.

- Always be faffing: check your *facts*, pay *attention* and ask what *follows*.

5

WATCH YOUR LANGUAGE

In every idea emanating from genius, or even in
every serious human idea – born in the human
brain – there always remains something –
some sediment – which cannot be expressed
to others, though one wrote volumes and
lectured upon it for five-and-thirty years.

FYODOR DOSTOEVSKY, *The Idiot*

'It's a perennial in philosophy for some philosophers to have
thought that what's letting us down are words: our grasp of our
words and our understanding of our words,' says the Cambridge
philosopher Simon Blackburn. Many of these philosophers
have concluded that straightening out our language is a powerful way to straighten out our thoughts, maybe even the best.

Ludwig Wittgenstein expressed one of the more bullish
versions of this idea when he wrote: 'Philosophical problems

arise when language goes on holiday.'[1] This thought echoes the core ideas of what came to be known as the ordinary language school of philosophy, born in Wittgenstein's Cambridge and later dominant in Oxford after the Second World War. Its adherents argued that philosophers generate puzzles and paradoxes about time, space, meaning, goodness and so on because they take concepts that have a perfectly intelligible everyday use and treat them as though they referred to abstract absolutes with some kind of pure, crystalline essence. So, for example, everyone knows what it means to say an apple is good, but philosophers generate problems by imagining there is something called 'the good' in itself. It would be an exaggeration to say that *all* philosophy is the result of linguistic confusion, but the ordinary language philosophers did us a great service by pointing out how many philosophical problems concern words, not the world.

A desire to get language right is not a foible of twentieth-century British philosophy. In the *Analects*, Kongzi (as Confucius is more authentically named) is asked what is the first thing he would do if he were to administer the government. His answer is 'What is necessary is to rectify names.' Unsurprisingly, he is told he is 'wide of the mark'. Surely a ruler needs to do things, not worry about getting words right? But Kongzi replies,

If names be not correct, language is not in accordance with the truth of things. If language be not in accordance with the truth of things, affairs cannot be carried on to success. When affairs cannot be carried on to success, proprieties and music will not flourish. When proprieties and music do not flourish, punishments will not be properly awarded. When punishments are not properly awarded, the people do not know how to move hand or foot.

Although the talk of 'proprieties and music' sounds odd to the modern ear, the general idea is clear. If the words used to instruct are not accurate, the instructions cannot be accurately followed. Getting language right, down to individual terms, is absolutely essential.[2]

Someone of a philosophical temperament is not in the habit of allowing more-or-less-right or imprecise statements to go unchallenged. They know that many big mistakes start from getting something just a little wrong. For example, recorded crime is not the same as actual crime, deaths attributed to a cause are not the same as deaths due to that cause, reported incidents are not the same as actual incidents. Yet our talk of crimes, deaths and incidents often doesn't distinguish between the phenomena themselves and the recorded data about them. 'Crime has gone up,' we say, not 'Reported crime has gone up.' A failure to make these distinctions can lead to major errors. More effective policing might lead to more reporting, making people think there is more crime when there is actually less. More accurate reporting in health care often leads to more reported cases of ill health, which people routinely mistake for there being more actual cases. When describing facts we should do so as accurately as possible, to avoid such misunderstandings. Nit-picking isn't wrong when your job is to find nits, and being precise with your words is entirely right when your job is to reason well. So how do we best ensure we get our words right?

There's an old joke, though not a terribly funny one, that if you ask a philosopher whether they agree with a statement, instead of giving you a straight answer they will ask what that statement means. Do you believe in free will? *What do you mean by 'free will'?* Is democracy the best form of government? *What do you mean by 'democracy'?* Would you like pudding? *What do you mean by 'pudding'?*

The call to 'define your terms' can be infuriating, but if we're talking about serious ideas rather than menu choices, it's basic cognitive hygiene. In too many arguments people talk past each other because they use the same words to mean different things. For example, much hot air has been wasted by people who think that calling an organisation 'institutionally racist' is a slur against its non-racist members. But as the UK's Commission for Racial Equality says, 'If racist consequences accrue to institutional laws, customs or practices, that institution is racist whether or not the individuals maintaining those practices have racial intentions.' This guideline takes its lead from the 1999 Macpherson Report into the death of the Black teenager Stephen Lawrence, which defined institutional racism as 'The collective failure of an organisation to provide an appropriate and professional service to people because of their colour, culture, or ethnic origin.' Any discussion of institutional racism is doomed to be confused if we are not clear about its particular meaning, which distinguishes it from ordinary racism.

Sometimes, however, it's not as simple as 'Define your terms.' In many debates, the whole dispute is about how to define the key terms. There would be no philosophical debate about what knowledge is, for example, if you could answer the question simply by looking in a dictionary. Here is a seeming paradox: in order to know what we're trying to define, we already have to have an understanding of the term in question; but if we have an understanding of the term in question, why can't we already define it? Take the nature of justice. Philosophers disagree about what justice is and what it requires. But how can they meaningfully discuss their differences if they don't know what 'justice' means and are talking about the same thing? And if they know what it means, why don't they already agree about how to define it? This is the paradox of analysis, formulated by the influential British philosopher G. E. Moore in 1903 and baptised by the American C. H. Langford in 1942.[3]

The answer starts with the realisation that you don't need to be able to define a word to use it correctly. Children could never learn how to speak if they had to know the definitions of the first words they used. Words have to come before definitions because definitions are made up of multiple words. Meaning comes from elsewhere. As Wittgenstein wrote, 'For a *large* class of cases of the employment of the word "meaning" – though not for all – this word can be explained in this way: the meaning of a word is its use in the language.'[4] To be able to use a word properly is to know its meaning.

The general approach has been given an empirical basis by the psychologist Eleanor Rosch. She says that we first learn how to use words by grasping their prototypical usages. This is how children learn words: we point at cats and say 'cat', sitting people and say 'sit', get close to the fire and say 'hot'. In each case the word is learned by its most prototypical, unambiguous uses.

But the meanings of words can extend beyond the core prototypes to other closely related things, activities or qualities. Hence a cat can also be any number of wild felines, or even an inanimate stuffed toy. Words can be used non-literally, which is why a bird can sit on a branch, even though it is technically standing. They are also used metaphorically, so that a person or product can be 'hot', irrespective of its actual temperature. When meanings move far enough away from the prototype we reach a word's borderline uses, where it may not be clear if it is correct to use it in that context. Is a fallen log in the woods a chair if I can sit on it? Is my coffee still hot when it has cooled to 60° or is it merely warm? It is foolish to demand precise answers to these questions because the legitimate scope of most words isn't precisely demarcated.

Sometimes, meaning *is* fixed by strict definitions – note how

Wittgenstein said the meaning-as-use principle did not apply to all words. In science, terms like force, mass and velocity are given precise definitions. We can also define words for legal reasons, creating absolute distinctions between minors and adults, employees and contractors, married couples and cohabiters, and so on.

All this explains why it is possible to have a genuine puzzle about what a concept like 'truth' or 'justice' means while being perfectly able to use the word in everyday speech. These concepts have prototypical uses that few would argue with. Gratuitously killing an innocent person is unjust, lying is not telling the truth. But away from these clear-cut cases there is more ambiguity, and we can disagree about how words should be used. Ordinary language has given us these loose concepts, and many have the desire to make them tighter.

This desire may sometimes be a quirk of personality that reflects the needs of the speaker more than those of the human community of knowers. Who cares whether a flatbread is a pizza or a man'oushe if it tastes good? But often, being as precise as possible with our words is essential, or at least very helpful, for effective communication and understanding.

Consider that many words have multiple meanings, and if we mistakenly or deliberately switch one usage for another we commit the fallacy of equivocation. 'Right', for example, can mean 'correct', 'a human or legal right', and 'the opposite direction to left'. Having a right to do something does not make it right to do it, yet many seem to elide these two meanings of 'right'. I have a right to be offensive, but it is often wrong to act on it. Less seriously (usually, at least), everyone has had the experience of trying to work out which way to turn in a car, making a suggestion and being met with the reply 'right', unsure if it means 'correct' or 'not left'.

Sometimes, the purpose of making a concept more precise

is not to identify its true meaning but to advocate for what that meaning should be. 'Justice' is not, as Plato thought, a universal, timeless concept waiting for us to discover its essence. Justice is for us to shape and form. The word doesn't tell us if it requires economic equality, the abolition of distinctions made on the basis of biological sex, mitigation for deprived childhoods, and so on. That does not mean justice can be defined however we want. It has to be rooted in the everyday concept or else we are just using the same letters to mean something else. But among the range of possible ways in which justice could be made more precise, nothing about the given concept itself can fix which definition we should settle on.

One of the cheapest rhetorical moves is to stipulate that a word means such-and-such and call an end to the debate. But advocacy requires arguments. You can't just say that you are using a word in a certain sense – you have to offer reasons why that's the meaning we should all use.

Very often, linguistic advocacy is surreptitious rather than explicit. Definitions are often stipulated, sometimes implicitly, and it is not noticed when the stipulations are questionable. The two main ways in which stipulative definitions work by stealth are by high and low redefinition. High redefinition *narrows* the usual meaning of a word. For example, populist politicians say they speak for 'the people', but on any normal understanding of 'the people' it is obvious they don't speak for them all. The meaning of 'the people' becomes implicitly narrowed, so that if you disagree you are not among the 'true people' but become their enemy. Similarly, when people talk of 'true patriots' the intention is to exclude many from the category of the patriotic on the basis that they don't agree with what the stipulators say patriotism requires.

Low redefinition works in the opposite way, by diluting the meaning of a word to make it more inclusive. For example, Humanists UK once used opinion poll data to suggest that there were 17 million humanists in the UK, around a third of the population. That claim required a flagrant diluting of what it means to be a humanist. A necessary criterion for being humanist is not believing in any gods or supernatural forces, but the poll didn't ask about that. Rather, humanists were counted as anyone who agreed with three humanist beliefs: the importance of evidence for understanding the universe, the possibility of explaining right and wrong by human nature alone, and the idea that moral judgements are based on the effects of actions on people, society and the world. It's like asking people if they agree with three beliefs about animal rights and concluding they are vegans, without asking them if they only eat plants. As a patron of Humanists UK, I'm afraid to admit that the desire to highlight the truth that there are more people in Britain who are humanist in outlook than self-identify as humanists led them to lower the bar for being a humanist, exaggerating their prevalence.

An important example of a debate (although that may be too genteel a word) which hinges on advocacy for the right scope of a contested word is the one over the best way to promote the rights of trans people. Although this is a question that goes to the core of how people perceive themselves, a lot hinges on a disagreement about how we should use words. Are 'woman' and 'man' categories determined by objective biological sex, or are they social constructs that could be used by someone with none of the prototypical biological markers? The obvious answer is that they are both: a person has both a sex (biological) and a gender (a socially constructed identity). If we agree with that, the disagreement then becomes not about how things are but how we should best socially regulate the use of these categories. In other words, in which situations, if any, should 'woman' and 'man' be understood as biological categories and in which should they refer to gender?

One reason why it's more complicated than this is that many people believe that only one of these usages is legitimate. Some argue that gender identity makes no sense, as it doesn't pick out any real quality of 'womanhood' or 'manhood', merely a personal feeling. Others believe that the biological categories 'male' and 'female' aren't objective, as all scientific concepts are human artefacts. Others believe that biological categories are real but irrelevant when considering how we should address and recognise people in the social world. In other words, they are legitimate only in the narrow domain of biology.

There can be no hope of resolving the issue of how best to protect trans rights unless all protagonists recognise that this is not, and never could be, a simple matter of people facing the facts. Both sides have to argue why their preferred usage is the best way for promoting the rights of both trans people and those who identify with their biological sex. Both sides are engaged in *advocacy* for their preferred usages of sex and gender language; they are not simply trying to show that one usage is objectively correct.

The power of well-defined words to sharpen our understanding explains why philosophers have always been so keen to make new conceptual distinctions. Take, for example, Gottlob Frege's distinction between *sense* and *reference*, which has been canonical in Western philosophy since the philosopher, logician and mathematician published his seminal paper in 1892. The reference of a noun is the thing or class of things to which it refers. So if you want to know the reference of 'cat', just point to some cats. The sense is the meaning of a word and this isn't exactly the same. For example, 'Rover' and 'your dog' could refer to the same animal. But 'Rover' and 'your dog' do not have the exact same sense. 'Rover' is a proper noun belonging entirely to this hound, while 'your dog' is a description that hinges on the relationship between you and him. If you gave Rover up for adoption, the sense of both terms wouldn't change and nor would the reference of Rover, but the reference of 'your dog' would either vanish or transfer on to the spurned hound's replacement.

In practice, human beings are instinctively good users of language and context tends to avoid most potential confusions that could arise from the sense/reference distinction. But sometimes the difference can trip us up, or even be used to intentionally mislead. For example, in April 2016 the UK government introduced a national living wage for everyone aged twenty-three and older. Until then, the sense of 'living wage' was 'the remuneration received for a standard work week by a worker in a particular place sufficient to afford a decent standard of living for the worker and her or his family'.[5] The UK government borrowed the term and used it to refer to the national *minimum* wage, essentially just rebranding it. Hence the Living Wage Foundation claims that the government's new, official 'living wage' does not refer to what they call the 'real living wage'. In 2020/21, for example, the government's 'living wage' was £8.91 per hour, whereas the real living wage, as calculated by the Living Wage Foundation, was £9.50, and £10.85 in London, where the cost of living is higher.[6]

This is Orwellian doublespeak in practice: using a word or phrase that has a clear sense to refer to something that doesn't match that sense at all. Many communicators use this tactic. Foods are labelled 'healthy' or 'natural' when the ingredients or the factory process would not remotely accord with your sense of what 'natural' means. Hyperbolic phrases like 'incredible value' are used to refer to things that are actually a rip-off. Sense is hijacked by an ill-matched referent and we don't always notice.

You could call this *semantic slide*: a word generally assumed to mean one thing is used slightly differently, but by a shift subtle or gradual enough to go unnoticed. Such sliding is easiest where words have ambiguous meanings. This is a common sales ploy.

Marketers use a word or phrase intending it to be understood one way when its true meaning is something else. Ambiguity is used as a deliberate strategy of deception. One of the most egregious examples is the use of the word 'farm' to conjure images of fields full of happy animals. But today a farm could, and usually does, refer to a fully enclosed feedlot where the animals can't even move, let alone go outside. This is not the kind of 'farm' that someone who sees a 'farm-fresh' label thinks of. In this context 'farm' captures no meaning, only associations. It adds no information, since until the day when food can be made and not grown, all food is from a farm.

Ambiguity is a constant threat to clear thinking and communication. The real-world implications of ambiguity can be deadly serious. A key reason why Derek Bentley was hanged in 1953 for the murder of a policeman is that he said to his accomplice, who was pointing the gun, 'Let him have it.' In English argot, this phrase can mean hit, kick or shoot him. But it can also mean 'Let him have the gun,' which would have been a sensible response to the police officer's command, 'Hand over the gun, lad.' Bentley's use of the ambiguous expression probably cost him his life.

When we fail to clear up potential ambiguities, our disagreements can end up being more about words than matters of substance. The Australian philosopher David Chalmers has a useful tip to help us get beyond 'essentially verbal disputes'. He says that the question we should start with is not 'What is the one true meaning of this word?' but 'What role do we need this word to play?'

Take his example of free will. Almost everyone believes that we have the capacity to make choices free from coercion, as a result of our internal decision-making processes – all, of course, under the influence of our history and environment. Some say that this amounts to free will, others argue that this is not enough. They believe it is also important that our choices ultimately originate in ourselves, and that it is in no way inevitable, given your history and environment, that you make one choice instead of another in any given situation. Without this escape from inevitability, they argue that our notions of responsibility, praise and blame make no sense.

There's no straightforward way of saying who is right about what 'free will' *really* means. It's more fruitful to ask: what role does the concept of free will need to play in how we make sense of our lives and selves? Should it be reserved for the second, stronger sense of acting freely or is it OK to use it to apply to uncoerced choices? We need to decide on this before we can say whether we have free will or not, otherwise we might agree about what degree of freedom we have and simply disagree about what the right name for it is.

Often, there isn't a right or wrong answer about the 'correct' usage. As Chalmers says, 'It may well happen, and I think that it does happen, that two different people are interested in totally different roles. [. . .] It takes quite a lot of work to figure out what the role you're actually interested in is.' We just have to be clear about which one is in play.

Think back to the transgender issue. The question isn't simply 'What do words like "man" and "woman" mean?' It's 'What role do we need them to play?' Do we need these words to make biological distinctions or some other kind of distinction? This illustrates how although getting words right is important, these disputes are not 'merely linguistic'. The language matters because when we choose which words to use, with what meanings, we are identifying what we think matters.

Despite the reputation of philosophers for being abstruse, I've found that the ones I have most admired are almost obsessed with being as clear as possible, and are meticulous in their use of language. The broadcaster Joan Bakewell, who has met many philosophers in her illustrious career, has also noticed this, saying, 'Philosophers use words that are current and that we all use, but they use them so exactly that if you listen to them and then try to interpret what they're saying loosely, that won't do.'

Roger Scruton, for instance, said: 'I lead a studious life and work extremely hard at getting the right word, the right sentence and so on, which I needn't bother with if I didn't have that sense that this is of intrinsic value. If I didn't do that but just wrote sloppily I wouldn't be able to propagate any message.'

Many philosophers value writing for a non-professional audience precisely because it forces them to be clearer. John Searle talked about the 'tremendous intellectual discipline' of writing for the general reader. 'I feel if you can't say it clearly you don't understand it yourself. So partly it's for my own benefit.' When you are forced to spell things out clearly, 'the intellectual weaknesses in your own ideas are much more obvious'.

Simon Blackburn laments that, too often, obscure academese crowds out clear language. He has a delightful put-down of his colleague Michael Dummett, famous for his intellect but notorious for his impenetrable prose: 'Clearly, Dummett swims in deep philosophical waters here. But whether he throws us a lifebuoy or pushes us under is a moot point.'

The impenetrability of much philosophical prose is, sadly, often purely a matter of bad writing rather than of any inherent difficulty in the ideas. The broadcaster Melvyn Bragg provides evidence for this when describing his friendship with the great Peter Strawson, one of the most respected post-Second World War British philosophers. 'There was an enormous precision and a weighting of words that I loved,' said Bragg;

With Peter, I never found it difficult to discuss or even to argue with him. But when I tried to read his books, I found myself stubbing my mind on it quite often. It was clearly in the English language and there were clearly beautifully balanced sentences, but it did require a particular sort of training which I hadn't had. Reading some [philosophy] books I soon feel there's a bigger tide coming against me than pushing me out to sea.

Sometimes it seems that philosophers are proud of how difficult it is to read them. Not so T. M. (Tim) Scanlon, the American moral philosopher whose first book *What We Owe to Each Other* inspired the TV comedy *The Good Place*. He recalls how his father, a lawyer and highly literate man, 'really looked forward to reading my book and then was terribly disappointed when he found it was unreadable'. Scanlon can't fault his father's judgement. 'It is in a way unreadable. One of the reader's reports for the press when it was published said "This book is written in ordinary English – there are no symbols, little of what could be called technical terminology – but this appearance is entirely misleading."' It takes an open-ended afterlife for one of the main characters in *The Good Place* to be finally able to finish Scanlon's book.

Some people mistake difficult prose for inherently deep and complex ideas; others see opaque sentences as sure signs of pseudo-profundity. Both equations are simplistic. Some excellent thinking is badly expressed, and some bad thinking is conveyed with deceptive eloquence and lucidity. Scanlon is an example of the former. He's an excellent philosopher, well worth the considerable effort it takes to read him.

The politician and philosopher Jesse Norman offered a good defence of difficult writing. 'I don't think it's the worst thing in the world for an idea to be slow in getting to its elevator pitch. The problem with the world is not that there are too many deep ideas lacking a snappy summary, it is that there are too many shallow ideas *with* a snappy summary.'

Timothy Williamson would surely agree. He is sometimes hard to follow, but not because he is being anything other than as clear as his subject matter allows. When I interviewed him, his answers sounded almost hesitant, and there were frequent pauses between clauses and even single words. Yet when I later transcribed our conversation I found, unusually for an interviewee, that almost all his sentences are perfectly formed, as are the thoughts they express. His speech reflects an important virtue of thinking: the desire to be as precise as is possible, not more and no less.

The desire for clarity can, paradoxically, be a reason why some prose is hard to understand. To be precise in your thinking you often have to make subtle conceptual distinctions, and this can require coining new terms. This 'jargon' can become off-putting and hard to decode, but it exists for a reason. Perspicuity and precision are sometimes in conflict: to be precise you may have to use technical words, or give familiar ones a more technical meaning. In philosophy, language is often not so much off on holiday as on a secondment.

Precision also sometimes requires sentences that may at first sight look circumlocutory. I have often found that when copy-editors are let loose on my work, the worst ones react badly to some sentences that seem a little too convoluted, but their more 'elegant' reworking subtly changes the meaning in ways that are crucial. Complex ideas sometimes require complex, awkward syntax that a poet could never tolerate.

The problem with much difficult philosophy is not that sometimes we have to use difficult language, but that 'the machine has started to go on on its own,' as Bernard Williams put it. This approach leads to 'scholasticism', which Williams defined as 'pursuing distinctions beyond a point at which they have anything to do which would worry any grown-up person about this kind of subject matter.' Tim Crane believes one reason for this kind of obfuscation, in certain specialisms at least, is that 'Everyone wants to carve out a little space for themselves so a lot of people make things spuriously technical.'

Williams concluded that 'Something can be over-distinguished or under-distinguished. The need for another distinction always has to show itself. You shouldn't do it just for the hell of it.' The best thinkers only use technical language when it is required to be more precise than the everyday variety. Like any piece of specialist equipment, jargon is invaluable when it it is strictly necessary and pointless when an ordinary word will do.

Some philosophers become too enamoured of their technical terms. Wittgenstein warned of 'the bewitchment of our intelligence by means of our language', and this spell can be cast by ordinary or specialised ways of speaking. Words shape our thoughts and sometimes that can make them misshapen. One way this can happen is by means of what the Oxford philosopher Gilbert Ryle called 'category mistakes' in his 1949 classic *The Concept of Mind*. These occur when we take a word to refer to one kind of thing when it actually refers to another. For example, when Basil Fawlty, in the TV series *Fawlty Towers*, told his dinner guest that he couldn't make him a Waldorf Salad because 'we just ran out of Waldorfs' he was mistaking *an ingredient for a salad* with *a way of composing a salad*.

Were I to be even more ignorant about technology than I am, I might make a category mistake when I think about how this document is being backed up in 'the cloud'. I could imagine that 'the cloud' is a single, unified thing: either a huge memory bank somewhere in the Nevada desert or perhaps an ethereal storage facility in the sky. These errors would be natural because 'the cloud' is a proper noun, and proper nouns are supposed to refer to specific things. But 'the cloud' is actually just a worldwide network of interconnected, physical storage facilities, and my data is stored in such a way that it is distributed among them, not just in one place. My category mistake would be to think of the cloud as a single thing when it in fact refers to a network of things and their configuration.

Ryle thought that many of us make a category mistake when we think about the mind. To say we have a mind is not to say we possess a non-material thing inside our heads. Rather, it is to say that we have the capacity for thought and consciousness. Like a song or a poem, a mind exists in physical substances but it is not itself an object.

The contemporary philosopher of religion Richard Swinburne, who holds the unfashionable 'dualist' view that mind and body are two distinct substances, continues to make this mistake. When I interviewed him about this, he began his summary of his argument by saying, 'There are things and they have properties. I am a substance, I have properties.'

This opening sentence begs the very question he is trying to answer: 'What is the nature of the self?' He asserts 'I am a substance,' putting his self into the category of substances. This rules out the possibility that the self is not a substance, but something that arises from the functioning of a substance, like music emerging from a speaker, or the software running on a computer. Clearly, whatever I am, I am 'embedded' in a substance, a human animal, but that does not mean the activities that make me *me* – such as thought and emotion – are themselves substances.

Our understanding of the world is often distorted by such bewitchments of language. Take one more example, from psychotherapy. Because words like 'treatment' and 'patient' are often used, many assume that mental health is just like physical health. So they believe that addiction can be treated like an illness, when addiction is not something that can be 'cured', nor can it be managed by the application of 'treatment' alone.

If, as many therapists do, we talk about 'working with clients' rather than 'treating patients' the differences between mental and physical health become more obvious.

The way to avoid such bewitchment is, as ever, to play close attention. Words bring with them associations and implications, many of which go under the radar of conscious awareness. The question we need to ask ourselves is 'Are there any ways in which these words, or the way they are arranged, are leading me astray?' Or, to put it even more simply, 'Does this mean what I think it means?'

One important aspect of meaning is how precise a given word or phrase is. Just as we can be too imprecise with our language, we can also go wrong when we try to make language more precise than it is. One way of doing this is to take something too literally. If you're told to read someone the riot act you should not literally recite the text of the Riot Act 1714 to them. In such cases, to interpret someone's words literally is to interpret them wrongly.

Literalness has become a key issue in debates about religion. Assertive atheists have sometimes been quick to argue that because the universe was created by the big bang and not in six days by God, and that the Bible is not the word of God but the work of human writers, therefore religion is false and that's all there is to be said. In response, many people have defended religion on the grounds that – in its best forms at least – it is not about such literal truths at all. As the philosopher and formerly ordained Catholic priest Anthony Kenny put it, 'Though I believe religions are not literally true, they have a great poetic value and philosophers have not really done enough reflecting about poetic kinds of meaningfulness and how they fit into science on the one hand, and how one should live one's life on the other.'

Although I agree with Kenny, it would be a mistake to assume that religious language is *always* non-literal. For many believers, possibly the majority, it is not only literally true that Jesus rose from the dead and that God hears their prayers, it really *matters* that these truths are literal. They don't want metaphorical life after death, they want to go to heaven. So you need to know *how* literally people are using religious language if you want to have a constructive discussion with them, neither assuming that they are literalists nor that they must be speaking poetically.

Sometimes the problem is not that we take other people too literally, but that we take ourselves too literally, without realising it. This was part of Mary Midgley's critique of approaches to philosophy and science that take there to be some unequivocal verifiable facts that alone are the proper objects of knowledge. From the 1970s to her death in 2018 she argued that many of these so-called facts are metaphors in disguise. 'What people take to be proper, official thinking is often a paired-down version of a myth and metaphor that they've been using,' she said. If we use these metaphors and forget that they are metaphors, we soon end up in a muddle. Midgley was particularly concerned about using mechanistic language to describe human beings, such as 'The human mind just is a computer made of meat.' Midgley argued that 'It's not just that people are using metaphors of which they are not totally aware but they use these metaphors explicitly as facts.'

Midgley's views are not universally popular among philosophers, many of whom argue that they know the difference between a metaphor and a literal statement, thank you very much, and are not at risk of confusing the two. The force of Midgley's argument is certainly diminished by the fact that she chose the wrong (metaphorical) hill on which to (metaphorically) die. In a famous, or perhaps notorious, paper she criticised the biologist Richard Dawkins for talking of 'selfish genes' when genes cannot be selfish, since they have no agency.

She thought the problem with this metaphor was that it led people to believe that human beings, not just their genes, are naturally selfish.

But Dawkins was very precise with his metaphor, aware that it was a metaphor and explicit that it did not mean whole human organisms – that is, persons – are necessarily selfish. Midgley's mistake, it seems, was a form of confirmation bias: she was so confident about the truth of her own theory that she saw evidence for it everywhere, even when it was absent. To a hammer, everything looks like a nail; to Midgley, everything looked like a misused metaphor.

The moral of this story is an important one: the problem with many theories is not that they are wrong, but that they are not Rosetta Stones for decoding everything. Good thinking requires that we do not run away with any ideas, even the best ones.

Even if it is true that our speech contains many hidden metaphors, when discussing ideas we are usually better off speaking as directly as possible. Digressions and gnomic utterances are to be avoided. 'Get to the point!' we say. But sometimes we express ourselves better by *not* getting to the point, or at least by getting to something which is not nearly as sharp.

This way of thinking is strongly evident in the Daoist and Zen traditions. In both, there is a kind of suspicion of words. The world always escapes full capture by language. According to the seventh-century Buddhist text the *Shurangama Sutra*, language is like 'a finger pointing at the moon'. If someone 'looks at the finger instead and mistakes it for the moon, he loses not only the moon but the finger also. Why, because he mistakes the pointing finger for the bright moon.'[7] Words point us towards that to which we need to attend; they themselves should not be the ultimate focus of attention.

Pointing at the moon is fairly straightforward. But sometimes we need to give verbal directions that are less clear. The nineteenth-century Danish philosopher Søren Kierkegaard was a master of this. Most of Kierkegaard's works are not straightforward treatises but fictions, written from the point of view of various pseudonyms, including a judge, a seducer and an editor called Hilarius Bookbinder. Kierkegaard believed that you could not critique any form of life from an entirely objective, external standpoint. World views had to be examined from within: that was the way to reveal most completely their internal strengths or contradictions.

The essayist, historian and philosopher Jonathan Rée sees this same spirit in one of Kierkegaard's successors. 'Like Kierkegaard before him, Wittgenstein realised that there are forms of philosophical intelligence that do not lend themselves to direct explanation or explicit communication. [...] Wittgenstein knew, as he once put it, that philosophy must be "written like poetry".'

Wittgenstein goes too far: not *all* philosophy *must* be written like poetry. But contemporary academic philosophy has made it difficult for anything resembling poetry to be accepted as philosophy at all. This is not the case in Japan, where poetry is a core philosophical genre. The thirteenth-century philosopher Dōgen, for instance, wrote both essays and poems. In Japanese philosophy, 'The important thing is to feel, not to conceptualise,' Kobayashi Yasuo told me. Sometimes it is not possible to convey what one has carefully attended to with the precision of prose and the only way to communicate is through more indirect, poetic language.

Despite the assumption that Western philosophy always requires precise terminology, it is full of words that point towards a meaning without nailing it down. Consider the thirteenth-century Scottish priest, philosopher and theologian Duns Scotus's concept *haecceity* or 'thisness', what it is that makes a thing the particular thing it is. What *haecceity* actually comprises is not clear from the word itself and over the centuries people have come to very different conclusions. The most popular now would seem to be that *haecceity* doesn't exist, since few philosophers have a theory of it at all.

Or take the more modern concept 'qualia' (the plural of quale), the subjective feel of experiences. The word exists because most people agree that there is something it is like to be conscious, and qualia refer to this 'something it is like'. But even as a technical term it lacks precision, with the *Stanford Encyclopedia of Philosophy* offering four different definitions. And like *haecceity*, some, most famously Daniel Dennett, deny qualia even exist. He argues that you can accept there is something it seems like to be conscious without positing the existence of these indefinable things called qualia.

I don't want to overstate the importance of vagueness and imprecision. Generally speaking, both are to be avoided. But the idea that we can and must always be precise is to make a demand that cannot be met. All the while that there are things which our minds or language cannot fully and clearly grasp, there will be a need to speak metaphorically, elliptically, poetically. To ban such language as unphilosophical is to say that there are some things we just should not talk or think about at all. Wittgenstein famously said, 'Whereof one cannot speak, thereof one must be silent.'[8] Wisely, he did not say, 'Whereof one cannot speak *precisely*, thereof one must be silent.'

It is not just that language has its limit; every particular language also has its own limitations. Words carve up the world and demarcate certain aspects of experience. Inevitably this means some things escape their capture, and that alternative ways of categorising are left unrealised. Anyone who speaks more than one language will have examples of this. Spanish and Italian have two words for the English 'to be' while English has only one. If you think about it, it is extraordinary that this most fundamental of verbs is conceptualised differently in such closely related languages.

Furthermore, if you've ever tried to explain what the difference is between, say the Spanish *ser* and *estar*, you'll know it's very difficult. You end up with something that reads very much like a philosophical distinction, such as: *'ser'* is used for the permanent nature and quality of a thing and *'estar'* for its temporary and relational properties. No rule explains every usage, however: death is a permanent state but in Spanish you'd say of the deceased *están muertos*. Time is ever changing, yet when it's time for your afternoon *churros con chocolate*, *'son las cuatro'*.

There's no reason why a language couldn't have even more verbs for 'to be'. There are at least four different core senses to the English word: to be an instance of something (Felix is a cat), to have a property (Felix is furry), to be located somewhere (Felix is in his basket), and to mean something else (to be a cat is to be free). Vietnamese has different words for each of these meanings. You could even further divide them: Japanese has two different words for the located sense of 'to be', one for animate and another for inanimate things.

In English, in some contexts the difference between having and being – possessing something and having a property – can be blurred. For example, we can say 'I am grey-haired' or 'I have grey hair.' I would not be surprised if there were a language in which certain possessions are so intimately tied with identity that they are always referred to with the verb 'to be' rather than 'to have'. The link between a people and the land they inhabit might be so essential that they say, 'We are landed' or 'We are homed', never 'We have land' or 'We have a home'. The concept of owning land could be so alien that they would barely understand what having land would mean.

These differences show that the meanings words have are in some sense arbitrary. Yet we often find ourselves using them as though they captured the one true essence of reality. Unfortunately, philosophers have been especially prone to this. For much of its history, Western philosophy's main subject matter has been big abstract nouns: 'What is Truth?' 'What is Beauty?' 'What is The Good?' This is pure folly. There is no one, timeless thing to which these words refer. Consider one of the most pointless questions in philosophy: 'What is Art?' It should be obvious that the single word 'art' applies to a wide and diverse number of things and that to expect to be able to draw a clear line between art and non-art is absurd.

That is not to say philosophers should not be interested in truth, knowledge, the nature of art and so on. It's just that none should come with capital letters. We need to think carefully about the different ways in which such words are used and to focus on the one or ones of greatest philosophical interest.

Take the biggest philosophical abstract noun of them all: meaning. Almost every philosopher will tell you that you can't answer the question 'What's the meaning of life?' without thinking about the meanings of 'meaning' and working through each in turn. To sum up the main ones, we can think of meaning in life as its purpose, goal, significance or value. Each of these terms then needs taking apart. Purpose can be given by a creator, a user or the thing itself. Frankenstein had a purpose for his creature, a slave trader might have a different purpose for it, and the creature himself might reject both and find his own. Your life may be cosmically insignificant, historically significant, and sadly of little consequence to family and so-called friends. It is only by breaking down the possible meanings of meaning that we can make any sense of the otherwise hopelessly vague question 'What is the meaning of life?'

One final way in which language can lead us astray is when we confuse words with the things they refer to. This sounds too basic a mistake to make, but it's clearly there in one of the worst arguments in the history of philosophy: the ontological argument for the existence of God (ontology being the philosophy of the nature of being). Strictly speaking, I should say ontological *arguments*, because they come in infinitely ingeniously different forms. But they all at root have the same basic structure. If we ask what the concept of God means, although we may dispute some details, everyone would agree that God is the most perfect being imaginable. If you then say that God does not exist, you are saying that something perfect does not exist. But if it doesn't exist, it isn't perfect. If I were to say I had baked you a perfect cake, it's just that it doesn't exist, you would rightly think I was talking nonsense. So, a non-existing perfect being is a contradiction in terms and therefore impossible. So – *voilà!* – the perfect being, God, must exist.

Volumes have been written showing why this argument is wrong, and volumes trying to argue that it isn't. But the fundamental flaw is clear enough: you cannot leap from saying anything about the meaning of a concept to the existence of what that concept refers to. I can have the concept of perfect justice, but that doesn't mean perfect justice exists. If a non-existent God is a contradiction in terms, then so is a non-existent perfect unicorn, and that doesn't mean it exists.

A word is a word, not a thing. Language is a tool, not the fabric of reality. We need to use words to help us understand the world, not become so fixated on the words themselves that they, rather than reality, become our subject matter. Words make distinctions, but there are always more and different distinctions than the words of one language make. Words have to be used with care, never taken at face value. When they seem to be telling you they are transparent mirrors of reality, don't believe them.

How to watch your language

- Define your terms.
- Where meanings are contested, argue for your definition, don't just stipulate it.
- Be alert to and avoid high and low redefinition: arbitrarily either broadening or narrowing the meaning of a word to suit your purposes.
- Be alert to and avoid the misuses of ambiguity. In semantic slide, word meanings shift imperceptibly from one appropriate usage to an inappropriate one. This can involve misleading confusions of sense and reference, when words with one sense are used to refer to things that correspond to the word only in another sense.
- Rather than ask what the one true meaning of a word is, ask what work that word has to do in the context in question.
- Use technical words and jargon when it is necessary to make essential distinctions, but not otherwise.
- Beware of category mistakes: thinking that a word refers to one kind of thing when it actually refers to a different one, or not any kind of thing at all.
- Don't read the literal and the non-literal in the same way. Each has its place and each has to be read differently.
- Don't end up getting more bogged down in debates over words than the things the words are about.

6

BE ECLECTIC

> All mankind in our age have split up into units,
> they all keep apart, each in his own groove;
> each one holds aloof, hides himself and hides
> what he has, from the rest, and he ends by
> being repelled by others and repelling them.
>
> FYODOR DOSTOEVSKY, *The Brothers Karamazov*

Etymology tells us that philosophers are lovers (*phili*) of wisdom (*sophia*), but that does not mean others aren't equally enamoured. Good critical thinking requires us to draw on knowledge wherever it is found, and to synthesise information from a wide range of sources.

Say you want to assess the impact of competing economic policies on inequality. You might assume that the only relevant experts you need to consult are economists. But although they can model different scenarios, they can't tell us what kinds and degrees of inequality should matter to us most. Is income equal-ity more important than equality of wealth or equality of access to public services? Economists might have good information on which welfare policies are most financially efficient at targeting the poorest, but they have nothing to say about which system provides more dignity. Indeed, generally speaking, the more tar-geted a welfare policy is, the more it stigmatises. As citizens, we have to decide whether a less 'efficient' system might be better for social cohesion. That's not a question for economics. A prop-erly holistic assessment of competing policies also requires some knowledge of political science, history, sociology, anthropology and philosophy, and probably also psychology.

For almost every question we have to answer, listening to a narrow range of experts limits our abilities to come to a good answer. If you want to know what's good for your health, you need to listen to more than oncologists because they may know little about anything other than cancer. If you want to know about art, consult a range of critics because each has their own tastes and biases. And if you're worried about damp in your house, speak to more than one damp specialist, who is highly incentivised to sell you their solution.

Likewise, don't aspire to think like a philosopher, if that means thinking like someone who is *only* and *narrowly* a phil-osopher. This warning has only become necessary relatively recently. Descartes wrote books on anatomy, Hume was a historian, Spinoza ground lenses, Aristotle did *everything*. Specialisation is a result of the relatively recent academicisation of philosophy and its effects have been profound.

For instance, if I tell a dozen people that I wrote my PhD on personal identity, the chances are that they will have twelve different ideas about what my thesis was about. Every discipline or tradition has its own interest in or angle on the question. If you're steeped in classical Indian philosophy, you might think I was exploring what, if anything, distinguishes *ātman*, the individual self, from *Brahman*, the universal self or world-soul. From a psychodynamic perspective, you might primarily be asking about the role of the unconscious in the formation of identity. As a psychologist, you could be most interested in the sense of self, while a neuroscientist wants to know how the feeling of 'I' is created in the brain. Sociologists and anthropologists might think more about the role of society in shaping identity. In recent Anglophone philosophy, the question has been more squarely on identity as a logical relation: what it is that makes a person the same person over time? So that was the question my PhD addressed.

It is often legitimate to pursue just one of these questions. But in doing so you have to remember that you are investigating *one* question of personal identity, not *the* question. If you are interested in understanding as fully as possible what it means to be *you*, you're not going to be able to come up with a decent answer by approaching it from only one angle.

Most questions that matter do not fall within any one intellectual discipline, and those that do tend to be of interest only to specialist researchers. For most purposes, it is not a good idea to think like a typical contemporary philosopher – or a historian, psychologist, chemist or linguist. The ways in which the disciplines have been organised does not reflect the most compelling ways the world is divided. For instance, whenever I meet a sociologist or an anthropologist, I ask them if there is any compelling reason why the two disciplines are separate. I have yet to hear a persuasive explanation. Most say that the division is a result of a historical accident, which has led to two different families of methodologies and literatures. But in any rational world, they would at least be two more or less distinguishable aspects of one discipline, not two different ones.

Even when disciplinary boundaries are justifiable, their thickness and impenetrability are not. As the former long-serving Labour MP and political theorist Tony Wright said, the academic world has become 'increasingly disaggregated', and 'even disciplines that the outside world think are cognate [such as political philosophy and political science] are not. People just work in these different bunkers.'

I agree with Ziauddin Sardar, who says: 'I do not believe in disciplinary boundaries – that this bit is physics and this bit is chemistry – because I don't think nature behaves like that. [...] For me, you pursue a question and you need to do whatever you need to do to answer that question. If you need to go and learn geology then you need to go and learn geology.'

That, of course, is what philosophers did before the disciplines took on their own modern academic identities. Aristotle studied nature in a lagoon on the island of Lesbos, not reclining at home in Athens. Descartes dissected animals as well as concepts. Hume was better known in his day as a historian than as a philosopher.

It's easy to lambast the academic balkanisation which has made such polymathy a thing of the past. Who could not be against intellectual 'silos' and 'ghettos', and be all for 'joined-up' thinking? But specialisation exists for reasons, many of them good. Most obviously, the global explosion of learning over the last several centuries means that the big picture has become too vast and complex for any one person to be able to paint it by themselves. They might be able to do something original in a small corner, but the whole will mainly be the work of teams. As social animals, we can gain more expertise collectively if different people develop different specialisations. But that does not justify being a myopic and monomaniacal dweller of a narrow intellectual niche. No knowledge or understanding exists in isolation; no discipline is an island, entire unto itself. Specialisation works as a division of knowledge labour, not when it results in a division of knowledge itself.

The efficiency of such a division is evident in the world of ethics committees. Bioethicist John Harris has served on many and says, 'We're all contributing different things, and as long as there is somebody there who can, for example, articulate clearly issues of autonomy, or whatever, I don't think others need to do that.' He brings philosophy to the table and others bring 'detailed scientific knowledge, or in some cases detailed knowledge of social science research, of how to consult the public without prejudging the issues, or about how the operation of something like our own system, the National Health Service, is going to effect the delivery of therapies and preventive strategies'. Only a group could do all that.

Ideally, ethics committees would be just one of many kinds of intellectual collectives in which expertise is shared. Academic life would incentivise some researchers to work on the pieces of the jigsaw and others to put them together. Instead, the biggest academic rewards are for originality and rigour, which means people get promoted and hired for creating little dots, not joining them up. As Tim Crane explains, 'In order to make progress and in order to make your ideas public, you have to focus on something very specific and say something original about that. That means that the old idea of the general philosopher, someone who could say a little about everything, and publish papers on a variety of subjects, is to some extent less common than it was.' The same goes for any kind of academic generalist.

Even if you simply want to paint a slightly bigger picture by joining a cluster of dots, the dilution of expertise this requires often results in a dilution of quality. Crane says witheringly, 'A lot of what counts as interdisciplinary work in philosophy of mind is actually philosophical speculation backed up with certain, probably out-of-date, *Scientific American*-style summaries of research in psychology or neuroscience, which tends to support the philosophical preconceptions of the authors.'

Onora O'Neill, a model eclectic thinker, agrees that 'The great risk of being very interdisciplinary is that rather than meeting the standards of all these disciplines you meet the standards of none of them.'

Another risk of thinking outside of your silo is that you can end up trying to reinvent the wheel without realising that automative engineers already exist and have not just made one, but have refined it countless times. I fear John Searle did this when he said, 'I think we need to invent a new branch of philosophy, which I want to call the philosophy of society.' He confidently said: 'This subject doesn't exist. I'm trying to bring it to birth.'

This sounded odd to my colleague at *The Philosophers' Magazine*, who had a sociology PhD. To him Searle's *The Construction of Social Reality* (1995) sounded very much like *The Social Construction of Reality* (1966), a book written forty years earlier by Peter Berger and Thomas Luckmann. It's not that Searle said nothing that these sociologists hadn't said before. It's just that he waded into the intellectual territory as though it were virgin territory, without engaging with what others had said first.

I don't know what Searle's thinking was, but in many cases, ignoring what other experts have to contribute is the result of pure ignorance. I'm convinced that if academics knew what their colleagues in other departments were working on, they would find plenty to fuel their own thinking. I have a fantasy of universities appointing readers and professors of Synoptic Studies to facilitate these interchanges, but I'm not holding my breath.

Sadly, ignorance is often wilful. I have heard philosophers put down certain other disciplines as less rigorous than their own. The attitude is something like: 'What could sociologists possibly teach philosophers?' Narrowness of vision is not a unique vice of philosophers, but I suspect that the self-congratulatory image of philosophy as the 'Queen of the Sciences' makes them especially prone and that other academics are more open.

For much of the twentieth century, Anglophone philosophy almost prided itself on its smallness. 'One of the real problems in philosophy is that people can be a little bit myopic,' says Daniel Dennett. The 1960s probably saw the nadir of this narrow insularity, when Dennett was a graduate student. 'It was comically cautious and unambitious. I mean, the very idea of trying for a large view of anything! This was miniature little piecework stuff. I thought it was dreadful.'

Perhaps the most unashamed on-the-record embrace of philosophical narrowness I've witnessed came in the form of six short words from Michael Martin. I asked him, 'Are there any key books in the latter twentieth century which are of interest to academic philosophers which have not been written by academic philosophers?' He replied, 'Not that I can think of.' When pushed, he defended himself robustly:

> I don't think there's a general answer about who you should be reading. On the whole, you ought to be reading as broadly as you can, but also in as much depth as you can and there's a limited amount of time that you can study. [...] There are good examples of brilliant philosophers who paint with a very small palette of figures with whom they engage. So general prescriptions here are, I think, foolish.

Martin's concluding remark should be taken seriously. There is always room for narrow specialists and not everyone ought to read widely. But my conviction is that narrowness is a vice more often than it is a virtue, and that the risks of breadth are worth taking more often than they are not. Most of time, the issue is not *whether* to think eclectically but *how* to do so well.

Onora O'Neill is a model of how to balance the virtues of specialisation and breadth of scope. 'I suspect I've always been an awful trespasser,' she says, revealing in one self-deprecating sentence the humility required to go beyond what you know best. I like it that she has 'always made a point of lunching with people who weren't necessarily in my own discipline', although sadly this is not an option for those of us who don't live Oxbridge college life.

We can emulate her more easily by being careful not to try to run before we can walk when treading on unfamiliar ground. She said that, for a long time, 'I kept my philosophy and my bioethics quite strictly separate' because 'it was hard to achieve philosophically rigorous standards doing bioethics.' To cast your intellectual net wide requires a constant awareness of how much you *don't* know, to avoid diving in too soon and finding yourself out of your depth. However, over time O'Neill became more confident that she had something to say, and in 2000/01 she gave the prestigious Gifford Lectures on Autonomy and Trust in Bioethics and in 2002 the BBC Reith Lectures on 'A Question of Trust' in public life more generally.

You don't always have to be an expert to make a valuable contribution to a debate. Sometimes it is an advantage to be an outsider, as it enables you to notice what insiders take for granted. But you should always do your best to understand what it is you're getting into, so you can be confident your contributions are pertinent. That's why it is no coincidence that some of the most powerful critiques of philosophy have come from those within it. The American pragmatist Richard Rorty, for instance, became a leading late-twentieth-century critic of the idea that philosophy holds up a mirror to nature, simply describing how reality is. He launched his attack as someone deeply rooted in the tradition he was in the process of abandoning. So when he attacked the idea of 'truth' he did so intelligently, insightfully, unlike the many sloppy relativists who think the possibility of objective truth is so silly it doesn't even need serious arguments to defeat it.

The view from within, however, can be as partial as the

view from without. When I was an undergraduate, we students were thrown head first into many of the greatest philosophical works Europe and its most enduringly colonised nations had produced – 'head first' because we invariably got stuck into analysing the arguments with little to no historical scene setting. 'Modern' philosophy – by which is meant everything from the seventeenth century onwards – seemed to start with Descartes, as though philosophy had taken a near-two-millennia sabbatical after the Ancient Greeks. The historical background we were given was minimal. Most of our reading was *ahistorical*, with no reference to history at all.

My education was not abnormal. I was educated in the 'analytic' tradition of philosophy which has been dominant in the English-speaking world for over a century. In practice this is a broad church and the term is used loosely to cover pretty much all Anglophone philosophy except that which draws mainly on modern continental European philosophy. The family resemblance shared by all analytic philosophy is an emphasis on conceptual analysis, inspired by, but not necessarily using, the methods of logic and natural science. Analytic philosophy has had little time for history, and even less for biography. This ahistoricity is often conscious and wilful. As Michael Martin defended it, 'When you've got an argument there and the argument works, and you've clearly identified that the conclusion seems to follow from the premises, then there is no particular role for the historical context to come into play, other than to possibly explain why that argument became salient.'

I'm not convinced. One mistake this insensitivity to context can lead to is what we might call *the fallacy of domestication*. This is when you understand a writer or an idea so entirely through the lens of your own tradition or background that what you see is not authentic, but a domesticated version in which much has been lost in translation. Take Plato. When you read him today, many of his arguments sound as though they could have been made last week. But with inconvenient frequency, Plato has his protagonist Socrates discuss the deeds of the gods and other myths. For example, *The Republic* concludes with the Myth of Er, the story of a man who dies in battle but whose body does not decompose, and ten days later comes back to life. Er then tells everyone of his journey through the afterlife. Many modern readers ignore this, treating it as little more than a creative adornment to the 'proper' philosophy. But all the signs are that Plato was serious: it is a fairly long passage, one that ends the book, and is used to support Plato's argument for the immortality of the soul. To set aside such passages is to avoid confronting the challenging truth that Plato was not a timeless philosopher who would have been as much at home in twenty-first-century Oxford as in classical Greece, but an Athenian very much of his time.

Simon Glendinning also experienced the distortions of domestication when he first got interested in Wittgenstein. He found himself getting frustrated with the 'gulf between what I was trying to read in the *Investigations* and the secondary literature which, as I thought about it then and still to a degree think about it today, domesticated it'. I had a similar experience with Kierkegaard. His work was the subject of my undergraduate dissertation, and at the time there wasn't a large secondary literature in English. It was only later that I realised that what little there was had extracted from Kierkegaard arguments of a comfortably familiar kind, rather than fully embracing his incredible difference and originality.

Anthony Gottlieb, the author of a brilliant two-volume history of Western philosophy, warns:

You must keep in more than the back of your mind the historical contexts of the questions they were trying to answer, which were often completely different. That's the only way to really understand their arguments. It seems to me quite often that the arguments of a philosopher have been misunderstood because we think he's answering a question we're now interested in whereas in fact he's answering another one.

The historian of ideas Jonathan Israel pulls no punches in his critique of philosophers' wilful neglect of history:

> If the philosopher pays no attention to the context in which things are being said, I don't see how you can then interpret them accurately, because everybody had to fashion what they said in order to accommodate the constraints and pressures at the time. [...] I think it's even a contradiction in terms to imagine that there can be a real philosophy which answers to basic universal human questions and values, which is not historically based. It's an idea that doesn't make sense, even if some people hold it.

To make matters worse, in the absence of serious history, most of us have some kind of ersatz version that goes in its place, providing the implicit background to our understanding. Israel thinks this bad history is at least as much of a problem as is a lack of it. Take the period Israel has been most concerned with: the European Enlightenment. Israel argues that most people have a simplistic idea that natural science and British empiricism lit the torch of secular, naturalistic reasoning, which the French then enthusiastically carried, helping to spread the word across the continent. This reading of history reinforces crude nationalist stereotypes and ignores 'a relatively large body of often illogical or conservative writers'. If you know this, the image you have of the Enlightenment becomes 'dramatically different'. It shows that 'our accepted, official, conventional notions about the history of philosophy are completely distorting everything'.

Israel paints a pretty dismal picture: philosophers with warped vision because they lack a historical lens, historians with gaps in their understanding because they leave philosophy well alone, and everyone with an inaccurate history of ideas which leaves them believing comforting myths instead. One of the most self-serving is that to do philosophy, you only need to know about Greeks and Europeans. Even if you are only and proudly interested in Western philosophy, the neglect of history means that most people are unaware of how important the Islamic world has been in its development. When you're not taught about that, you've had an 'unjust education', according to Ziauddin Sardar. 'What you've missed is from the eighth century to the seventeenth century, a thousand years of philosophy, which is a hell of a lot of philosophy.'

If you need any further encouragement to make history a part of your critical thinking, Kwame Anthony Appiah presents a good case for its positive benefits. In his book *The Honor Code*, Appiah argues that the titular virtue has been given very little moral significance in Western philosophy and makes the reader see its virtues as well as its drawbacks. Unlike much moral philosophy, this is achieved by a careful analysis of how the concept of honour has worked in three specific historical contexts: foot-binding, duelling and slavery. The stories he tells do not just provide illustration and colour; rather, his key claims 'are made plausible by the historical examples'. Without a deep appreciation of context, the contemporary Western reader would not even take the idea of honour as a major moral value seriously since it seemingly 'runs against morality and religion, law and reason'. Appiah believes that the 'normal methods of philosophy', namely 'sitting around in your study thinking', are not up to the job. You need rich, real-life examples to understand how it can be that a practice can be 'wrong in some sense and yet, nevertheless, required, in another sense'.

According to Appiah, you can't even understand what philosophy is unless you understand it as a discipline shaped by its history. Philosophy is 'a historical object, its shape changes over time, but there are continuities. In that sense philosophy is like families and various other things. It grows through time, it changes over time.' Those who learn from history about philosophy know that its shape and borders are constantly shifting and that change and evolution are inevitable.

To be fair to philosophers, they have always been interested in the philosophical history of the problems they are concerned with, citing long-dead thinkers when discussing live problems. Daniel Dennett points out one obvious reason why this is important. 'The history of philosophy is the history of very tempting mistakes made by very smart people, and if you don't learn that history you'll make those mistakes again and again and again. One of the ignoble joys of my life is watching very smart scientists just re-invent all the second-rate philosophical ideas because they're very tempting until you pause, take a deep breath, and take them apart.'

Philosophy has also changed a little in recent years and history is not so egregiously ignored as it once was. But it is still not given as much attention as it should. I would put my own hand up and say that a relative ignorance of history impedes my own thinking.

This is not just a problem for philosophy. You can't begin to understand the situations in places like Palestine, Russia or Afghanistan if you know nothing of their histories. Nor can you have an informed view about the pros and cons of new technologies if you are ignorant about why some past innovations have been used to benefit the powerful and others to serve humankind. The past is a huge repository of data about how human beings and societies work which we ignore at our peril. That's why when David Hume wrote his *History of England* he thought he was continuing his philosophy, not abandoning it.

The neglect of history is part of a wider problem of insensitivity to context. So often we misunderstand people's problems, beliefs, practices and questions because we are blind to the circumstances in which they occur. Consider how many political situations look baffling because we don't even try to understand what would make them more comprehensible. For example, to understand why so many Americans voted for Donald Trump as president, you have to understand just how profoundly disillusioned and cynical many were about the political mainstream, which they believed held them in contempt. For many Trump voters the election was not just another choice between competing political programmes. It was an opportunity to 'drain the swamp' and kick out a political elite perceived as being out of touch with middle America.

Nothing exists in a vacuum, yet too often we think about things as though they do. Context matters and historical context often matters a great deal.

Not all intellectual borders are drawn at the boundaries of disciplines. One of the most important is the distinction between facts and values. This was first explicitly articulated in the West by David Hume in the eighteenth century. He observed that when people reason about morality, they start by talking about 'the nature of things, be that God or human affairs', when

> of a sudden I am surprised to find, that instead of the usual copulations of propositions, *is*, and *is not*, I meet with no proposition that is not connected with an *ought*, or an *ought not*. This change is imperceptible; but is, however, of the last consequence. For as this *ought*, or *ought not*, expresses some new relation or affirmation, it's necessary that it should be observed and explained; and at the same time that a reason should be given, for what seems altogether inconceivable,

how this new relation can be a deduction from others, which are entirely different from it.[1]

Hume's point is a powerful one: you can't logically leap from statements about *how things are* to *how they ought to be*. To put it another way, you can't leap from mere *description* to *prescription*. The 'normative' – how things ought to be – is distinct from the factual.

Ignore this distinction and you risk committing the 'naturalistic fallacy': jumping from facts about what is natural to judgements about what is right or good. People do this all the time, but few as crassly as the actor turned purveyor of quack health products Gwyneth Paltrow, who told *Cosmopolitan* in 2013 that 'I don't think anything that is natural can be bad for you.'[2] Tell that to Nicholas Evans, author of *The Horse Whisperer*, who nearly died and needed a kidney transplant after eating the poisonous webcap mushroom.

The 'natural = good' move is common in reactionary arguments against feminism, in which people claim that certain natural differences between men and women justify treating them differently. The argument is weak, not only because we don't even know how many of these so-called differences – such as assertiveness, empathy and sexual promiscuity – are rooted in nature rather than culture. Even if all sex differences were natural, that wouldn't settle the moral and political issues. For example, we might want more women in boardrooms even if it were true that men are more naturally competitive and so would claim more seats at the table if we didn't stop them. Indeed, male competitiveness might be a very good reason for intervening to stop it getting in the way of cooperation. As Janet Radcliffe Richards said, 'The Darwinian world has no harmony or purpose of its own. If we want to achieve any good at all, trying to leave things to nature is not the way to do it.'

However, the take-home message of the is/ought gap cannot be that we should never combine thinking about facts with thinking about values. If you want to think seriously about the impacts of climate change, food justice, poverty, digital exclusion and so on, you have to be concerned with the facts. But if facts aren't values and you can't get from an *is* to an *ought*, how do you root a moral discussion in facts?

To answer this, start with the most fundamental question of all: if *oughts* can only be grounded in other *oughts*, where does the first *ought* come from? Hume's answer is that the primal *ought* is sympathy, or fellow-feeling. The vast majority of humankind is gifted by nature (or we might now say evolution) to feel the pain of others and to delight in their happiness. This is what motivates us to do good, not any rational or logical principle.

But doesn't this commit just the fallacy Hume himself identified? If 'natural' does not mean 'good', how can he root morality in natural instincts? Hume commits no fallacy here. Hume is not saying that the reason why we ought to be good is that we have natural instincts to be good. He is saying that we can only be good because we have a natural sympathy. He's offering a *causal explanation* for our moral sense, not a *rational justification* of it.

But don't we need a rational justification for moral sympathy? Hume thought not, and I agree. We'd better be right, because no one has convincingly managed to provide a purely rational basis for morality yet. Being able to recognise that pain and suffering are to be avoided is a basic condition of being fully human. If you do not have any moral sympathy, you cannot be argued into feeling it.

If we accept Hume's argument, then often the is/ought gap can easily be plugged. If I argue that 'Factory farming causes needless suffering to animals, therefore it is wrong,' a philosopher will immediately notice that the conclusion doesn't follow:

'therefore' is being misused. It *seems* to follow to most people because, perfectly understandably, they assume a premise which is unstated – an 'enthymeme' – which in this case is 'causing needless suffering is wrong'. That is not a factual statement but a basic moral commitment all decent humans should share. If someone wants to disagree with that, your best response is not to argue but to steer clear of them.

To live with the is/ought gap we have to give up the idea that rationality forms the basis of ethics and accept that it is simply a tool to help us think more clearly about it. If we do that, we soon see that doing the right thing requires a combination of basic moral sympathy and the ability to attend carefully to each particular situation to see how best to act. You cannot treat people with kindness, sympathy, charity or benevolence unless you know what they need, what they want, what is good for them. These are factual matters, ones that we determine mainly by closely attending.

Mary Midgley understood this. 'We are always treating people in ways which we think are appropriate to them as we see them – we think we've got the facts about these people,' she told me. 'If we attend more closely we may often realise that these were not the relevant facts, the facts are more complicated. One's business is not only to respond to the situation in which one finds oneself, but also to make sure that *is* the situation by attending.' When we do this, 'The fact/value distinction is dissolved because if you have a full appreciation of reality you come to know what is the right thing.'

I was talking to Midgley about her peer, the novelist and philosopher Iris Murdoch. 'On Murdoch's view of ethics, we learn what is the right thing to do – the good – by attending to what is the case and increasing our understanding of reality. That's why she thinks art is important, because art increases our sense of reality.' The suggestion is that if you want to think philosophically, you should watch films and plays, and read books, philosophically.

The idea that art is inevitably morally improving is obviously false, as opera-loving Nazis showed. But someone who engages with narrative art forms in the right spirit can learn a lot about ethics from them. Take, for instance, the films of the Iranian director Asghar Farhadi. Farhadi's highly naturalistic films masterfully explore the moral dilemmas and ambiguities of ordinary life, as well as the difficulties of establishing the truth when each person's partial perspective is very different.

Farhadi shows rather than tells us important truths about morality. In *A Hero* there is a scene in which a charity has to decide whether to cover up an embarrassing incident in order to protect its reputation and so go on to do more good work, or to be truthful. You could give a philosophical commentary on this and talk about the conflicting priorities of utilitarian, Aristotelian or Kantian ethics – the best outcome for all, being of good character or fulfilling one's duties respectively. But it is the specificity of the circumstances which makes the dilemma so difficult, preventing the film from reaching a neat, tidy conclusion. Theory is less useful than carefully attending to the situation, as Farhadi does. Proof that you don't need the three-theory framework to get to the heart of this dilemma is that as an Iranian, Farhadi's philosophical sources, if he had any, were likely to be different anyway.

Farhadi's characters are neither heroes nor villains. They are all ordinary people who would not wish to harm anyone. His films show us how easy it is to justify small lies and misdemeanours to ourselves, often in the name of a good cause, and how this can take us down a treacherous path. If you're interested in the nature of morality, Farhadi's movies will teach you as much, if not more, than a theoretical text. These films do not merely illustrate philosophy, they do it.

Martha Nussbaum has been one of the keenest recent advocates of the uses of literature and the arts in philosophy, often drawing on both in her own writing about ethics and politics. 'I imagine a partnership between philosophy and the arts, in which philosophy would provide a focus on ethical issues and the works of art would direct the imagination in a more concrete way. [We] need texts that arouse the sympathetic imagination, if we want not just to talk about it but also to cultivate it.'

Nussbaum talks of the importance of art not only for the sympathetic imagination and emotional empathy, but also for nurturing *cognitive* empathy: the ability to get inside the thought processes of others. This kind of intellectual imagination is sorely needed today. As she says,

> When you deal with situations where in addition to political polarisation you have ethnic and religious polarisation, listening requires not just arguments but a cultivation of imagination. You need to understand where other people are coming from, what their history is, what their experience of life is. [...]Before you condemn you try to imagine and understand where different people are coming from. If you don't do that, it's much easier to engage in hatred, even violence against people.

It is because I believe that we need to draw on a variety of ways of thinking, including the creative, that I decided all the epigrams in this book should not come from recognised philosophers. In the end, I chose quotes from one of the most philosophical writers of all time, Fyodor Dostoevsky. I want to make the point that while it is good to be eclectic, many a single intellectual source is rich enough by itself to merit a lifetime's mining. The tension between depth and breadth can never be removed, only managed.

How to be eclectic

- Approach an issue from more than just one angle so that you're thinking about the whole of it, not just a part.
- Remember that disciplinary boundaries are not nature's boundaries.
- Putting the pieces together is as important as making each one: piece-joiners and piece-makers are both essential.
- Check whether someone has already thought about something before treating it like virgin territory.
- There is always a trade-off between depth and breadth, so be aware of what you're sacrificing when you choose one over the other.
- Respect narrow specialists and be aware of what you don't know before pronouncing on their areas of expertise.
- Be sensitive to context, including the historical, the biographical and the social.
- Do not assume that the question you are asking is the same as the one others have asked. Under the surface, the superficially similar can be very different.
- Avoid *the fallacy of domestication*: thinking about the unfamiliar in ways that are familiar, remaking it in your own image in the process.
- Avoid *the naturalistic fallacy*: arguing from what is natural to what is good or right.
- Respect the is/ought gap. Facts inform our value judgements but they do not ultimately justify them.
- Engage with the arts to develop the emotional and cognitive empathy required to be able to see things differently and to reason ethically. The narrative arts actually do philosophy by showing rather than telling, getting us to attend more carefully – always the cornerstone of good thinking.

7

BE A PSYCHOLOGIST

We must never forget that human motives are
generally far more complicated than we are
apt to suppose, and that we can very rarely
accurately describe the motives of another.

FYODOR DOSTOEVSKY, *The Idiot*

If you were to draw a family tree of academic disciplines, almost all would trace their roots back to philosophy. One by one they left the nest and gained their independence: biology, physics, zoology, rhetoric, psychology, linguistics, economics, politics, meteorology, geology.

One of philosophy's youngest children is psychology. For most of our history, psychology was done by what we now think of as philosophers. David Hume is perhaps the greatest example. Human nature was his main subject and his writings on causation and ethics were at least as much about how we think as how the world works. Even as late as 1890, the author of *The Principles of Psychology*, William James, was identified primarily as a philosopher. At that time psychology was just beginning to separate itself from philosophy, a process begun in 1879 when Wilhelm Wundt opened the first laboratory dedicated to psychological studies at the University of Leipzig.

The separation of psychology and philosophy has come at a price for both disciplines, and philosophy has paid the highest. To oversimplify a little, psychology has taken ownership of how we *do* think while philosophy concerns itself with how we *should* think. For psychology, this has led to a discomfort with 'normative' questions, those concerning how we *should* think or feel. More than once it has taken for granted what is 'healthy' or 'normal' on the basis of often questionable assumptions that time has shown to be prejudices or fashionable theories. This contributed to dreadful mistakes such as the American Psychiatric Association classifying homosexuality as a pathology until 1973, and the persistence of the 'refrigerator mother' theory, which blamed lack of maternal warmth for autism in children. At other times, psychology's unwillingness to grapple with normative issues for fear of compromising its status as a science has left it for others, perhaps less informed, to do this for themselves.

For philosophy, the problem is that to learn how we *should* think you need to know a lot about how we *do* think. Without a proper understanding of how the human mind works, prescriptions for how to use it better can be impractical at best, completely misguided at worst. The human mind rarely proceeds on the basis of pure rationality, without taint of emotion or prejudice. This may be possible when considering the most abstract questions of mathematics and science, but anything involving human affairs must and should involve more than pure logic.

Consider the ways in which philosophy has long made use of thought experiments. Broadly speaking, thought experiments are imaginary, hypothetical scenarios designed to test beliefs or theories. For example, imagine a teletransporter which anaesthetises you, scans every cell in your body, destroys it and creates a perfect copy on Mars that wakes up exactly as you were. It would seem to that person that *you* have just woken up millions of miles away. So is the person on Mars you? This thought experiment is designed to see if we think continuity of mental life in a physically identical body is enough to preserve personal identity, or whether we need continuity of the exact same body, made of the same atoms.

Or imagine a world physically identical to ours in which the *Homo sapiens*, also physically identical to us, were 'zombies', meaning they had no consciousness. If you can do this, does this show that consciousness cannot be explained by our physical properties alone?

I love thought experiments. I've written a whole book based on a hundred of them. But they have serious limitations, flagged up by Daniel Dennett's name for them: intuition pumps. Thought experiments are excellent at eliciting our intuitions, but we cannot assume that these intuitions tell us anything true about the world. They are not arguments, just tools to get arguments going, by forcing us to ask why we have the intuitions that we do and why we think they are right.

For example, if you think you would survive the kind of tele-transportation described above, you have to explain why you believe a person can continue to exist when very clearly that person is a physical replica of an earlier self. That's a bit weird. If you think you wouldn't survive, you have to explain why you believe it is so important for a person to continue to be made out of the exact same stuff. After all, the cells in your body are changing all the time.

In some thought experiments, it is not clear that our intuitions provide any useful steer. The ex-philosophy PhD and musician Mylo says that the problem with many is that 'You don't really know what you're imagining' and 'We don't even know if it's possible.' With the bluntness a career in the music business licenses, he concludes: 'A lot of these thought experiments are a load of bollocks really, aren't they?'

The neuroscientist Anil Seth makes this case a little more subtly against one kind of thought experiment: 'conceivability arguments'. Take the zombies thought experiment above. Seth's synopsis of the argument based on it is 'If you can imagine a zombie, this means you can conceive of a world that is indistinguishable from our world, but in which no consciousness is happening. And if you can conceive of such a world, then consciousness cannot be a physical phenomenon.'[1] In other words, the mere fact that we can imagine physically identical humans, some of which are conscious and others are not, shows that humans' physical characteristics are not enough to account for whether they are conscious or not. But as Seth says, 'Whether something is conceivable or not is often a psychological observation about the person doing the conceiving, not an insight into the nature of reality.' I can imagine a jumbo jet flying backwards, but that doesn't mean it can. I can't imagine that most of what quantum physics says is true, but that doesn't mean that it's false. Being able to imagine a physically identical world in which no one is conscious tells us nothing about whether it is possible. At most it tells us that the concept of a zombie isn't incoherent. But then neither is the concept of a healthy diet comprising only doughnuts. The mere fact that a thought experiment shows us we can or cannot imagine or coherently conceive of something tells us little to nothing about whether that something is the case.

These lessons apply equally to the kinds of hypothetical reasoning we employ in everyday life. We often have to ask ourselves what it would be like if we changed job, ended a relationship, hadn't made *that* awful mistake, elected so and so for president. We can't live without imagining such scenarios, but we need to be careful that we don't mistake the bounds of our imaginations for what is actually possible or likely. Our gut feelings about alternative possibilities need to be subjected to rational scrutiny. The strength of our convictions should not simply follow from the apparent ease with which we can or cannot imagine something.

Thought experiments are especially common in moral philosophy, where they are often used to elicit general principles by means of a concrete example. In Onora O'Neill's seminal paper 'Lifeboat Earth', we are asked to imagine what we would do if we were in a crowded lifeboat with sufficient space and rations for all. Any decent person would say that no one should be thrown overboard or denied their share of the rations. 'Aboard a well-equipped lifeboat any distribution of food and water which leads to a death is a killing and not just a case of permitting a death,' says O'Neill. This established a general principle, 'To deny available resources so as to lead to death is a killing.' So any global economic or political system that denies sufficient resources, with the result of death or serious illness, is also effectively killing people. Even though the world's relatively wealthy do not set out to kill, by participating in a system that deprives people of basic goods 'we nonetheless kill and do not merely allow to die'.

But why should we assume that our reaction to this specific case reveals a more general, robust principle? The psychologists Daniel Kahneman and Amos Tversky tell us that in emotionally laden situations such as the lifeboat, when we are encountering people face to face we decide quickly, intuitively and unconsciously using what they call the mind's 'system 1'. This works very differently to the slow, rational, conscious deliberation preferred by philosophers that they call 'system 2'.

Thought experiments like 'Lifeboat Earth' seem to assume that the best way to work out what we should rationally think is not to rely on cold and rational system 2, but to use hot, emotional system 1 to generate an intuitive response, and then get system 2 to extract a rational principle from it. But why should philosophers, champions of system 2, allow themselves to be led by system 1?

Indeed, many of them do not. Some moral philosophers start with system 1 thinking and go on to argue that if that clashes with the intuitions of system 2, so much for intuition. Their goal is to come up with a rational ethics which bypasses the 'distortions' of emotion. For instance, communists argue that the optimal use of resources would be to distribute from each according to their abilities to each according to their needs, while utilitarians argue that we should act for the greatest good of the greatest number. Both principles entail that although it might seem to a parent that they are justified to pamper their children while others starve, this is wrong. Their favourable treatment is a bias that ought to be overcome.

The problem with this hyper-rational approach is that it does violence to what morality essentially is. As I said earlier, I tend to the view that morality is rooted in psychology, what Adam Smith called 'moral sympathy'. Reason by itself provides no motivation to be kind. To let intuition dictate moral principles may be wrong-headed, but to hand the task of principle formation entirely to the logical mind also seems misguided. What we need is a better way to understand the relationship between what we too neatly call 'reason' and 'emotion'. In a well-ordered mind, these forces are not opposites that compete. Rather there is a dialogue between them, one which recognises, as T. M. Scanlon argues, that emotions can be reasons.

For Scanlon, the category of emotion is too often 'a basket into which people put things as a way of saying you can't argue about it any more, or it's arbitrary or something'. He believes that, in fact, 'to experience most emotions, such as anger or resentment, is to see oneself as having reasons to do various things.' These emotions-as-reasons are not always rationally justified, but they are open to criticism and analysis. 'You know, I resent something, I take myself as having a reason to take revenge,' says Scanlon. 'Well, do I?' Check. Sometimes resentment is justified: someone has taken credit for your work or been rewarded for performing worse than you. Sometimes resentment is unjustified and is nothing more than envy. Emotions are bound up with judgements that are open to such rational scrutiny. Hence Scanlon says, 'I think the idea of a province of reason that's more logical, and emotion which is independent or personal or something, is something we should get away from.'

The seventeenth-century French polymath Blaise Pascal may have been right to say that 'The heart has its reasons, of which reason knows nothing.' But many of the heart's reasons can be known by reason and even moulded by it. Prejudice can be overcome by the realisation that it is baseless, love diminished by knowledge of what is unlovable, sympathy increased by greater understanding. We need to be careful not to create too simplistic a distinction between thinking and feeling, as though only the heart can move us and the head is a kind of disinterested, analytic observer. The ideal we should strive towards, without ever being able to fully arrive at it, is for our emotions and beliefs to be in harmony. When they are not, that is a failure of thinking as well as of feeling. You are not thinking as well or as clearly as you could be if your thinking doesn't motivate you to act in the ways that your beliefs should. For instance, if you're still treating women as inferior to men, even though you don't for one minute endorse the view that they are, you haven't really understood the equality of the sexes at all. There is some kind of short circuit that you need to fix.

That isn't always easy. We can change, we can learn from our past mistakes, we can make choices, we can surprise. Human beings may be 'biological machines', but we are not preprogrammed robots. However, perhaps we overestimate the extent of human plasticity. Wishful thinking and the desire to deny that human action is as subject to laws of cause and effect as the rest of nature can lead us to ignore the wealth of strong evidence that, given how people are, the ways in which people have behaved in the past is one of the best guides to how they will behave in the future.

This is most evident when we think of human groups. Take the Second Gulf War. The Americans and their allies should have known from history that invading a foreign nation, riven with ethnic divisions, and trying to establish a democratic government there from scratch was never going to end well. Yet they managed to convince themselves that this time it would be different.

Or ask yourself: given that non-binding agreements have always failed to slow greenhouse gas emissions sufficiently in the past, is it rational to expect them to suddenly start doing so in the future? If the parties at an intergovernmental conference proclaim, 'This time it's different', aren't we right to disbelieve them?

When anticipating the future, we have to identify what is relevantly different from past precedents. When it comes to human beings, en masse or as individuals, I tend to the pessimistic view that the burden of proof is for people to prove that they have changed. Giving people the benefit of the doubt is an act of generosity, not rationality.

Consider a mundane example. Imagine Jo has set up a business three times and failed every time. She now has a fourth venture. Sceptical friends and bankers look at her track record, and have no reason to think her fortunes will change. Jo says that she has learned from her mistakes and this time she'll succeed. Jo risks self-deception and wishful thinking while others risk judging her too much on her past record rather than on the merits of the current plan. There is no general principle of learning from the past that tells us who is right. But if we erred towards the sceptical, we would be right more often than we were wrong. The onus of proof is on Jo to explain why it should be different this time. People can change, but I think an honest look at the evidence suggests that they do not do so as much or as often as we'd like to think they can.

This is not the only way in which a knowledge of psychology leads us to a wary assessment of our ability to overcome our entrenched habits of thought. Thanks to the popularisation of the work of brilliant psychologists like Dan Ariely, Daniel T. Gilbert, Daniel Kahneman, and others not called Dan, such as Elizabeth Loftus, there can be few people left in the world unaware that our thinking is systematically distorted by myriad cognitive biases.[2] In some ways we have become *too* aware. Steven Pinker laments, 'In social science and the media, the human being is portrayed as a caveman out of time, poised to react to a lion in the grass with a suite of biases, blind-spots, fallacies and illusions.'[3] It is common to hear people say that rationality is a mirage, no more than a set of rationalisations for our prejudices, instincts and prior beliefs.

We need not be so pessimistic. The fact that psychologists have uncovered so many of these biases is itself evidence for the power of reason to expose error and illusion. While it is naive to think we can ever fully overcome our limitations, it is possible to become more aware of the tricks our minds play on us and so think better.

Take confirmation bias. This is the tendency to take note of evidence and arguments that support our beliefs and gloss over those that challenge it. This has recently been renamed 'myside bias' to emphasise the extent to which the confirmation we seek is that which suits ourselves.[4] An all-too-typical example is when someone who believes in the efficacy of an unproven herbal medicine latches on to every anecdote of someone getting better after taking it while ignoring those who don't and the studies that show it's no better than a placebo. They also ignore the obvious fact that most people get better in time anyway. The simplest explanation of their recovery is the natural 'regression to the mean': the tendency of any system to go back to its normal state of equilibrium. This regression tends to begin soon after symptoms near their worst, which is precisely when most start their 'remedies'. People prefer the weaker theory that the treatment worked, because this is the explanation they want to hear. When we assume we know what the right conclusion should be, bad arguments in favour of it tend to look stronger than they are.

You might think that a rigorous thinker, such as a philosopher, should be able to overcome this obvious weakness. But philosophy can actually make it worse, since advanced reasoning skills can enable people to come up with ingenious arguments to explain away any apparent conflict their views may have with reality. David Hume spotted this centuries before modern psychologists did. 'The passion for philosophy', he wrote, 'may only serve, by imprudent management, to foster a predominant inclination, and push the mind, with more determined resolution, towards that side, which already draws too much, by the bias and propensity of the natural temper.' The result is rationalisation rather than rationality: the 'natural indolence' of the mind 'seeks a pretence of reason, to give itself a full and uncontrouled indulgence'.[5]

It's difficult to identify indisputable examples of this, because such is the cleverness of philosophers that their rationalisations can be better than some people's unmotivated reasonings. I'm fairly convinced, however, that Richard Swinburne's solution to the problem of evil can only be a rationalisation. The problem of evil is that it seems impossible that the world could be governed by an all-loving, all-powerful, all-knowing God given how much pointless suffering there is in it. It must be that God doesn't know about it, doesn't care about it, or can't stop it. Whichever it is, that would cease to make him God as we know it.

Attempts to answer this are called theodicies. The most popular theodicies argue that suffering is unavoidable and necessary, so even the best possible world has to include it. Hence Swinburne called the suffering caused by disease 'the grit that makes possible the pearl of different kinds of reaction', creating the opportunity 'to show courage, patience and sympathy'. As for those who die in pointless battles, like the mass slaughter of conscripts which served no strategic benefit in the Somme, Swinburne pointed to the supposed benefit to those who ordered them over the top: 'It's only because some people will suffer if they make the wrong decision that the possibility of big wrong decisions is open to them. And so the soldier on the Somme, his life is of use because by its availability he makes the possibility of big decisions open to many, many other people.'

In other words, it's good for everyone that we live in a world where people can take responsibility for their actions and do dreadful things. We should be glad that our lives are useful in this way, even when terribly misused, because it's 'not just a good for others, it is a good for *me* if I am of use for others'.

I find this chilling. As he presented his arguments to me, I felt a sense of moral disgust that he was able to reassure himself in all sincerity that dreadful suffering was all for the good and to be sanguine about it. Think of the really awful things people and animals have endured, such as torture, sexual abuse and appalling illness, much of which has nothing to do with allowing wrong decisions to have their consequences. For me, this is the power of reason at its worst. It rationalises atrocity to ourselves in order to preserve our pre-existing beliefs. I admire much more the religious believers who cannot make sense of evil in the world and live with the contradictions their belief in an all-loving God entails, deeply troubled by it.

Fighting confirmation bias is difficult, but self-awareness can at least reduce its potency, even if it can't eliminate it. We need to get into the habit of asking ourselves the question 'Is this argument really as good or as bad as it seems, or is it that I want it to be so?' If we do this, I think we can easily tell when we want an argument to work or not. We get ready to scoff before someone we tend to disagree with has even opened their mouth, and wait expectantly to hear or read what those we admire have to say. Challenges to our opinions make us defensive, support for them gives us pleasure. These telltale signs should alert us to check our reasoning again, to try to imagine what someone without bias would make of it.

Another distortion we can do something about is implicit bias. Although there is some controversy about how deep and wide this is, there is very strong evidence that we are influenced by stereotypes and prejudices, usually at an unconscious level. Such is the power of bias that it can even negatively affect a person's self-perception. For instance, 200 women were put into two groups and given a maths test. One group was told the test was part of an experiment to see why men generally did better at maths than women, while the other group was told it was simply an experiment about maths performance. The group primed with the stereotype that men were better at maths scored around 80 per cent while the other group scored nearly

90 per cent. In other words, simply being aware of a negative stereotype turns it into a self-fulfilling prophecy.[6]

You might think that smart people like philosophers would never fall for such crass stereotypes, but the answer to the titular question of the horror show website 'What Is It Like to Be a Woman in Philosophy?' is clearly 'to be constantly confronted with sexism'. Take this all-too-typical testimony from a female philosophy PhD student (which is far from the worst):

> Regarding classroom dynamics, I notice that questions and comments are received much more favourably when they are presented by a student who is a man. When a woman asks a question or raises a comment, it tends to be a) misunderstood b) not deemed interesting enough to warrant attention/ development, or c) briefly discussed only to be brought up again by one of the men, which somehow changes it into a point worthy of more attention. Rarely do I hear a professor (who is a man) praise any of the women for their contributions to discussion.[7]

The professors were not consciously discriminating. They were unconsciously taking women less seriously. The woman who reported this also had to challenge the internalised stereotype of a 'whingeing woman' when she complained, which made her wonder if she was a victim of confirmation bias, misinterpreting harmless actions for discrimination when it wasn't there. 'I often feel like I might just be looking for things that aren't there, or seeing patterns where there really aren't any. I think that, deep down, I know this isn't true, but I don't trust my personal experience enough.' The slogan 'Check your privilege' tells only half the story: we also need to check the effects of our lack of any privilege.

Philosophy has historically been a laggard when it comes to gender equality. I strongly suspect that part of the reason has been that philosophers are so confident in their ability to reason clearly that they haven't taken seriously the possibility that they might be falling for implicit bias. Such lack of self-awareness is precisely what unconscious prejudice thrives on to operate unchecked.

Correcting for implicit bias is difficult because, like confirmation bias, it is by its nature unconscious. But in my experience, once you are aware of the pervasiveness of such distortions, you can monitor yourself and spot them much, if not all, of the time. If I find myself critical of a woman, for example, I ask myself whether I would talk in the same way about a man with the same failings. Imperfect though such checks might be, they are better than the alternative.

In short, no amount of knowledge about what makes for a strong argument or a fallacious one can, by itself, protect anyone against cognitive biases. Self-awareness and self-knowledge are also required, gained only with effort. You can't rely on what seems transparent to you about yourself. You need to see yourself from the outside and learn from what psychology has taught us about the hidden springs of thought. Know thine enemy, especially when that enemy is within.

However, there is one way in which it is important to resist drawing too much on psychology. This is the temptation to psychologise: to assume that people are arguing on the basis of their supposed psychological motivations, often hidden. The temptation is strong because it is indeed true that we are prone to motivated thinking: believing what we want to believe, finding arguments for the conclusions that we want to be true. And it is also true that our motivations are often unconscious and driven by emotion. But that does not mean we are good at knowing what those unconscious drivers are in other people.

To appreciate the attractions and perils of psychologising, take Simon Critchley's explanation of the appeal of the nihilistic pessimism of both Schopenhauer in the nineteenth century and John Gray today. 'It's an incredibly seductive diagnosis of the times, which allows us to feel some sort of thrill out of the dismal situations in which we find ourselves. Nothing is more exciting than being told that things are completely awful and impossible to reform. [Gray's] *Straw Dogs* is an exhilaratingly depressing book and I think that's the reason for its success, that people, in a sense, want that comfort of despair.'

There's something to this. But Critchley's reading says nothing about whether or not Gray's arguments are good ones. All attempts to psychologise dodge the point in this way. Although it is a reasonable hypothesis to assume that most people are engaged in motivated thinking a lot of the time, it is no argument against any specific instance of reasoning. If the argument is a good one, it doesn't matter if it is the result of motivated thinking or not. If it is a bad one, its faults should be evident, even in the absence of knowledge of its psychological motivations.

I was once rightly put straight on this by Richard Swinburne. He holds several philosophical positions which today are held almost exclusively by theists, such as that we have immaterial souls and that the evidence points to the existence of an all-powerful, all-knowing, all-loving God. So I put it to him that his arguments look very much like motivated thinking, since without certain theistic Christian commitments it would seem unlikely he would have come to hold the views he did. Arguments that lead him apparently inexorably to certain conclusions don't lead others there.

As it happens, I still think this is true. But Swinburne was right to object that this is no way to argue. 'I can also play that card in reverse and say that the only reason that people deny what stares them in the face is that they are captured by the physicalist dogma current in our time. We can all play that game and it doesn't get us anywhere. We have to consider the arguments on their strengths.'

Swinburne in effect accused me of committing the *ad hominem* fallacy: attacking the arguer rather than the argument. This is a version of the *genetic fallacy*: criticising an argument on the basis of its murky origins rather than the argument itself. For example, Soviet science was hampered by Marxist-Leninist ideology, but that would be a poor reason to dismiss the work of some scientists, like the Nobel Prize-winning Nikolay Semyonov. Attacking the arguer or the origins of the argument fails to deal with the substance of the argument itself. I could be full of malicious intent, but if I come up with a good argument, it's a good argument.

Everyone knows that arguing *ad hominem* is fallacious. That doesn't stop even philosophers doing it. When they do, I find it is almost always in its psychologising version, where people believe they have identified motivations that undermine the credibility of the argument. For instance, when Ray Monk wrote a critical biography of Bertrand Russell, many complained that Monk had some kind of hidden agenda. He denied this, and pointed to a 'particularly nasty' review by one of his peers, A. C. Grayling, who said that Monk 'found himself in the ghastly situation of being offered lots of money to write about a man whom – as he already knew when he banked the cheque – he loathed'.[8] 'It's just not true,' said Monk. 'Most of the things that I was appalled by were discovered during the research.'

Amia Srinivasan, a recently risen star of contemporary philosophy, also offered an astonishing piece of psychologising in an interview, in which she said:

> Trans-exclusionary women are very often cis lesbians who, for very good reasons, have issues with their bodies precisely

because they are going to be read in a particular way in a deeply lesbian-phobic, heteronormative culture. They've learned to deal with their frustrations with this in a particular way, and they dislike the idea of anyone dealing with it in a different way.[9]

As her interviewer Rachel Cooke said, 'It seems extraordinary to me that someone so interested in equality and freedom would generalise about an entire group of people (lesbians) in this way.' In Srinivasan's defence, you could say that this is not her *argument* against trans-exclusionary lesbians but a psychological explanation for their errors. Psychologising in this context provides a kind of speculative 'error theory': an explanation for what led people astray, not an explanation of what they have got wrong. Even so, Srinivasan's suggestion is evidently too speculative, implausible, generalising and untestable. It would have been better not to have made it.

There may sometimes be a legitimate role for a kind of psychologising. When writing her classic book *The Sceptical Feminist* in the late 1970s, Janet Radcliffe Richards developed a way of thinking that is similar to the principles of cognitive behavioural therapy (CBT). The idea is that you can make sense of what people say or do by asking what assumptions would make their actions or conclusions rational. That gives you a hypothesis, one to test, about what a person really believes. Radcliffe Richards gave the example of people's resistance to equal rights for women, despite their professed belief in equality. This makes sense only if you assume that they still believe in some fundamental differences between the sexes which justify differential treatment. However, as in CBT, where it is not for the therapist to tell the client what their automatic or implicit thoughts are, all this method generates are possible explanations to be explored and tested.

This limited and legitimate use of psychologising explanations suggests that an absolute bar on *ad hominems* is misguided. What's more, I think repeated breaches of the 'no *ad hominems*' convention show that people know that it is. For instance, several years ago I spoke at a conference on animal ethics in which I was trying to articulate the ways in which people who kill and eat animals can at the same time have a deep and respectful relationship with them. One of my examples was the fictional protagonist of Hemingway's *The Old Man and the Sea*. When it came to the discussion, one of the most senior philosophers there raised a hand, but before posing his question he pointed out that 'by the way' – signalling by this phrase and other similar ones that he knew this wasn't an admissible objection – Hemingway had once mixed broken glass with meat, fed it to a dog and boasted about how he watched it take a day or more to die in agony. So don't take Hemingway to be any kind of authority on a respectful relationship to animals. Then he raised his 'real' objection.

What struck me was that not only was this an egregious example of the *ad hominem* fallacy – since my argument drew on the example of a fictional character created by Hemingway, not Hemingway himself – the objector *knew* it was not a legitimate objection. Yet he said it anyway. Why? I can't know. But in general, I think that despite official disavowals of *ad hominem* arguments, most of us sense that, sometimes at least, the character of the arguer *is* relevant data when assessing their arguments. And I think we're right to think this. In this case, the suggestion is that although Hemingway's book might seem to exemplify a deep connection to nature, we should doubt that Hemingway is a reliable witness and wonder whether we are simply being reeled in by some skilful prose. There is no *ad hominem* fallacy here because this isn't an attempt to show the argument is wrong. It simply raises a flag.

This distinction is subtle but important. At the end of the day, arguments and evidence have to stand on their own merits. But it would be foolish to ignore warning signs that the person offering the argument may have a strong agenda, or may not be as reliable as we think. Similarly, people's deep psychological motivations are too obscure for us to dare to think we know them. But being interested in why people believe what they do, when it seems obviously false, is not only natural but healthy. It's only a problem if we confuse this with genuine counter-argument.

We need to consider motivations *and* assess arguments, but separately. A good illustration of this is provided by the both useful and potentially distracting question '*Cui bono?*' Who benefits? 'Following the money', literally or otherwise, is often the best way of working out what's really going on. If the people arguing that a ban on tobacco advertising won't cut smoking are manufacturers of cigarettes, beware.

Sometimes the mere fact that something is in the news at all raises questions about who is benefiting from it being on the agenda. The Australian political strategist Lynton Crosby has become notorious for his advocacy of the 'dead cat strategy', described here by one of his more Machiavellian clients, the then British Prime Minster Boris Johnson:

There is one thing that is absolutely certain about throwing a dead cat on the dining-room table – and I don't mean that people will be outraged, alarmed, disgusted. That is true, but irrelevant. The key point, says my Australian friend, is that everyone will shout, 'Jeez, mate, there's a dead cat on the table!' In other words, they will be talking about the dead cat – the thing you want them to talk about – and they will not be talking about the issue that has been causing you so much grief.

The then Conservative Defence Secretary Michael Fallon is credited by some for winning his party the 2015 general election by throwing just such a dead cat on the table at a judicious moment. The opposition Labour Party had been making inroads in opinion polls until Fallon said that it was preparing to get rid of Britain's nuclear weapons to secure a coalition deal with the Scottish Nationalist Party. No matter that he had no evidence for this. The charge got the headlines and made people focus on defence, the very issue that has traditionally been perceived to be Labour's weakest. Not only that, but Fallon linked his false claim to broader question marks over Ed Miliband, who had defeated his own brother to become leader of the Labour Party: 'Miliband stabbed his own brother in the back to become Labour leader. Now he is willing to stab the United Kingdom in the back to become prime minister.' In defiance of the opinion polls, the Conservatives went on to win. Even if the impact of Fallon's cat-throwing is overstated, it's a clear example of the strategy at work.

Simply knowing who benefits tells you nothing about the truthfulness of the claim. The risk of asking *cui bono* is that, like *ad hominem* attacks, it doesn't address arguments head on, and it carries the risk of committing the genetic fallacy, damning something by its origins rather than by its nature. Consider the opioid crisis in the US. Who benefited from the massive increase in prescriptions of pain-killing drugs? The pharmaceutical companies, of course. But pharmaceutical companies benefit from increased use of any of their drugs. Since all pharmaceuticals are made by pharmaceutical companies, does that mean we should assume none of them are therapeutic? *Cui bono* can quickly become an argument for vaccine hesitancy, and a very bad one at that.

The habit of asking *cui bono* would have alerted us to the fact that Fallon had a strong vested interest in getting his slurs against Miliband out there. But of course in an election campaign every claim is designed to benefit the claimer. No one says anything they think will hurt them. That does not mean everything they say is untrue. So in the context of politics, *cui bono* should make us suspicious of everything, dismissive of nothing. 'They would say that' does not entail 'That is false.'

When people talk as though knowing who benefits automatically leads to the smoking gun, they are applying the principle lazily and selectively because to apply it consistently leads to contradiction. Pharmaceutical companies say that their vaccines are 85 per cent effective. Well, they would say that, wouldn't they? But when vaccine sceptics claim they are killing people, they would say that too. Biotech companies would say that genetically modified crops are safe, but environmentalists would say that they aren't.

Being alert to the psychological drivers of arguments is a useful way of drawing our attention to reasons to be cautious, or of helping us to understand why arguments that seem to us so weak are so attractive to others. But because our hypotheses about motivations are so often by their nature speculative, we should generally avoid them. We are too confident that we can spot what drives other people when we often don't even know what's driving ourselves. Speculating about hidden motivations is probably best reserved for private conversations and our own thoughts. A better way to draw on psychology is to be alert to the myriad biases and distortions that interfere with our own thinking.

How to be a psychologist

- Test your intuitions, don't test your beliefs against them.
- When thinking hypothetically, don't confuse what you can imagine with what really is.
- Don't keep emotion and reason separate. Recognise the judgements implicit in emotions and use your reason to help regulate them.
- Give people the opportunity to show that they've changed, but remember the onus of proof is on them. If you expect human beings to continue to be fundamentally the same you'll usually be right and only sometimes surprised.
- Guard against confirmation bias: looking for and remembering evidence that supports your view and ignoring anything that is too challenging.
- Check your privilege and lack of it. Implicit bias affects us all, whether we are perpetuators or victims of negative stereotypes.
- Don't psychologise. Many of the springs of thought and feeling are hidden, but it is always speculative to say with confidence what they are. Wonder what's driving people, but deal with what they actually say and do.
- Avoid the *ad hominem* fallacy: attacking the arguer rather than the argument. It's fine to use an arguer's character or motivations as warning signs, but not as a concrete argument against them.
- Avoid the genetic fallacy: attacking the source of an idea rather than the idea itself.
- Follow the money, but remember that 'They would say that' does not entail 'That is false.'

8

KNOW WHAT MATTERS

He is a man of intelligence, but to act
sensibly, intelligence is not enough.

FYODOR DOSTOEVSKY, *Crime and Punishment*

Philosophy frequently flirts with pointlessness, and every now
and again the flirtation turns into a deep affair. Such moments
can suffocate the will to live. I remember one such low when
sitting through a lecture based around a paper entitled 'House-
cleaning and the Time of a Killing'. Its first dry-as-dust
sentence reads: 'Judith Jarvis Thomson has pointed out that
there is a difficulty in specifying the time a killing takes place.'
Here's the so-called problem.

Say Bugsy shoots Babyface. Babyface is rushed to hospital,
the cops chase Bugsy and shoot him dead. A few hours later,
Babyface dies. So when did Bugsy kill Babyface? Not when
he shot him, because Babyface hadn't yet died. But not when

Babyface died, as Bugsy was already dead, and how could a dead man kill someone? So it looks like there is no time when the killing took place. But there was a killing. How could such an event have taken place at no time?[1]

If you're intrigued by when Bugsy killed Babyface, it could be because you enjoy logic puzzles, which is fine. For me, however, the problem is obviously generated by language. There is no fundamental puzzle about what has happened and when. You can describe the timeline of events completely. A problem only arises if you insist that somewhere on this timeline we have to locate something called 'the killing'. If you do that, it's then a matter of who can suggest the most plausible way of doing so. Jarvis Thomson, for instance, proposes that actions can have among their parts events that are not actions. So the killing is an event that extends over time from the shooting to the dying.

But there is only a problem to be solved if we make the baseless assumption that every time we use an event noun such as 'a killing' it must refer to an event at a determinate time. Not everything we refer to with an event noun has precise time boundaries. The Enlightenment did not begin at a precise time on the day in 1651 when Thomas Hobbes published his *Leviathan*, in part because there is no specific second when a book can be said to have been published. 'Publication' is not a discrete event but a process with an indeterminate beginning and end. There is no need to agonise over when exactly Bugsy killed Babyface when we know everything that happened and when. This looks like a classic category mistake: language has tricked us into thinking a killing is an event at a determinate time when in this case the word is being used as shorthand to describe something that unfolded over time.

I could be wrong about this. Maybe there is a good reason why we need to be able to be more precise about when actions such as killings take place, and it's not obvious to a metaphysical bumbler like me. But if anyone is to take the puzzle seriously, it should be because they have some understanding of why it does matter. Otherwise, it's just a 'crossword puzzle work writ large', as Joan Bakewell described much contemporary philosophy, adding 'Some of it is brilliant game-playing, and there are people having a wonderful time doing that.' Ray Monk was so dispirited by 'the feeling that nothing serious was being said or entertained, but a series of intellectual games being pursued as a career' that he actually left academe for a long while in the early 1980s. Echoing Bakewell, he said: 'I found myself thinking that the pleasure one derives from those kinds of problems has no more depth to it than the pleasure one derives from a crossword puzzle.'

Many of the philosophers I rate most highly have confessed that they find a lot of philosophy pointless. I'm not sure you'd encounter that in other disciplines. People may decide that their passions lie in theoretical rather than experimental physics, Aztec rather than Norman history, human rather than physical geography, but few would describe the subfields they lost interest in as a waste of time. It seems that hot air is to philosophy what rats are to cities: never more than a few feet away.

Monk is not alone in questioning the value of a lot of philosophy. Mary Warnock was frustrated by a certain 'trivial' kind of moral philosophy she encountered in Oxford during and after the Second World War. 'I'm particularly thinking of H. A. Pritchard, who was a very influential philosopher in Oxford just before the war and whose books on moral philosophy were full of questions like whether you had a right to family news, whether you had fulfilled your duty by posting the letter or only if the letter had been received at the other end.'

Philosophers like Warnock, Philippa Foot, Mary Midgley and Iris Murdoch helped bring moral philosophy down to earth. Did being women have something to do with this? If so, it need not be because of any essential biological sex differences. 'Macho culture' is not something you find by looking at chromosomes under a microscope, but it is nonetheless real. 'It's a male peculiarity to wish to go right up in the air and go round in circles without relating them to anything else,' said Warnock. 'I do think that women are less likely to be prepared to spend their time playing games in philosophy and that's what I think a great deal of philosophy is doing.' Similarly, Mary Midgley complained that universities were full of 'young men who have to make their way. Inevitably things are competitive. The business of winning arguments becomes very important, the lawyerly side of philosophising is bound to come out. I think it is true that if you have some more women around, less of this happens.'

We can play intellectual games if we like. Just don't confuse these with serious work. As the philosopher Nicholas Rescher has said, 'It is clear that without the distinction between the important and the unimportant at our disposal, mankind could neither adequately understand, successfully teach, or effectively practice science.'[2]

Mistaking the trivial for the significant, the empty for the substantive, the inconsequential for the important is something anyone can do in any domain, not just philosophy. Take business. Assumptions about priorities often lead managers and workers to devote too much time and mental energy to things that don't matter. Hours are spent thinking about design details of the new website when core issues of functionality are given little thought. Pointless meetings suck up time because having meetings is what people do. Much restructuring causes more damage through disruption than it creates benefits in the form of new and better systems.

Just as some things are taken to be more important than they are, sometimes what matters is missed because everyone assumes it is trivial. Before Ignaz Semmelweis developed antiseptic procedures for medics, whether or not surgeons washed their hands was considered unimportant. Apparently minor changes to home loan rules turned out to have catastrophic consequences when sub-prime mortgages fuelled the 2008 financial crisis.

A key thinking skill is working out what deserves more thought and what needs less. Momentum and habit often stop us doing this and misdirect our energies. Genuinely important problems can also give birth to other questions that take on their own life and don't matter for the original problem at all. Getting into the habit of asking, 'Is this really what I should be thinking about?' is the simplest and most effective antidote to such diversions.

One warning. 'Important' does not always mean 'useful'. Physicist Alan Sokal became famous for publishing a hoax academic paper which parodied broadly postmodernist approaches to science. However, he was never against all philosophy of science, which theorises the nature of the scientific enterprise. He quoted Richard Feynman's famous comment that the 'philosophy of science is as useful to scientists as ornithology is to birds'. But, as Sokal says, 'Ornithology is not intended to be useful for birds.' Hence the Feynman quote need not be pejorative towards the philosophy of science. 'It clarifies what scientists do, whether or not it helps scientists. If philosophy of science didn't help working scientists at all, it would still be useful as a contribution to philosophy.'

Understanding for its own sake has value, but not if we are only understanding how a few concepts work in a highly artificial philosophical system. Good thinkers don't think about everything with the same intensity. They understand what matters and what doesn't.

No one wilfully sets out to think about things that don't matter. But sometimes we accept too readily what matters to others when it is not important for us. We forget that people have different judgements or assumptions about what really matters. Take climate change. For many, the priority is to stop and preferably reverse global warming. If this is what matters, then you would consider anything that might help, including nuclear power, carbon capture and storage, and carbon taxes. So why are many 'deep greens' opposed to some or all of these? Because for them something else matters too, perhaps even more. They want a fundamental change in how human society fits in with the rest of nature, so they reject measures that in any way protect the global market economy, even if they halt climate change. If we allow ourselves to believe that what matters for these people is the same as what matters for others, our discussions about climate policies will be at cross purposes.

There's no algorithm for determining what matters in any given debate since 'mattering' is relative to the issues and our interests in them. As is often the case, determining what matters is primarily a matter of playing close attention and checking that the terms, history or context of the debate haven't distracted you.

Daniel Dennett provides a great example of this in his writings on free will. The subtitle of his first book on the subject, *Elbow Room*, was *The Varieties of Free Will Worth Wanting*. That phrase captures so much. There are different conceptions of free will out there, and as Dennett says, 'It's child's play to define varieties of free will that we can't have. Then the question is why should we care?'

For example, in his review of Dennett's *Freedom Evolves* Jerry Fodor wrote: 'One wants to be what tradition has it that Eve was when she bit the apple. Perfectly free to do otherwise. So perfectly free, in fact, that even God couldn't tell which way she'd jump.'[3]

'Why would you want that kind of freedom?' asks Dennett. 'It's like wanting the kind of freedom that allows you to defy the laws of physics and influence events outside your light cone.' What Fodor calls 'perfect freedom' is to be able to have and act on desires that are not formed by your history; to be unconstrained by your character, settled values, beliefs and so on. That sounds less like free will and more like a capricious random decision generator. For Dennett, the freedom that really matters is the ability 'to act for reasons that are our reasons'. That is why he believes the greatest threats to freedom are political, not metaphysical.

The question of free will is a huge one and I don't expect you to be sold on Dennett's view on the basis of this short summary.[4] The example merely illustrates how apparently deep disagreements about how the world is can often actually be disagreements about what matters.

When we're not clear about what is really at stake for different parties, we can get sucked into talking on the wrong terms. Take the referendum campaign on whether the United Kingdom should leave the European Union. In retrospect, remainers spent too much time warning about the impact that leaving would have on the economy. But who really thought that was the be-all and end-all? Most leavers wanted the UK to have more sovereignty, even if that made the country a little poorer. Most remainers wanted a more united Europe, even if it slowed down economic growth. If you don't know what matters both for yourself and for others, you end up spending a lot of time thinking well about the wrong things, and that is as much of a mistake as thinking about the right things badly.

Seeing an issue from the point of view of others can also be a good way of sharpening and testing our own beliefs about what matters. 'If you can't explain why your questions are interesting questions to people who are outside the field, then probably you're simply taking each other on a wild goose chase,' says Dennett.

Institutional structures and incentives can also lead us to think about the wrong things. Critical-thinking guides rarely mention these. They assume that as long as your arguments are valid, you're interpreting the right facts correctly, avoiding fallacies and so on, you're reasoning well. However, a truly critical thinker would question whether all this formally rigorous thinking is in the service of the right goal. Structures and incentives may not mess with the mechanics of reasoning, but they can lead to its improper application.

Nigel Warburton, the author of numerous popular introductions to philosophy, struggled with this in academe. He believed that requirements placed on academics by the Research Assessment Exercise to 'churn out four articles in five or seven years' led people to write nothing but 'footnotes to footnotes'. People jump through hoops, writing about 'things which will be good for their career rather than what they're interested in'. Warburton eventually got out.

I admire anyone who has looked closely at the profession they have entered, concluded that what matters most for them isn't best for their careers, but have followed their convictions anyway. More often than not, they benefit from the decision as it allows them to align their energies with their talents. Anthony Kenny is a good example of this. He got to know Donald Davidson, one of the towering figures of twentieth-century Anglophone philosophy. 'It became clear to me that he was a much better philosopher than I was,' says Kenny. 'But also I felt that the system he was producing was a kind of artificial system, which really had very little relation to the philosophy of mind and action as I understood it. It would sparkle and be exciting for a while but it wouldn't be a fundamental contribution to the subject.' This strikes me as an incredibly prescient judgement, one which took confidence to make. Davidson was emerging as a giant, but Kenny saw – accurately, I believe – that within a generation or two he would be almost forgotten.

Kenny understood what this implied for his own career. 'I thought, well, if he's so much better than I am and he can't make a contribution to the subject, I would be much better employed not trying to make a contribution myself.' He focused instead on interpreting and explaining the works of people like Plato, Aristotle and Aquinas. 'I could just wallow in the great minds of the past and I found that much more pleasant.' It was also very fruitful. Kenny wrote several excellent books which, although they may be as relatively short-lived as Davidson's, have helped people understand philosophy enormously. Had he been less alert to the ways in which academic life was set up to channel his energies in other directions, he could easily have ended up becoming a second-rate Davidson rather than a first-rate Kenny.

Outside of philosophy, our reasoning is misdirected by many institutional factors. In business, the corporate culture might lead you to spend too much time thinking about communications and not enough about the substance of what you're communicating. This is most obviously a risk with corporate and social responsibility, where the demands of green reporting can divert attention from green acting. Or you might be so dedicated to research and development that you're not working hard enough on thinking about commercial realities. Think of the late Clive Sinclair and his ingenious but unpopular inventions, most notoriously the C5 electric recumbent tricycle.

Subtle social pressures can also stop us thinking well. We tend to mix predominately with people fairly similar to ourselves, and read media that has a world view close to our own. So we have incentives to come to certain opinions and we are constantly being nudged to think about some issues and not others. How much time a person thinks about Palestine rather than China, or vice versa, is often a matter of how important those regions are in their peer networks, not a matter of which is objectively more in need of thinking through. We tend to read only to add more and more information to support our views rather than challenge them. Even if our views don't need challenging, there comes a point when expending more mental resources yields diminishing returns. If you have a well-informed and settled view on Palestine, you don't need to keep reading voraciously about it. Maybe you could use that time to get more informed on another issue you are largely ignorant about.

On an even more general level, the practicalities of life can leave little room for the kind of reflection many feel is important. I experienced this recently when I moved house, in protracted, multiple stages. I became frustrated at how much head space was taken up by logistics, decisions about paint, storage, whether to make or accept offers and so on. At times I felt that if I had any pretence of living the life of the mind, that was now a complete sham.

The phrase the 'attention economy' has come to prominence in recent years, as media of all kinds try to capture our time. But there is also an internal attention economy, in which we divert the precious resources of time and cognitive effort. The market in this economy is affected by many external factors, often subtle, social ones. Our challenge is to make this attention economy more efficient, so that we're thinking about what our all-things-considered judgement thinks we should be thinking about. We need to step back from time to time and ask ourselves what that all-things-considered judgement is. If we don't, our wants, including what we want to think about, can become too influenced by social and chance factors. Our attention economy is being run too much like a consumer economy, in which our desires are moulded by marketing and advertising, not our deepest desires.

The ancient Indian Sanskrit text the *Nyāya Sūtras*, written sometime between the sixth and second centuries BCE, supposedly by Akṣapāda Gautama, sets out some of the key principles of debate, dividing them into three kinds. In *jalpa* and *vitanda* the aim is victory, but in *vada*, good or honest debate, the aim is truth. Gautama saw that, too often, what is taken to matter in a debate is winning. I've seen this in academic philosophy, where 'getting' someone primarily means catching them out rather than understanding them: 'Gotcha!', not 'I've got it.' The goal of reasoning should be truth or better understanding, but no one likes to be a loser and if we start out asserting one thing, our desire to be right is often stronger than our desire to find out what is actually the case.

This competitive instinct often leads us to seek out the weaknesses in positions different from our own. There is of course something good about testing any argument as much as possible. But for such a test of weakness to be genuine it should test the best version of the argument, not the worst one. Hence the millennia-old tradition of formal debate in Indian philosophy in which interlocutors are forced to address the strongest counterarguments and even play devil's advocate.

This requirement is intended to stop them committing the straw man fallacy. A straw man argument gleefully demolishes a claim or belief, but it isn't actually the one the opponent holds. The argument defeats a feeble straw man version while the real, stronger one is left untouched. For example, some have argued that vaccine mandates are a violation of human rights because to forcibly interfere with someone's bodily integrity is in legal terms assault and battery. But most vaccine mandates do not entail that people are forcibly injected. They simply mean that if you choose not to be vaccinated your movements are limited or, in extreme cases, you are fined. There is an argument that this is an infringement of human rights, but it is a hard one to make. If you oppose vaccine mandates, it is easier to make a case against the straw man version in which they amount to assault and battery.

The principle of charity, widely embraced by philosophers, takes the requirement to avoid straw men further. It requires us not only to avoid easy, bogus targets, but to make sure we tackle the best, strongest version of an argument. For example, many now argue that the case for meat-eating has been destroyed on environmental grounds. Since it always takes more land to create a calorie from meat than it does to create a calorie from a plant, meat-eating is an inefficient use of resources. This seems obvious, and that's an important clue. If it were that obvious, how could an intelligent person think otherwise? The principle of charity nudges us to ask: don't the more thoughtful defenders of meat-eating have a response to this?

They do. Much grazing land is unsuitable for arable agriculture and many animals can be fed on waste from the food system that is inedible to humans. That's a good argument against the idea that we should all go vegan on environmental grounds. (Animal welfare is another matter.) But the meat defenders, too, should adopt the principle of charity. They may have defeated a poor argument against them, but have they defeated the best ones? At the very least, it should be obvious that this is not a defence of business as usual in the meat industry, since it gives livestock feed grown on land that could be used to produce plants edible for humans, not just pasture-roaming cows and waste-eating chickens and pigs.

This little summary shows that when you look for the best arguments on the other side, you can make real progress. Each party is forced to adapt their claims, drop the sloppier ones and concentrate on the best. The principle of charity encourages us to approach thinking things through as a joint enterprise to reach the truth, not a competition in which one side is out to win. This is important for creating a constructive, civil space for discussion. 'The tendency is to see people on the other side of an issue as just demonic forces that you need to defeat,' says Martha Nussbaum. 'Our talk radio and our internet culture encourage this. You don't listen to what they say, you just want to talk louder and win the battle.' Nussbaum argues that if you have a good humanities education 'you learn that each person has reasons. You learn to listen to those reasons.'

Our understanding of others' beliefs is also deepened if we think about *why* people believe what they do. For example, in the United Kingdom many people have falsely believed that immigrants receive more welfare benefits and get higher housing priority than UK-born citizens. If you thought the only thing that mattered here was the truth or falsity of the belief, you'd just be dismayed at the prevalence of these myths and assume that their only explanation is xenophobia. But if you attend to the question of why people are so ready to believe such falsehoods, you can see that many people believe that their communities have been neglected by politicians who talk more about the needs and rights of minorities than they do about the problems of white working-class communities. The false beliefs can then be seen for what they are: symptoms of a dissatisfaction, not their cause.

Too often, when we are clear that a conclusion is false we lose interest in why others have reached it. It should be the other way around: when intelligent people believe false things, it is especially interesting to work out why. More often than not we'll find truths in play. For example, I have little patience for anti-vaxxers, but even they have some truth on their side. Summing up an argument in his book *Antifragile*, Nassim

Nicholas Taleb claimed that 'Medicine is for the very ill, never the healthy,' and that 'there has been practically *nothing* made by humans to "improve" on nature or help with shortcuts that did not end up harming with *unseen* side effects.'[5] His basic idea is that because every medicine carries risk, you should not take any unless you really ought to. You might dismiss this out of hand once you realise its logical conclusion is that we should not have used the vaccines that have completely or nearly eradicated smallpox, polio, TB, cholera and the bubonic plague from our lives, let alone the ones that are helping us come to terms with Covid-19.[6] But if the evident falseness of this conclusion ends your interest in the argument, you deprive yourself of the opportunity to think harder about when you should or should not undergo elective medical treatment.

Sometimes the most fruitful insights arise when one party is able to see a better argument for something than the one its advocate came up with. Take 'forest bathing': the fashionable, Japan-inspired practice of walking in the woods for therapeutic benefit. Over-zealous advocates of forest bathing talk a lot about research that has attributed some of its benefits specifically to the inhalation of antimicrobial volatile organic compounds called phytoncides produced by conifers. The science is sound, but the health gains are too marginal to justify seeking out woodland walks. But it is also, more importantly, true that walking in the woods does us good simply because it involves being outside, relaxing, exercising and enjoying the natural world. Applying the principle of charity, we can see that there are better reasons for forest bathing than those offered by people over-impressed by the impact of phytoncides.

Anthony Gottlieb is a model user of the principle of charity. His brilliant two-volume history of philosophy covers several ideas that to modern eyes look eccentric, to say the least. There's Parmenides, who argued that one could never talk of what is not, or Anaximenes, who thought the earth was supported by air. 'A lot of these ideas appear quite barking,' he says. 'But then I tried to dig a little deeper to understand why Parmenides, to take an example, said what he said. When you try to do that you almost automatically in most cases come up with a sort of justification. [...] A lot of the ideas that appear silly only appear silly because you've just looked at the surface of them.'

I may have given just such an example already. Earlier, I quoted Michael Martin saying that he could not think of a single book written in the latter twentieth century by someone who is not an academic philosopher which is of interest to academic philosophers. It is a striking claim, and it would be easy to think it betrays nothing less than an astonishing narrow-mindedness. But Martin has his reasons, and even if you don't agree with them they are not silly. He argued that there is a distinction between philosophy and academic philosophy, and that 'academic philosophers have an interest in key texts, the canon of philosophy and that canon shifts and changes over time.' It is in the business of 'handing down certain traditions and skills of thought, and problem-seeking as well as problem-solving, from generation to generation'. In other words, it now has a very particular, narrow role and that is why today contributions to the discipline come overwhelmingly from within it.

Applying the principle of charity requires one of the key philosophical virtues: cognitive empathy. Whereas emotional empathy is a feeling-with-others, cognitive empathy is the ability to think-with-others, to understand their beliefs and the reasons they have for holding them. You can be the cleverest person in the world, but if you don't understand what people think and why, your critiques and questions will miss their targets.

You can give too much as well as too little charity. I spoke to Daniel Dennett soon after he had debated the notable Christian philosopher Alvin Plantinga. Dennett admitted that he found it difficult to attribute reasonableness to the work of Plantinga and many other philosophers of religion. You can take the principle of charity too far, in other words, I suggested. 'Yes.' There are limits to how respectful you can be to another's position. 'There is no polite way of asking somebody, "Have you considered the possibility that your entire life has been devoted to a delusion?"' says Dennett. 'But that's a good question to ask and of course it's going to offend people. Tough. Some people need a pail of cold water in the face and some people need very gentle treatment.'

The withdrawal of the presumption of reasonableness is rare in philosophy, as it should be in all civil debate. But that does not mean it isn't sometimes justified. Myisha Cherry has argued in *The Case for Rage* that norms of civil disagreement sometimes work only to protect the comfortable status quo and to keep the underprivileged in their place. Martha Nussbaum has also written about the validity of the right kinds of anger as a politic emotion. When issues really matter, showing emotion is at least understandable and at times necessary. Sometimes we need to signal the seriousness of the dispute and not to present it as a polite drawing-room debate.

Sometimes, the principle of charity requires us to set aside some of the things people say as unfortunate mistakes. For example, Kant argued that we are morally required to do only those things that we could consistently will everyone to do. You don't steal because you can't in good faith desire that others steal as well, and the same goes for murder, adultery and so on. It's common to argue that Kant himself showed how this leads to absurd conclusions. He wrote that if a would-be murderer knocked on your door and asked if you knew the whereabouts of his intended innocent victim, you should not lie, as lying is not something you could wish everyone to do.

You're not employing the principle of charity if you take this to be the smoking gun that destroys Kant's whole philosophy. Rather, you should accept that even the best philosophers sometimes slip up and say daft things. That does not undermine the whole. Onora O'Neill has never been able to make much sense of Kant's refusal to lie to the murderer in terms of his wider philosophy. Yet she remains a Kantian, saying: 'You can always find silly examples in any philosophy so I'm on the whole inclined to look for structure, not examples.'

O'Neill is talking about what we might call the *fallacy of the telling slip*. We're too quick to assume that when someone says something silly, outrageous or just wrong, it undermines everything else they have said. I suspect this is partly due to a collective swallowing of a cod Freudian world view in which our slips are more revealing than our ordinary words and actions. But just as Freud said sometimes a cigar is just a cigar, not all slips are Freudian. As O'Neill says, we should pay more attention to the patterns of people's speech and behaviour, not occasional aberrations.

The most common examples of the fallacy of the telling slip concern offensive language. In the recent past, more than one British member of Parliament has been caught using an old-fashioned idiom that contains the N-word, which is rightly judged to be an offensive racial slur which demands an apology. But does a single use of that word prove someone is racist? I don't think so and can use myself as evidence. I grew up when certain words were routinely used as insults which are now judged offensive, such as 'poof' and 'spastic'. These words are deeply lodged in my brain and I would not be confident that I would never, perhaps in an agitated or mildly drunken moment, find myself using one or other, not intended as a slur against homosexuals or people with learning disabilities but as ill-chosen words plucked from my internal lexicon when trying to say someone is weak or stupid. Indeed, in my early twenties I was mortified when I described myself as 'a bit of a poof about spiders' in the company of some gay men. Fortunately, they employed the principle of charity and saw that the pattern of my behaviour was more telling than this stupid verbal slip. Likewise, if someone uses a racial slur, we should ask whether this fits in or clashes with their general behaviour before we draw conclusions about what this reveals about their moral character. I stress: using such words is wrong, but a single use is not enough to warrant negative generalisations about the user.

Some slips *are* telling. When Hillary Clinton called Trump voters 'deplorables' she was probably expressing a real contempt she had been trying to hide. But our reasons for thinking this (or denying it) are based on everything else we know about Clinton. By itself, the slip says very little.

One way to apply the principle of charity is to come up with a plausible 'error theory'. If people are wrong, and they are not stupid, why are they wrong? What explains the widespread acceptance of an error? Error theories are especially important when we propose ideas that go against established or expert opinion. It's not enough to argue why you are right. You have to explain why so many others are wrong.

Unfortunately, the error theory most of us reach for first is that people are stupid, corrupt or fanatical. We say that people are gullible, they are taken in by smart-sounding good talkers, they want to be reassured, they want to feel important, they're just following fashion. Sometimes any of these might be true. But, generally speaking, such explanations are too quick and dismissive.

A good error theory should explain why a wrong view seems plausible and rational. Does Richard Swinburne's error theory for why so few people believe in immaterial souls pass this test?

Science has found out that we used to hold some very primitive beliefs which we now know aren't true and we used to be religious, so religion probably is not now true, which you'll recognise is hardly a valid deductive argument. People have been rather overwhelmed, and therefore rather over respectful of science. I am a great believer in science but we mustn't attribute to science an ability to make claims beyond its particular field.

In other words, people have become too respectful of science, they believe science leaves no room for souls, therefore they don't believe in souls. Some people do indeed grant scientists more authority than they should. But the idea that people reject religion because they thoughtlessly lump it together with other 'primitive', pre-scientific views seems to me to be uncharitable and false. Most non-religious people do not *assume* that (at least some) religious views are primitive and unscientific, they *conclude* that they are, and that's why they reject them. Furthermore, Swinburne's error theory might explain why a relatively unthinking person might assume that religion is a relic, but it doesn't explain why professional philosophers and neuroscientists reject the idea that minds and bodies are composed of different substances, a belief which does not require any religious conviction. So for me, Swinburne's error theory is weak. Not only does it not explain why people have gone wrong, it doesn't even explain why it is understandable that they have gone wrong.

What if we turn things around and ask – assuming that we believe there are no good arguments for an immaterial soul – why a supposedly intelligent person like Swinburne can be so wrong? Here, our error theory is in some ways simple, in others complex. Its essence is that beliefs are not held in a vacuum. If you believe certain things about God and creation, some beliefs fit more naturally with them than others. Belief in immaterial souls fits very nicely with many of the theistic commitments a Christian like Swinburne has. Given that no argument or evidence can prove beyond doubt that they cannot exist, Swinburne therefore has more soul-friendly beliefs than he does anti-soul ones. So the source of the error is not to be found in the arguments Swinburne advances for the immaterial soul – which are evidently weak by themselves – but the wider set of theistic commitments that buttress these arguments.

In ordinary life, many error theories can be quite simple. People may not understand the science, they may be getting their information from unreliable sources, their distrust of certain authorities may be prejudging them, accepting the truth might be inconvenient or embarrassing. It's not always difficult to understand why people go wrong, if you are in the habit of asking yourself why an intelligent person could be mistaken.

Another way to understand people we disagree with is to focus less on *what* they believe than on *how* they believe. For example, many people in the free will debate agree completely on what kinds of agency human beings do or do not have. They think that human beings make choices, but that these are determined by circumstances and their life histories to such an extent that, at any given moment, they could not have done otherwise. Some are relaxed about this and see that it affords us enough autonomy to say we have free will, while others think it's terrible, and *that* degree of autonomy isn't real freedom at all. They agree on the basic facts but have very different attitudes towards them.

I sometimes call this the overlooked importance of intonation. The belief that 'At any given moment, we cannot do other than what we do' can be said in shock and horror or with calm acceptance. (A related idea is 'the philosopher's *just*'. Inserting the word 'just' into a claim makes it sound less believable, even though it doesn't change the core claim itself. Compare 'Human beings are biological machines' and 'Human beings are just biological machines.' Whenever you hear something being described as 'just' this or that, try removing the 'just' and see what differences it makes.)

Think about the belief that those who are not saved by Jesus will be sent to hell for eternity. This is horrible. There is a case to be made that anyone who thinks a good God would make this happen is evil, since they are saying it is good to torment fallible human beings forever for the crime of not being wise enough to believe in a sadistic God.

However, the vast majority of people who say they believe this are not evil. They are often very kind. It's tempting to think that they don't *really* believe that people like me are going to hell. It's more accurate to say that the way in which they hold this belief is different from the way they hold many others. The psychologist Hugo Mercier distinguishes between intuitive (or affective) and reflective beliefs. Intuitive beliefs are the ones that we use to get around in the world and that we deeply feel to be true. You believe that drinking petrol would make you sick, so you don't do it; you believe fire burns and you keep your distance; you believe you love your partner so you treat them well and spend time with them. Reflective beliefs, on the other hand, are beliefs we assent to but which don't affect our actions much, if at all. We believe that cakes are unhealthy, but we eat them without suffering much cognitive dissonance. We believe that people starving to death is terrible, but we don't often get upset or make any effort to feed them. I even know a lot of people, including some philosophers, who tell me they believe eating animals is immoral, but they still enjoy a nice steak.

Belief in eternal damnation is more reflective than intuitive. It is a sincere belief but it's kept compartmentalised, away from affective beliefs about the value and lovableness of human lives.

We might find this odd, but we ought to remember that we all have such beliefs and that, awful though this one is, it's usually more harmless than it seems.

Philosophers talk of the 'semantic content' of beliefs and their 'truth value'. This reflects the 'logocentric' – word-centred – assumptions of Western thinking, which tends to assume that the contents of beliefs are their most important features. Semantic content matters when we are trying to get our descriptions of the world right. But in daily life, language functions more diversely. If we think too much like philosophers in everyday conversations we risk taking what people say at face value. Rather than trying to get our heads around only *what* people believe, we ought to think more about *how* they believe. If we do that, we are more likely to come up with a good error theory when they are wrong.

To get to the heart of what matters you need to be able to do more than process arguments and understand the reasoning of others. The P-factor requires *insight*. This isn't a mystical capacity to see beyond appearances, but the ability to notice what others have missed, to put your finger on what really matters, to clarify what is obscure.

'The great philosophers are those with insight, insight into something important,' says Ray Monk. 'When one's teaching students, one says, "Don't just give me your conclusion, give me arguments." But who reads Nietzsche, who reads Wittgenstein, who reads Kierkegaard, laying it out as if it were a piece of propositional calculus, and says this argument goes through or it doesn't. It would be impossibly boring and would miss the point.'

Michael Martin seems like the epitome of the contemporary, hyper-rational, analytic philosopher. But he is also clear that being a kind of high-performance processor isn't enough to make a great thinker. He cites Elizabeth Anscombe's classic book *Intention* as an example of 'an excellent piece of philosophy which contains virtually no arguments'. Rather, it is an analysis of what it means to act intentionally which points out such facts as that by doing one thing, such as running your finger across your throat, you can intentionally be doing another, such as instructing that someone be killed. Martin says that in that paper, 'you get a real sense of insight into certain aspects of what the nature of intentional action is, what's special about practical reason. [...] I defy anyone who has any taste at all for philosophy not to get excited by reading that piece.'

Philippa Foot is a great example of a philosopher of tremendous insight into the relationship between morality and our understanding of facts of human nature. Her patient, slow way of working results in writing that gets to the heart of things and contains nothing superfluous. 'I don't think it could be shortened much,' she replied with fitting economy when I asked her about her book *Natural Goodness*. She eschews the flashy mental gymnastics found in much philosophy but has instead a perceptiveness about what is at stake and what is important.

The novelist and bioethicist Alexander McCall Smith suggested that insight involves 'an ability to place theoretical constructs in context, to moderate them with a sense of what actually will work or can work in human society'. This in turn requires insight into human nature. As A. C. Grayling says, 'If you try to plan everything on purely rational, geometric grounds that would begin to run across the grain of human nature. So in fact the better and more rational thing to do is go with the grain.'

People are often frustrated by talk of wisdom and insight because it sounds nebulous. As Martin says, it is impossible to specify exactly what the ability to make good judgements consists of. 'I can't describe for you a Turing machine which enables you to sort the good pieces of philosophy from the bad ones.' Here precision is elusive and trying to pin things down is as futile as trying to nail jelly to the wall. But sometimes the most important things are those that are hardest to capture. It is precisely because there is no algorithm for good thinking that insight and wisdom require skill that can only come from practising the virtues of good reasoning.

Genuine insight is rare, which is why, as Bernard Williams said, 'Ninety per cent of philosophy at any time is not much good.' But then again, 'Ninety per cent of any subject is not much good.' Knowing what matters is what enables you to distinguish that 10 per cent. (It also enables you to realise that what matters here is not whether the 10 per cent figure is literally correct; 10 per cent stands for the small minority of really good stuff, whatever the actual proportion is.)

If you develop a good nose for what matters, you might find yourself ignoring whole chunks of a subject, even some of those that have historically been considered core. For instance, most contemporary theists agree that the traditional arguments for the existence of God are weak and irrelevant. Peter Vardy, for example, has written whole books about them as a service to students, but he thinks 'They're a waste of time. I actually think they're boring because I don't think religion rests on them. You do not get someone saying, "Well, I thought there was a 68 per cent chance that God exists but I've just read an article in *The Philosophers' Magazine* which has increased the probability by 7 per cent so I'm off to be a Jesuit." That's ludicrous.' You may, like Vardy, find the arguments interesting for philosophical reasons, but if you thought they mattered for deciding whether you believe in God or not, you'd be wrong.

Mattering is always situational. Considered *sub specie aeternitatis* – under the aspect of eternity – nothing matters at all. Within the human realm, there are times when no matter how philosophically significant a problem is, it just doesn't matter in other contexts. This is arguably the case for metaphysical arguments about free will. Oliver Letwin, the philosopher and Conservative politician, says that it is 'blindingly obvious' that we cannot have social life without blame, anger and responsibility. He accepts that there is 'a profound philosophical nexus of issues' around reconciling this with 'the brute fact that we are machines and that there are laws of physics'. But he doesn't have to resolve these in order to do politics. 'It's not a practical issue for moral life or political life.' That is why even most people who argue that humans don't have free will say that we cannot but act as though we do, and that it makes little or no difference to the assumption of responsibility in law.

On other occasions, deeper reflections might be relevant but they are unhelpful. The politician and political theorist Tony Wright said that in the thick of government, 'Intellectuals are unhelpful people on the whole, because they'll always tell you about there being many sides to a question and how things are all very difficult.' The time to engage in genuine discussion is 'usually away from the sharp end of power. It's often when parties and political traditions are trying to think through what they are about, or redefine or reorientate themselves.' Philosophy has its time and its place.

Sometimes what matters most isn't philosophy, or intellectual activity of any kind. For many years, hardly anyone knew that the philosopher Michael Dummett was incredibly active in supporting refugee rights. As one of his then-students, drug-dealer-to-be Howard Marks, recalls, sometimes that trumped philosophy. On one occasion Marks had skipped a tutorial with Dummett to speak in court on behalf of someone who had been arrested on a demonstration against Enoch Powell, the Conservative MP whose notorious 'rivers of blood' speech inflamed anti-immigration feeling. Marks felt less guilty about playing hooky when he discovered that Dummett was also there, speaking for another arrested demonstrator. 'It's a wonderful combination, the right morals, a brilliant mind and someone who smokes himself to death. I found that very comforting.'

How to know what matters

- It's OK to play intellectual games if you like. Just don't confuse them with serious work.
- Don't assume the difference between the trivial and the significant is what everyone thinks it is.
- Value understanding for its own sake. What matters isn't always a practical matter.
- If you want to understand people you disagree with, try seeing whether different things matter to them than to you. Many apparent disagreements about facts are at bottom disagreements about values.
- Guard against having your priorities skewed by institutional incentives and structures.
- Question what your peer groups believe to be most important.
- Avoid straw men. It's a hollow victory when there's a hollow opponent.
- Apply the principle of charity: assume others are not stupid and consider the best versions of their viewpoints and arguments, better even than the ones they offer.
- Don't just think about *what* people believe but *why* they believe.
- Think also about *how* they believe. Many beliefs are merely reflective: we sincerely agree with them but they don't impact on how we generally think and live.
- Don't assume a slip or a mistake is indicative of deeper or wider failings. Sometimes it is, sometimes it isn't.
- Have an *error theory*, an explanation for why people believe something when you are so sure it is wrong.
- Remember what matters in some contexts doesn't matter at all in others. Mattering is situational.

- Try to develop insight, not just cleverness. Always be on the lookout for the nub of an issue, what really matters.

9

LOSE YOUR EGO

People with new ideas, people with the faintest
capacity for saying something *new*, are extremely
few in number, extraordinarily so, in fact.

FYODOR DOSTOEVSKY, Crime and Punishment

With the worldwide success of *Zen and the Art of Motorcycle Maintenance*, Robert Pirsig became an international superstar. The book was a one-off blend of fiction, memoir and philosophical musings. It was a genuinely inspirational intellectual ride and one that set many a reader's philosophical motors running.

However, Pirsig thought that *Zen* was merely an introduction to his fully fledged philosophical system, which he called the 'metaphysics of quality' or MoQ. According to MoQ, 'quality' or 'value' is the fundamental constituent of the universe, yet it is also largely indefinable. He set out his MoQ more completely in the sequel, *Lila: An Inquiry into Morals*. But the world was not moved, the philosophical one especially so.

Many years later, in an ill-conceived written interview with me that did not produce any genuine engagement, Pirsig wrote, 'It does bother me that *Lila* is not as successful as it should be among academic philosophers. In my opinion it's a much more important book than *Zen and the Art of Motorcycle Maintenance*. My feeling is like that of someone trying to sell five-dollar bills for two dollars apiece and hardly making a sale.'

Instead of having the satisfaction of writing one of the most significant books of the twentieth century, Pirsig lived with the bitterness of being the Great Thinker the world spurned. Perhaps more importantly, instead of continuing to deepen his understanding throughout his life, he spent decades doggedly defending the position he had developed as a young man. Perhaps Pirsig is an unacknowledged genius. More likely, his ego inflated his justifiable sense of achievement. In his mind, his ideas were big – it was philosophy that got smaller.

Pirsig's case is exceptional, but the power of the ego is not. It affects us all and is an insidious obstacle to clear thought. Some, however, are able to loosen its grip. Take the late, great American philosopher Hilary Putnam. 'I make no secret of changing my mind on one or two important issues,' he once said. 'I've never thought it a virtue to adopt a position and try to get famous as a person who defends that position, like a purveyor of a brand name, like you're selling corn flakes.'

Putnam's views on changing your mind are hardly controversial. No one thinks that bone-headed obstinacy is a hallmark of a good thinker. Yet the uncomfortable truth is that most of us rarely change our minds, at least on the big issues. In philosophy Putnam had a reputation for his regular shifts in position only because they are so unusual.

A fear of this single-track intellectual life was one reason why the DJ and musician Mylo gave up a PhD to pursue a music career. 'In any kind of academic field, people seem to reach their position in their twenties or thirties and then bang on about it for another two decades until they eventually get a *Festschrift* in their honour or something. If you're not careful, it can be a rather boring way to spend your life.'

Few philosophers express concerns about this. An exception is Christine Korsgaard, who candidly admitted, 'As I get older, it becomes more unnerving to me, the way my own work seems to be unpacking a box that I got in graduate school. After a while you think, OK, I've been a professional thinker for thirty years and I don't seem to have changed my mind about very much, and there's something alarming about that.'

There is something to be said for 'relentless unpacking'. It has certainly reaped dividends in Korsgaard's work, which has been continually exploring the ways in which we create our identities through our lives and actions. As I suggested to her, aren't some of the most interesting things precisely the result of taking an idea which, if you think about it, is inescapably true and then unpacking it, because it's in the unpacking that the surprises come? 'I hope so,' she replied.

There are good reasons why our beliefs don't oscillate from day to day. If you are remotely rational, your beliefs form a more or less coherent set. If someone believes that reiki doesn't work, for instance, it is usually not solely because of views they have on reiki in particular. They may know nothing about it other than its claims to heal at a distance. Their rejection of reiki will relate to broader views about how the world operates. These connect with such things as the existence of God or an afterlife, which in turn link to their values and life goals. These beliefs form a mutually reinforcing set. You can't change one without that having implications for many others. If you were to come to believe that reiki does work, many other beliefs would fall like dominos. Each of our beliefs helps keep the others in place.

So if you face a challenge to a particular view you hold, even if you do not have a direct rebuttal, the totality of your beliefs will often indirectly testify against it. Any apparently strong study that seems to show reiki does work will justifiably be met with scepticism if it is incompatible with many other beliefs that we take to be well founded.

So it makes rational sense that it takes a lot to make us change our minds on big issues. It is little wonder that, as philosopher of science David Papineau says, 'Switching to a new way of thinking isn't a simple process. If you already have a view, you will naturally resist the alternatives. You need to be softened up first, to be forced to think about the new options. Only then will you be ready to be converted.'[1]

Still, if there is a perfect balance between flip-flopping and rigid constancy, most of us err towards the unbending. Being properly open to change requires habitual self-doubt, which is not something people find natural or comfortable. Nor is it likely to earn respect. We talk of people having the 'courage of their convictions' and see 'backsliding' or 'doing a U-turn' as weakness rather than as an admirable willingness to change our minds.

We tend to become very attached to our beliefs since they form a real part of our identities. You are what you think and do, and so to give up a core belief is to disown a part of yourself. Having a belief is more like having a body or a life partner than a car or a watch. Our relationship to beliefs is intimate. It takes humility to accept when we are wrong. It is an affront to our ego.

Changing your mind is no more an intrinsic virtue than standing your ground. The point is to change your mind when the reasons for doing so become strong enough and to stick to your guns when the counterarguments are weak, even if they are numerous and popular. Yet because there are so many barriers to changing our minds, we have to compensate more for attitudinal inertia than for inconstancy. Being 'open to change' in the casual way most people claim to be is not enough. We need to 'soften ourselves up', as Papineau put it, by seriously doubting ourselves and seeking challenge. To do that, we need to overcome pride. But modesty is fast becoming an unfashionable virtue. In our age, self-confidence goes hand-in-glove with ambition and success. The meek will not only fail to inherit the earth, they won't even claim a decent corner of it.

In my experience, people tend to take excessive pride in their own ideas. This morning, for instance, I received the kind of email that finds its way to my inbox with wearying regularity. It was from a '25-year-old guy' who wrote, 'I have a theory that I think you will find quite interesting. I have developed a philosophy that argues for the absence of objective truth in reality.'

I sigh. I am sympathetic. Most of the people who write such emails are intelligent and earnest, but they lack the peers or teachers who can rein in their excesses, point them to the right reading and provide constructive critique. I don't want them to give up, or suggest I'm a better thinker than them because I have a PhD and a list of publications. But I'm also a little irritated by their arrogance. Here is another person who thinks that they have single-handedly made a major philosophical breakthrough that none of the great minds of past millennia have managed, usually without having deeply engaged with their works.

Philosophers are not immune from vainglorious pride. Few say it explicitly, but I have often heard the echoes of a gripe that not enough people are interested in their work or appreciate the significance of their contribution to the discipline. It could even be that overconfidence is a professional asset.

Rebecca Goldstein observes that 'Sometimes the most successful philosophers are ones who have such strong intuitions and convictions on one side that it's very, very hard for them to entertain, to even wrap their heads around those who don't see it that way.'

A cautionary tale is Jerry Fodor's ill-conceived 2010 attack on Darwin's theory of natural selection, in a notorious late-career book which many felt tarnished his reputation. Fodor, whose major work was on mind and language, told me: 'I've never done philosophy of biology and I don't know much serious straight biology,' and 'I make no claim to extensive knowledge of the actual data and experimental results in biology.' He thought this didn't matter because 'What philosophers are taught to do in graduate school is, in some very loose sense, worry about conceptual relations or quite simply about the soundness of arguments. It's a kind of training which can make a characteristic kind of contribution to a thoroughly empirical programme,' even biology. He thought he was able to identity 'a sort of conceptual incoherence in the foundations of the Darwinian picture' despite knowing very little about its details. He relied on his biologist co-author to flesh out the science.

I won't attempt to summarise his arguments, because it would require several paragraphs on what almost everyone who knows their evolutionary science believes is hopelessly misguided. Take this withering summary by philosophers Ned Block and Philip Kitcher: 'Apparently unshaken by withering criticism of Fodor's earlier writings about evolutionary theory, they write with complete assurance, confident that their limited understanding of biology suffices for their critical purpose. The resulting argument is doubly flawed: it is biologically irrelevant and philosophically confused.'[2]

In other respects Fodor is very modest. 'I could be wrong,' he said about his attack on Darwinian theory. 'I've been wrong before. I'm wrong very, very frequently. Sometimes I can't even find the cap to the toothpaste. It doesn't matter about me. What matters is whether the arguments are any good.'

It's true that many successful people, including intellectuals, scientists and artists, are arrogant. But that does not mean their arrogance is necessary for their success. Correlation is not causation. Determination, talent and hard work could have been enough, without the swagger. Arrogance is almost always unwarranted and the few exceptions who are as good as they believe themselves to be prove the rule.

We have no reason to think that genius requires or merits arrogance. I asked Rebecca Goldstein if she had ever met a genius and she said yes: Saul Kripke. 'To listen to him was to listen to somebody taking you some place you would never think to go. When I was a graduate student, he gave these seminars with no notes, nothing, and it was like music, it really was.' But Kripke wasn't arrogant. He was just ferociously intelligent and uninterested in anything other than philosophy.

The best philosophers I have come across have not been arrogant, while the few really conceited ones have been second-rate. I don't think this is a coincidence. Overconfidence makes us less likely to check and test our ideas, to see their flaws and improve on them. It encourages us to fall in love with arguments and concepts that are not as smart or as useful as their creators think they are.

Proper modesty is not a matter of self-deprecation. It is rather about seeing clearly where your own weaknesses and limitations lie. I don't think I've met anyone who exemplifies this better than Philippa Foot. She freely accepted that she was no scholar. 'I just don't read and I can't remember all these books and all their details. [...] I couldn't give a five-minute lecture on dozens of philosophers. I couldn't tell you about Spinoza. I'm very uneducated really.' More surprisingly, she said: 'I have a certain insight into philosophy, I think. But I'm not clever, I don't find arguments easy to follow.' This would sound ludicrously self-deprecating to anyone who knew Foot and her work. She is evidently both learned and clever. But by 'clever' I think she was referring to a logical agility and ability to process complex calculations quickly. I can believe Foot wasn't especially clever in that sense and that she was not as good a scholar as many of her peers. Foot's recognition of these weaknesses required acute self-awareness.

Foot knew her talents were more subtle. She had great insight and a penetrating mind but wasn't quick. She had a good nose for what's right but not the eyes to see it clearly straight away. 'I know who's good, I think. Often if I hear a paper I know where it went wrong, it sounds wrong. I know it intuitively.' One of her colleagues used to say she would drop flares but didn't know how to respond to them. To bring her thoughts to fruition she needed time and care. 'Forests were felled for that book,' she says of her only monograph, *Natural Goodness*, which argued that morality is rooted in our understanding of what human beings need to live well. She wrote in notebooks every year, keeping one just for the anecdotes that would help make her ideas concrete for the reader.

The way she conducted her philosophy reflects her modesty. She spent hours in conversation with the philosophers she wrongly thought better than herself. She recalled John Campbell. 'He was a wonderful person to talk to because the egos just went on the fire. Either of us was pleased if the other showed us we were wrong.'

Mary Warnock is another philosopher with a humility that is far from false: 'If what I've done is of rather modest value, then that, I think, is an absolutely just judgement. [...] I haven't done very much work and I haven't done it very well. I think of myself as a very, very second-eleven, even third eleven member of the profession.' Again, there is potential absurdity in this remark because Warnock did great work. But her excellence was not as an original thinker. She was a great explainer of others' ideas and, most importantly, a brilliant chair of ethics commissions which helped bring experts together to make public policy. This work may score less highly in philosophical terms, but it left a greater legacy than much work by 'better' philosophers.

Foot and Warnock are models of intellectual modesty. We should become self-aware about where our strengths and weaknesses lie so that we don't rush to an opinion on a matter of statistics if we're not strong on numbers, or complain about the verdict of a court case when we know little to nothing about the law. As I write, commentators and social media users are expressing opinions about the decision to acquit four people on charges of causing criminal damage by pulling down the statue of Edward Colston in Bristol in 2020. Many are convinced that their opinions, based on a superficial following of the news coverage, are more legitimate than those of a jury who have heard days of evidence, aided by expert lawyers. It seems that the temptation to opine over and above our competence is strong.

Knowing your abilities cannot be separated from knowing your limits. This is heresy in a culture in which we are told we have to 'believe in ourselves' to excel. Doubt is poison. But knowing your limits should not mean settling safely within them. Bernard Williams puts it succinctly: 'It's a basic feature of all our lives that not only can nobody do everything but nobody can do as much as they need to do. As T. S. Eliot said somewhere, unless you go beyond what it is sensible to do you're not going to get anywhere.' We should stretch ourselves, in full awareness of our temerity. But if we have no idea where our limits lie, we might well end up pushing fruitlessly in the wrong places.

To paraphrase Winston Churchill, we are a modest species with much to be modest about. We have achieved great things and have expanded our understanding enormously. Yet error and plain silliness are never far away. Pride cometh before a fall, in reasoning as well as in life.

Egos are easily inflated when you're the biggest fish in a small pond. Unfortunately, academe is full of such puddles. The smaller the niche you try to fill, the larger your chances of filling a significant part of it. Hence we become proprietorial not only about our own views but about our own small fields of interest. This is natural because these become parts of our identity. When people join humanist, sceptic, Buddhist or environmental groups they often have a sense of belonging that makes them attached to the dominant ideas within those groups. When these are challenged, that can seem like a threat to who we are.

Small ponds bring other dangers too. For example, a few decades ago, applied ethics – bringing moral theory to substantive, real-world issues – was a growth area. Roger Crisp, then a rising star in British moral philosophy, was concerned by one unfortunate side-effect of this expansion:

> These little areas of applied ethics become little fiefdoms and people gain notoriety within those areas who are not particularly knowledgeable about philosophical theory as a whole and it gives those areas something of a bad name. Because they're new, they attract a lot of interest and it's also easier to make a name for yourself because the standards haven't yet been developed for judging what's good and what's bad.

There's a lot more to this short diagnosis than small-pond syndrome. There is the allure of novelty. 'Such is the nature of novelty, that, where any thing pleases, it becomes doubly agreeable, if new,' wrote David Hume. But at the same time, 'if it displeases, it is doubly displeasing, upon that very account.'[3] In our contemporary culture both of these factors make novelty attractive. Because people tend to love or loathe it, having a new idea generates attention, which in an age of social media influencers, reality TV, likes and shares is always a boon.

Novelty is also attractive because Western culture prizes originality. Consider how the Enlightenment and the Romantic period are often thought to be in conflict because the former prizes reason and the latter emotion. But what both have in common is the elevation of the individual. For the Enlightenment it meant individual rights and thinking for yourself, for the Romantics it was authenticity and self-expression. On both counts, to have your own ideas, rather than someone else's, is a badge of honour. 'To go wrong in one's own way is better than to go right in someone else's,' as Dostoevsky has Razumikhin say in *Crime and Punishment*.

But gratuitous iconoclasm is as intellectually lazy as slavish conformity. This is A. C. Grayling's criticism of John Gray, who had built a career attacking liberal triumphalism and optimism. Grayling sees this as a contrarian attack, 'anti liberal values, anti the idea of human rights, anti the idea of human values, anti the idea of rationality, and so on'. He calls it 'a kind of pose, something to do. "Let's combat the orthodoxy, to get a debate going, to kick up the dust." It seems to me utterly irresponsible, because people live and die, and kill, on the basis of their beliefs, and this is not a matter for messing around with.' You may think Grayling has picked the wrong target, but it is evidently true that some people are too fond of being contentious for contention's sake and become too attached to their status as mavericks.

Over-identifying with ideas may be widespread, but it is far from inevitable. For example, David Chalmers is famous for positing with Andy Clark the 'extended mind' hypothesis, which suggests that things outside of the skull, like notebooks and smartphones, can literally be extensions of the mind. Several years later, he told me: 'I've always been very, very sympathetic with the idea, but at the same time just a little bit ambivalent about it. So when Andy and I first published the piece, there was a footnote that said that the authors are listed in order of their degree of belief in the central thesis.' Those authors were Clark and Chalmers.

Such is the assumption that people are fully committed to what they argue for that Chalmers says many took this footnote to be a signal that he 'didn't believe a word of it' and was just 'a gun for hire'. Note that Chalmers's ability to hold views more or less tightly doesn't stop him being an ambitious philosopher, one who, he later told me, wants to 'swing for the fences'.

Ideas matter, and what matters most is whether they are true or not. It should not matter if the beliefs I have are mine or someone else's, or whether my tribe agrees with them. Given a choice between believing my own false ideas and the true ones of others, I know which I would opt for.

You'd be hard pressed to find a philosopher who would disagree with that. However, philosophy's dirtiest secret is that no matter how much they parrot Socrates' hoary saw that we must simply 'follow the argument wherever it leads', no one actually does so. The way reason takes you depends to an embarrassing degree on factors of temperament, personality and prior beliefs. This hit home when I was researching a paper on philosophical autobiography. It became apparent that people invariably end up holding philosophical views that they are instinctively drawn to. People who by disposition like neat, logical distinctions end up – surprise, surprise – making neat, logical distinctions. Those who are attracted by ambiguity and mystery avoid such tidiness. People who live in their heads do philosophy in their heads; those more curious about how the world works are more empirical. Ambitious people come up with ambitious, bold theories; more modest ones do not dare.

Yet, as Stephen Mulhall says,

> Philosophers seem to have an almost inveterate tendency to forget that they're human beings too. For perfectly understandable reasons, philosophers, not specifically but including analytical philosophers, tend to forget that they are situated human beings, they are inheritors of a particular tradition, of a particular historical and cultural context, they're responding to questions and deploying methods that themselves have a history of a more or less interesting kind.

Striving for objectivity *is* laudable. Philosophy should not be about opinions, but reasons. That's why many philosophy students have stories to tell about their teachers putting a red line through every instance of 'I think' in their essays. But the systematic erasure of the first person in philosophic language creates the illusion that reason is totally detachable from reasoners, that arguments are free from influences of personality or biography. As the writer and moonlighting philosopher Michael Frayn says, it is more honest to 'accept one's own idiosyncrasies and write in one's own voice and from one's own outlook in the world than try to adopt a completely impersonal one'.

Arguments never exist without arguers. I agree with Hilary Putnam, one of the finest American philosophers of the twentieth century, when he said: 'I think that the philosopher should to some extent disclose himself as a human being.' Putnam's work on meaning and the nature of mind wasn't autobiographical or obviously personal. He believed in 'the authority of intelligence' but said, 'it's always situated, it's never anonymous.' He quoted Walt Whitman: 'who touches this book touches a man.'

Iris Murdoch remarked: 'To do philosophy is to explore one's temperament, and yet at the same time to attempt to discover the truth.' In his podcast series *Five Questions*, Kieran Setiya takes Murdoch's statement as the inspiration for one of his questions. He asks each guest, always a professional philosopher, 'Does your temperament influence your philosophy, and if so how?' The philosophers will almost always accept that it plays some kind of role – how could it not? Some say that their temperament affects their motivations. Scott Shapiro said, 'What draws me to philosophy is my abiding sense of confusion,' while Zena Hitz identified in herself 'a visceral hatred for deception, delusion'. Others acknowledge that their temperament affects the *way* they do philosophy, usually positively. Tommie Shelby said: 'I like to think I'm pretty fair to those I disagree with.' Jennifer Hornsby conceded 'I'm sure there are features of my temperament which influence my style, how I present thoughts, whether in speech or in writing.'

However, hardly any accept that temperament influences the philosophical positions they come to hold. Hornsby insists that 'I don't think of my personality, if that's what is meant by temperament, as determinative of what I think, in so far as the questions are philosophical and what I'm doing is philosophy.'

Nancy Bauer is a rare example of someone who says that temperament isn't merely an influence, it *'determines*, almost, my philosophical work'. A significant minority of others acknowledge a link between their temperament and their ideas, although not always explicitly. Cora Diamond told Setiya, 'We can be drawn to ideas which may not hang together, and that's certainly something that I feel.' This would clearly impact on what views she holds. Similarly, Gideon Rosen said: 'I'm suspicious of depth in philosophy, I'm suspicious of mystery in general.'

The problem with accepting that temperament plays a large role in our thinking is that it casts doubt on the idea that the views you hold are not just ones that appeal to you, but the objectively strongest. Rosen bites this bullet. 'Philosophy tends to leave everything where it was except that you come out the other side with a deeper, more articulate, more clear-headed view of the world view you started out with.'

Is this shocking? It depends on whether you believe thinking can and should be free of subjectivity. It should be uncontroversial that no thinker can fully escape their biases, preconceptions and preferences when reasoning. In certain disciplines, such as maths and science, the criteria for a theory being correct are sufficiently clear that in the long run this doesn't matter: the right ideas will out. In arenas where there are no agreed ways of determining the correct answer – which includes most of philosophy – it does not mean that the positions you hold merely reflect your character, or that there are no means of distinguishing stronger from weaker positions. But where more than one theory is a contender, and where there is no decisive flaw or set of flaws in any, the view that anyone holds is going to be at least partly determined by temperament.

I don't think this is anything other than exactly what you'd expect. If there are no purely logical or evidential grounds for determining which of a number of positions is correct, then which one a person holds must be due to something other than logic or evidence. That something will involve character or personal history. This is not a failure of reasoning or philosophy: it is inevitable, and we have to accept it honestly. That is why Miranda Fricker was right to welcome Setiya's question as a good reminder that 'philosophy is authored.' She said that although there are benefits in the 'self-effacement' and 'posture of impartiality and objectivity' typical of analytic philosophy, she did not like the way it 'encourages the fantasy of non-presence, of non-authorship, of ahistoricism'.

Because reasoning is a collective endeavour, it could even be a strength that people contributing to the great conversations of humankind bring a variety of temperaments, particularly when reasoning about politics and ethics. If we tried to work out the best way to live based on the thinking of only one kind of personality, we'd end up with a solution that didn't work at all for many.

We do not fail when we bring our idiosyncrasies to our reasoning. It is a failing, however, to pretend we're doing no such thing, and make no efforts to allow for them. If you know, for example, that you are temperamentally drawn to neat, clear-cut solutions, you should question your willingness to accept one which others claim is *too* neat. I see little evidence that philosophers routinely make such attempts. 'Know thyself', the ancient injunction inscribed on the Temple of Delphi and affirmed by Socrates, is no longer a philosophical axiom.

One reason for this is that many seem to think self-knowledge is no longer even a possibility. The most common response to Setiya's question about how temperament influences their philosophy is: how am I supposed to know what my temperament is?

Take these answers, all just from series one. Helen Steward: 'I'm not completely sure quite how to identify what temperament I have.' Miranda Fricker: 'Your asking me that question presumes that I'll have the slightest idea about how my temperament is expressed in my philosophy, but of course I might have no idea about that.' Susan Wolf: 'I'm less confident that I know my own temperament or how it shows in my work. [...] Other people might actually be in a better position to see than I am.' Richard Moran: 'Maybe I'm not the best person to ask

about how my temperament influences my philosophical work.'
Barry Lam: 'I'm not quite sure how to characterise my own
temperament. That's one of those things that other people are
a lot better of knowing than yourself.'

You might think this just shows appropriate modesty and
self-awareness. Hasn't psychology taught us that we are not
transparent to ourselves, that much of our motivation is unconscious, and that the idea you can 'know thyself' by introspection
is naive? But, as several answers acknowledged, none of this
means we can't have *any* self-knowledge. Realism only demands
that we accept we can't get it purely and directly from looking
within. To learn about ourselves we have to observe what we
do and say as if from the outside, and ask others who know us
to tell us what they see. We may not even need to ask them: we
just have to pay more attention to what they are already telling
us. We get feedback from others all of the time, in workplace
evaluations, peer-review reports or more informally. This is
free information too few study with care.

We can also learn a lot by nurturing the habit of careful and
critical self-monitoring. 'You can find out a lot about yourself
by finding out which arguments you fudge,' Janet Radcliffe
Richards told me. 'The real test, when you're defending something you feel strongly about, is to produce a parallel argument
about a neutral subject, and see whether that looks plausible.
When you feel strongly about something you can easily make
mistakes in argument that you'd spot straight away in other
contexts.'

I found it a little dispiriting that so many of the philosophers
on *Five Questions* were unwilling to acknowledge the full extent
their personalities had on their philosophising, disinterested in
trying to understand those influences better, and too quick to
assume that self-knowledge can't be had. I'm fairly confident
that the best thinkers know their own quirks and biases and try

to allow for them. You can't be carefully monitoring your own thinking while not also monitoring the nature of the thinker. 'Know thyself' remains a key philosophical injunction.

A lack of self-knowledge may not always get in the way of clear thinking, but at the very least it hinders our ability to think about ourselves and the problems of our personal lives. Sometimes, good logical reasoners are bad at this kind of inner reflection because they cannot deal with anything that isn't clear-cut and calculable. Ray Monk believes that Bertrand Russell

> was to a certain extent hampered by his philosophical abil-
> ities, or at least by his philosophy, which drew too rigid a
> distinction between affairs of the heart on one hand and
> reasoning on the other. Russell felt, I think, that anything
> that couldn't be satisfied by a valid deductive argument was
> just settled by the whim of feeling. That is to say, he is too
> ready to assume that feelings are just irrational and there's
> no doing anything about it. So if he wakes up one morning
> and discovers that he's not in love with Alys, that's it.

Another example of when *not* to think like a philosopher.

Many philosophers also provide warnings against taking yourself too seriously. Philosophy is a serious subject. It doesn't contain many jokes, and those it does tend to be not very funny. Philosophers who can make you laugh stand out, like Sidney Morgenbesser, who once responded to J. L. Austin's claim that there is no language in which a double positive implies a negative with the words 'Yeah, yeah.' On another occasion a student once interrupted him, saying 'I just don't understand,' and Morgenbesser replied, 'Why should you have the advantage over me?'

Professional philosophy has become highly performative and it doesn't usually pay to project self-doubt, even less self-ridicule. Even writing in a popular, accessible style can arouse suspicion. Daniel Dennett says: 'There are some philosophers who object to a light-hearted approach to philosophy. They want you to take it seriously! I do take it very seriously, but not solemnly.'

Christine Korsgaard uses wit effectively. One of her academic papers opened with the withering put-down, 'G. E. Moore, always ready to volunteer when a straw man would otherwise be wanted ...'. She thinks there are 'some good philosophical reasons for' such levity, 'since often humour is a form of stepping back or distance, and stepping back or distance sometimes gives you a view'. She also thinks that 'philosophy is the most fascinating subject in the world and yet most of it is a chore to read. These two things fit badly together. It has to be possible to write philosophy in a way that makes it fascinating because it is fascinating.'

Roger-Pol Droit is a rare example of a philosopher who relishes being playful. At the beginning of his book *How Are Things?* he wrote, 'Take none of the assertions in this book seriously? An exaggeration. Take all of them seriously? More exaggeration.' Explaining this to me he said, 'I personally prefer texts, books or ideas where you are never totally sure if they are serious or not. And that's the case of some philosophers. Very often in Nietzsche you can't tell if he says something seriously or not.' This suited the aims of the book he had just published, which was 'not intended to deliver any theory, but to produce the feeling of how the world may be strange, step by step, object by object'.

Slavoj Žižek, sometimes accused of being a clown, is prepared to laugh at himself. When I asked about the psychoanalytic foundations of his philosophy, he interrupted to say: 'I'm not a practising analyst. You know why not? After meeting me, let's imagine that you were to have psychic troubles, would you come to me?'

Taking yourself too seriously interferes with good reasoning because it requires forgetting all the ways in which even the most intelligent human beings are always only a step away from being ridiculous. Newton's fascination with alchemy is well known, as is the Nobel Prize-winning chemist Linus Pauling's evidence-defying obsession with high-dosage vitamin supplements. Intellectual honesty requires not only an admission that we might end up believing something silly, but the realisation that we might unwittingly already do so. When modesty is absent, pomposity soon fills the gap.

How to lose your ego

- Don't just be open to changing your mind, be actively interested in doing so.
- The courage of your convictions is often the cowardice not to change them.
- Always think about how changing your mind on one thing might require you to change your mind on others.
- Modesty without ambition is enfeebling, ambition without modesty is hubris.
- If you find yourself thinking you're the first person to have had an idea, remember you're probably wrong. Seek out and study the precedents.
- Know your limitations, all the better to push at them.
- Resist the temptation to opine above your pay grade.
- Neither fear nor fetishise novelty.
- Don't overestimate the size of the pond you're swimming in.
- Don't be proprietorial or tribal about your opinions. What matters is whether they are right, not whose they are.
- Don't be a contrarian for contrarianism's sake.
- Cultivate self-knowledge but don't rely on introspection alone to find it.
- Be aware of how your own temperament affects your thinking and try to allow for it.
- Don't take yourself too seriously. People who cannot laugh at themselves become laughable.

10

THINK FOR YOURSELF,
NOT BY YOURSELF

Everywhere in these days men have, in their
mockery, ceased to understand that the true
security is to be found in social solidarity
rather than in isolated individual effort. But
this terrible individualism must inevitably have
an end, and all will suddenly understand how
unnaturally they are separated from one another.

FYODOR DOSTOEVSKY, *The Brothers Karamazov*

Robinson Crusoe is more admired for his self-sufficiency than
pitied for his isolation. He is a hero born of an individualist
Western culture in which the less we depend on others the
better. (He is also a product of a colonial society in which this
autonomy is in no way compromised by having the service of a

dark-skinned man.) In the modern West, the life of the mind is portrayed essentially and ideally as a solitary one. Philosophy, science and the arts are popularly imagined as pursued by lone geniuses. In philosophy, the trope of the solitary genius is epitomised by Descartes' *ego*: the self as an inner, self-contained mind. 'Think for yourself,' we are told. If our instructors are more erudite, they might quote Immanuel Kant: '"*Sapere aude!*" Have courage to use your own reason!'

Were you to take this advice seriously and think about it carefully for yourself, would you really conclude that to think well you should find yourself a comfortable garret and retire to cogitate?

'When Robinson Crusoe moves back into society, is society making him dumber?' asks David Chalmers. In a way, it is. 'On the island, he can do more by himself; in society he can do less by himself.' But, on the other hand, back home 'he could do so much more by virtue of his connection to all the people around him.' In society, 'the sum total of his capacities are greater.'

Chalmers was talking to me at the World Congress of Philosophy in Korea, and he observed that 'the traditional Western way of looking at the cognitive system is that every person is a cognitive island. We think for ourselves and then we interact.' In Korea, he had been told, there's 'much more of a communitarian way of thinking about these things' which is deeply rooted in the culture. There, as across Asia, thinking is part of a 'much grander, much larger interconnection of thoughts, reasoning and action'.

The question of whether Crusoe is smarter on the island is like comparing a Swiss Army Knife with a toolbox. You can do much more with a single multi-bladed knife than with any one of the tools in the box. But you can do more and do it better with the whole toolbox. Thinking by ourselves is like trying to turn ourselves into Swiss Army brains, depriving ourselves of a greater variety of minds with diverse specialities. We gain cognitive autonomy at the price of reduced cognitive capacity.

The burgeoning field of social cognition has helped us to understand that reason likes and needs company. For many years, psychologists seem to have had fun showing how stupid we are, ironically, with clever experiments. But once they started comparing what happens when we think by ourselves and when we think with others, it became clear that we are smarter together than we are alone.

For example, the Wason selection task is a classic experiment designed to show how bad we are at abstract reasoning. You have to implement a simple logical rule of the kind 'If x, then y'. Sometimes this rule has a social context, such as 'If a person is under eighteen, they cannot buy alcohol.' Sometimes it is purely abstract, such as 'If one side of a card is yellow it must have a triangle on the other side.' The right way to implement the rule in social contexts tends to pop into people's minds. Around 80 per cent get it right. But in the abstract task, 85 per cent of people get it wrong. If that sounds unlikely, you can try it yourself online.[1] Even if you get it right, you'll almost certainly find the answer much less obvious. What's extraordinary is that in purely logical terms the tasks are identical. But if you give the same tasks to groups to solve together, 80 per cent get the abstract version right too. Leaving our cognitive islands really does make us smarter.[2]

Recent philosophy has also been remedially correcting its bias towards solitary thought. Social epistemology is the study of the social dimensions of the formation and justification of beliefs. It has become one of the most vibrant and interesting fields in the discipline. Before its emergence, it was common to think that the social generally undercut the rational. For instance, when scientists are heavily influenced by 'social factors' this interferes with their objectivity. Examples of this are legion. Just look at how the food industry funded research that supported the myth that fat, not sugar, was the big problem in people's diets; how fossil fuel companies supported research against climate change; how pharmaceutical companies have buried null and negative results in drug trials; how big 'agritech' companies promote technological solutions to farming problems over less intensive alternatives: the list goes on. The social interferes with the rational by introducing political and ideological motivations, culturally specific distortions, financial incentives.

All this is true, but Alvin Goldman, one of the pioneers of social epistemology, argues that it presents a one-sided view. It occludes the obvious truth that 'you can get more knowledge by using social sources, that is by drawing on the experiences of others and what they have to contribute. They have maybe better ideas, maybe better education than you do on certain subjects, or they have just read more about it than you have. There the social doesn't conflict with the rational, or with acquisition of knowledge, but complements it.'

Lone geniuses are not impossible, but they are exceptions, not the rule. They are also getting rarer, because there is now so much knowledge in the world that no single person can internalise enough of it to generate something genuinely original. A closer look at the history of ideas shows that solitary geniuses are elusive. The best philosophers have combined solitary reflection and writing with deep engagement with brilliant others. An early model was Aristotle, who always started his lectures by reviewing what others had said on a subject. Like Plato's Academy, his Lyceum was a place where philosophers talked endlessly together. Forerunners of the modern university, these were communities of thinkers, devoted to the advancement of understanding. Even Descartes' *Meditations*, which reads like a piece of private reflection, was published with a series of objections and replies from people whose criticisms Descartes actively sought out. Hume may have gone to isolated La Flèche to write his first masterpiece, but he conversed regularly with the town's scholarly monks and always valued intelligent company and correspondence. Today, peer review institutionalises the requirement to think with others.

Thinking outside of our own heads is advisable because that's where most of the world's great thinking has been done. If you loved music, you would be an idiot only to listen to your own compositions, or those of your nation. If you want to reason, you'd be just as foolish only to construct your own arguments or ignore those that hail from overseas.

We still have to think for ourselves because it is always our responsibility and choice to go along with the consensus view or to reject it, and sometimes it is the iconoclasts who are right. But we have confused the importance of thinking *for* ourselves with thinking *by* ourselves. Lock yourself away to think and you'll probably emerge with half-baked fantasies, not radical revelations. The knack is to think for ourselves, with others, not just going with the flow but using the mental power of others to help us forge our own path. How do we pull off that trick?

One way to broaden your mental engagement is to look beyond your own culture, whether that's a national or disciplinary one. The British political theorist and politician Bhikhu Parekh makes the case for multiculturalism on these grounds. He takes multiculturalism to be premised on the notion that 'no culture has a monopoly on wisdom, no culture embodies all the great values, and that therefore each culture has a great deal to learn from others, through dialogue. What the dialogue does is to enable each culture to become conscious of its own assumptions, its own strengths and own weakness, to learn things from others.'

History suggests that Parekh is right and that variety is the spice of thought. The great flowerings of philosophy have almost all occurred at times and in places where people were in movement and ideas flowed. Ancient Athens was a vibrant trading hub, as were eighteenth-century Paris, Amsterdam and Edinburgh. In all of these cases there were innumerable formal and informal gatherings of people with different intellectual histories thinking together.

Note that Parekh calls this 'interactive multiculturalism' or pluralism. The interactive element is crucial. Too often people assume that multiculturalism is about celebrating a diversity of different world views without challenge, that even to question the wisdom of another culture is to be chauvinistic and intolerant. For Parekh, sterile so-called 'respect' is anything but, because it does not treat the plurality of cultures as being capable of criticism or worth learning from.

Variety in thought can also be achieved by seeking out the company of intelligent interlocutors, a privilege not easily available to all. Many of my interviewees talked about how much they gained from wise peers. Michael Frayn recalled his enthralling conversations with his Cambridge supervisor, Jonathan Bennett, a man 'full of fire and energy' and 'the most argumentative and difficult man I've ever come across. [...]You'd say "Good morning" and he'd dispute it.' Frayn's supervisions would start at noon and often continue over lunch in the pub, in Bennett's room in the afternoon, and not concluding until after dinner. 'It was terribly hard work, but it was absolutely fascinating.'

When we can't literally think with others, simply imagining being inside their minds can help. Like many novelists, Rebecca Goldstein loves being surprised by her own characters. Her first novel, *The Mind-Body Problem*, was written in the first person, from the point of view of a protagonist very different from the author herself. Around the time she wrote it, Goldstein recalls seeing a minor incident on the New York subway. 'First *I* reacted,' said Goldstein, 'and then I heard *her* reacting. She's much funnier than I am, she had a very amusing thing to say about it all. What a weird situation that is. And it leads me to things I would never think of on my own.' For instance, she says she only came up with her idea of the 'mattering map', a tool for thinking about all the things that matter to you in your life, because she was inhabiting her protagonist's point of view.

We're not all gifted with a novelist's imagination. But we can all see things from some other perspectives. Most of us experience this when we have unintentionally internalised another person's point of view. People find themselves acutely aware of what their father would say, what their colleague would think, how their partner would react. Sometimes we consciously try to conjure such voices. Christians ask, 'What would Jesus do?' (without apparently being aware of the blasphemous hubris of thinking they could imagine the mind of God). Trying to think about what a wiser friend would say or do is natural and often helpful. In a strange way, it means we can think with others even when we are by ourselves.

Sometimes, however, the collective mind can be more of a prison than a liberation. In May 1978 an article was published in the prominent Chinese newspaper *Guangming Daily* headlined 'Practice Is the Only Criterion for Judging the Truth' and signed by 'The Special Commentator'. As the Chinese philosopher Ouyang Kang wrote twenty years later, 'The article argued that for all forms of knowledge, including Marxism, their nature of truth must be judged and proved by practice. All scientific knowledge, including Marxism, should be amenable to revision, supplementation, and development in practice in accordance with the specific conditions under which they apply.'

For Chinese philosophers, this was a moment of 'thought liberation'. 'It used to be the case that academic philosophy was always subordinate to the leaders' thoughts and did not have any independent status. Since 1978, however, philosophical research has won a relatively independent academic position.'

Editing Kang's article for *The Philosophers' Magazine* in 1998 was both sobering and startling. It was a stark reminder that the freedom of thought so many of us are lucky to enjoy should never be taken for granted. Kang went on to say that although 'one would think that a new edition of a textbook is a matter of pedagogy' in China, because 'it is only the Marxism embodied in the textbook that is regarded as the orthodox Marxism', a change in what the textbooks say marks a change in the accepted philosophy of the country.

In the West, the threat of stifling conformity comes not from state oppression but from groupthink. Thinking with others brings huge benefits but also the risk of too much consensus, so that alternative viewpoints no longer even register. Groupthink has been blamed for a number of major corporate failures. One of the early developers of the concept, psychologist Irving Janis, used the disastrous US invasion of Cuba's Bay of Pigs as a case study. President Kennedy and his team uncritically accepted the CIA's view of the legitimacy and potential success of the invasion while doubters were brushed aside. The Challenger Space Shuttle disaster of 1986 has been blamed on NASA uncritically accepting a collective judgement that the launch schedule had to meet, meaning that when key team members raised serious safety concerns they were not taken seriously. Groupthink can not only harden opinions but push them in a more extreme direction.

Groupthink does not describe a neat, discrete phenomenon. It is not a kind of mental illness that always has the same causes and symptoms. It is better understood as an umbrella term for the myriad ways in which group thinking can create too much consensus and conformity. It would be reassuring to believe that critical thinking is a prophylactic against it, but that would be to fall prey to another cognitive bias: wishful thinking.

Take philosophy. Can anyone seriously believe that it is immune to groupthink when its history is full of movements such as the Vienna Circle, American Pragmatism, British Empiricism, Cambridge Platonism, the Scottish school of common sense, not to mention the Budapest, Ionian, Kyoto, Lwów–Warsaw and Frankfurt schools, to name but a few. Today university departments are still associated with different styles and approaches to philosophy, so that even in the English-speaking world you'd get a sometimes subtly, sometimes obviously different image of philosophy if you studied at Harvard, Oxford, Chicago or Essex.

It would be pleasing to believe that philosophers are by nature freethinkers, yet time and again we see that the philosophical ideas a person holds depends to a large extent on where they have done their philosophising. Our chances of escaping groupthink are tiny if we allow ourselves to believe that we are immune to its pressures. No one likes to think they follow the herd, but it is frighteningly easy to do so unintentionally. Within any community of interest consensus has a tendency to form, and once it does it can be hard to see beyond it.

This is a particular peril for political conservatives, who believe that the justification of many social practices and norms is that experience has shown they work, even if they don't always seem rational. The Conservative politician and philosopher Jesse Norman concedes that 'It's certainly true that there's no sure-fire way of distinguishing between idiotic received opinion and a widely shared common view that comes from the wisdom of crowds.' A sensible conservative does not assume that established traditions and beliefs must be optimal, but nor do they assume we should get rid of them if they don't seem to make rational sense.

Groupthink is not an irresistible force we inevitably succumb to. Janis believed it was because the Kennedy administration learned its lessons from the Bay of Pigs fiasco that it was able to get through the Cuban Missile Crisis one year later. Active strategies can counter conformity. In groups, leaders need to minimise their involvement and encourage criticism. Problems should be discussed by different, independent groups. External expertise should be sought and all alternatives considered.

As individuals, we need to resist groupthink by similar, less formal means. Actively seek views that differ from your own and come from people outside your circle. Don't get all your information from the same source, or those with a similar stance. Be prepared to challenge friends and colleagues and learn to do so without being aggressive or confrontational. Loyalty should be reserved for people, not ideas.

Loyalty to people and ideas gets mixed up when we allow ourselves to become acolytes. In Germany, explained Michael Dummett, it used to be that 'Each professor had his system which students were expected to study and accept.' He then told me a story about a man who went to Freiburg to study under Husserl:

He described arriving at Husserl's house and presenting himself as Husserl's new student. Husserl answered the door himself, asked him to wait, went back into the house and came back carrying a pile of books and he said, '*Hier sind mein Lebenswerke*' [here is my life's work]. The student was expected to go away and read them all before he came back.

'I rather disapprove of that tradition,' said Dummett. However, discipleship in philosophy has a venerable tradition. In both China and the Indian subcontinent it has historically been assumed that you study at the feet of a master (alas, it

THINK FOR YOURSELF, NOT BY YOURSELF

would rarely be a mistress), metaphorically, if not literally. Discipleship teaches humility and the need to study at length before having the temerity to come up with any of your own ideas, which would probably be expressed with deference as mere interpretations of the ancient sages.

In contemporary Anglophone philosophy, this reverence has been upended. Students are expected to rip the arguments of the greats to shreds from day one. Classic texts like Descartes' *Meditations* are used as 'target practice' for students to sharpen their critical skills. Deference is most definitely out.

I'm too much of a product of the Anglosphere to lose my commitment to independent thought and open criticism. However, this spirit could probably be tempered by a greater appreciation of the need to really spend time understanding a position before launching in with attacks. Students get mixed messages when they are presented with what are supposed to be the greatest philosophical works in history on the assumption that even novices can spot the glaring holes in them.

Both gratuitous iconoclasm and slavish conformity are to be avoided. Just as we need to relinquish a sense of ownership of our ideas, we need to give up misguided feelings of loyalty to a particular thinker, theory or school. We need to be non-partisan. Reasoning well is not about taking sides.

One of the most striking examples of the dangers of partisanship was the cult that built up around Wittgenstein, a bona fide genius who was charismatic and eccentric to boot. For many years, Cambridge philosophy came almost entirely under his sway. Students would even mimic his mannerisms and ways of speaking, perhaps not intentionally, but simply because they were so in awe of him.

Stephen Mulhall, a great admirer of Wittgenstein, was acutely aware of the trap of ending up doing philosophy that was 'some kind of ventriloquising' of the Austrian. 'It is very difficult to see how to go on with and from Wittgenstein without getting your own voice completely submerged. You can find yourself doing no more than reiterating what he's already done.'

Acolytes will often take the methods and ideas of their favourite thinker and apply them as widely as possible. Mulhall accepts 'that holds certain attractions', but 'it also holds great risks of just being very mechanical in what you're doing.' Mulhall believes that too much of what first- and second-generation Wittgensteinian philosophers did 'seemed to teeter on the edge of parody'.

Mulhall's third way requires 'acknowledging what Wittgenstein has done and remaining indebted to that, but doing something that much more intimately expresses your own interests in the subject'. This is surely the best way to work with all good ideas. We need to recognise what they have contributed and move forwards without leaving them behind or treating them as unquestionable, eternal truths. This is also how Anthony Kenny developed his own Wittgensteinian approach to philosophy. 'Wittgenstein wasn't a philosopher I wanted to be looking at all the time, he was somebody who had given me a pair of eyes with which to look at the other things.'

Slavish devotion is fortunately not common in philosophy, but nor is it unheard of. The most extreme example I have come across was the Dutch philosopher Wim Klever. As an undergraduate, I was taught a course on Spinoza by him while on an Erasmus exchange programme in Rotterdam. It became clear that his life's mission was to show that Spinoza was right about absolutely everything. Realising that a critical coursework essay wouldn't go down well, I produced one that vindicated the great Dutch rationalist. Klever gave me 10/10, an absurd score in a subject like philosophy where perfection is impossible. If I was tempted to think the mark reflected my own genius, I was soon put to rights when all three of my fellow Brits used the same sycophantic tactic and also got full marks.

Absolute fidelity to one philosopher is less usual than allegiance to a school. In India, this is pretty much formalised. The philosophers of the past are organised into various schools and scholars today are generally expected to conform to one of them. At the Indian Philosophical Congress the plenary endowed lectures are all devoted to a particular school, and when I visited every speaker was speaking in favour of their own.

Such blatant partisanship would be frowned upon in the West, although it exists in more or less subtle forms. One of the most glaring examples is the division between so-called analytic and continental philosophy. This split opened up in the late nineteenth century and had become a canyon by the middle of the twentieth. The divide is best understood as a difference of opinion about how philosophy should proceed after Kant. Kant argued that our knowledge is confined to the *phenomenal* world, the realm of appearances. The *noumenal* world of 'things in themselves' is unknowable. In the Anglophone world, this was taken as a green light to get on with our essentially empirical, 'down-to earth' philosophising and forget all talk of ultimate reality as metaphysical nonsense. In Germany and France in particular, the Kantian legacy led to the rise of phenomenology, an approach to philosophy which made the analysis of our experience of the world primary. This made sense post-Kant because, if you accepted his philosophy, our experience of the world was in effect all there was to examine.

I don't think the distinction is as deep as many assume, but over the decades it led to institutional divisions that exaggerated the differences. Depending on where you studied and worked, you were presented with a different canon of post-Kant texts, different jargons, different problems or at least different ways of framing them. The language of philosophy started to develop two different dialects which in time became mutually incomprehensible.

According to Simon Glendinning, the divide also took on a symbolic meaning. He argues that, historically, philosophy has distinguished itself from sophistry. Philosophy is sincere argument with integrity, whereas sophistry is the display of reason without substance. With this division come other pairs of valorised opposites: 'logic and rhetoric; clarity and obscurity; precision and vagueness; literal language and poetic language; analysis and speculation'. In Glendinning's view, in order to bolster its own self-image, philosophy has always needed this 'other' to stand in contrast against. Hence for Anglophone philosophers, continental philosophy became 'the false per-sonification by self-styled analytic philosophy of a possibility which is internal to and which threatens all philosophising, that is the possibility of being empty, the possibility of sophistry'.

So partisanship led to Anglophones dismissing an entire tradition of philosophy that is so closely related it is most accur-ately thought of as a non-identical twin. And that's without mentioning the almost complete disregard Western philosophy has had for non-Western traditions.

Another way in which partisanship infects reasoning is by encouraging 'cluster thinking'. Cluster thinking is when we assume that certain beliefs form a natural set when in reality they are independent of each other. This is most obvious in politics. For instance, today I passed a car with a 'Lesbians for Socialism' sticker on it saying 'Gay liberation will never happen under capitalism'. This seems obviously false. Pure capitalism is *laissez-faire*. It doesn't care whom you sleep with as long as you are willing to spend. That's why there has been a corporate rush for the 'pink pound', with businesses loudly proclaiming their support for Pride festivals and LGBTQ+ rights. But if you are both lesbian and socialist it is tempting to believe that these beliefs form a natural pair and cannot be separated.

Michel Onfray gave as a controversial example of cluster thinking what he saw as the taboo in left-wing politics against criticising Islam:

> On the one hand there is capitalism, the bourgeoisie, the USA, George Bush, the state of Israel; on the other there is Palestine, Islam, the Third World, liberation movements. To choose Islam is to go against Bush and Western capitalism, but I reject this dichotomy. I don't want to take sides either with Bush or Bin Laden. It was a big mistake in the twentieth century that you had to take sides with either the Soviet Union or the United States, which affected Sartre as well as Raymond Aron. I side with people like Camus who refused to make that choice.

Many political discussions remain hampered by cluster thinking. The slowness of Republicans in the USA to accept the reality of climate change was largely due to it being identified as a Democrat cause. Although a carbon tax is almost certainly one of the best ways to reduce greenhouse gas emissions, many on the right are against it because creating new taxes looks too much like socialism, and many environmentalists don't like the way it works within the existing capitalist system. In Europe, left and centre parties have been dismissive of patriotism and the idea that immigration can cause any problems at all because they associate these with right-wing, xenophobic nationalism.

As Michel Onfray suggests, cluster thinking tends to create false dichotomies, in which a choice is presented as binary when in reality you don't have to choose at all. For example, some environmentalists argue that we face a choice between increasing economic growth and reducing our negative impact on the environment. This is a false dichotomy because some economic growth can be driven by increased efficiency, not more resource use. Highly efficient renewable energy, for example, could give us more power while reducing our greenhouse gas emissions and use of natural resources. The false dichotomy of 'growth or green' suggests green growth is an oxymoron when it is a very real possibility.

Jesse Norman told me: 'We've moved away from a rather boring period of cluster thinking in which you could allegedly know what someone thought overall by knowing one view about them.' I suspect that the 'we' in this sentence is a rather small group. It would be good if it grew to be less of an anti-cluster cluster and more of a zeitgeist.

Thinking can be both too independent and not independent enough. The ideal lies between an excess of solitariness and an excess of conformity to the group. But this ideal is not always at the neat halfway point and it can vary according to context. Sometimes, the right degree of independence is out on a limb, as a maverick. But when?

'Of course, I am in a significant minority,' says Richard Swinburne. Not many philosophers believe as he does in an immaterial soul, or that the rational case for God's existence is overwhelming. But he doesn't see this as a problem. He says: 'I am very interested in the truth and I hope I can learn from other people, but the arguments go where they do ... Any philosopher at any period is bound to be taking on people and some of the best philosophers have been in a minority to start with, so that fact doesn't worry me too much. Good arguments worry me.'

These words read like admirable independence of mind. In the abstract, it is hard to disagree with them. Yet I'm sure Swinburne isn't a lonely voice of reason. For all the romance of the iconoclast, the sober truth is that most mavericks are plain wrong, and most would defend their views using something like Swinburne's argument. We are left with what we might call the Maverick's paradox: mavericks are doing the right thing by trying to follow the evidence and the arguments, not the herd; but when they do so, most are led to the wrong conclusions.

The paradox is, however, only a seeming one. Truth isn't a democracy and it can't be identified by knowing who is in the majority or the minority. However, if you reach a dissenting opinion on an issue where there are competent experts, it is the dissension that needs justifying. The default explanation, all other things being equal, should be that the dissenter has gone wrong. If you've been given a maths problem along with twenty other reasonably competent others and everyone gets the same answer except you, it is almost certain that you have made the mistake.

Few issues are as clear-cut as a maths problem. But even when it's more complicated, as long as there are expertise and evidence, the onus of proof is on the dissenter to show why everyone else is wrong, not the other way around.

Imagine, for instance, that you are a tiler. You're looking for the best tiles to use and you know that almost everyone uses a standard kind for kitchens. But you then see another, slightly more expensive tile which is meant to be a lot better. It's been around for a few years but hasn't taken off. You wonder why. You suspect that the industry is conservative and not open enough to new materials. But you also know that there have been many supposedly wonder products launched in the past that have turned out to be poor or too expensive. How do you decide if this one is different?

The onus of proof is on the makers of the new product to show it is better, since the old one has been tried and tested. This isn't prejudice against the new but a reasoned demand, since by necessity the established products have an evidence base for their quality built up over years and the new one doesn't.

Part of this onus of proof is to provide an error theory for why the majority are wrong (see p. 177). Maybe they lack a key piece of information that has only recently come to light. Uncharitably, you might think they are just conservative, and if they all said it's rubbish without any evidence, your cynical explanation would gain credibility. If, however, they have stories of people they know having tried the new tiles without satisfactory results, the error theory looks weak.

As a customer of the tiler, the same principle applies. That nine out of ten tilers agree that the more expensive ones aren't worth it is a good reason to assume that they aren't. Of course, that assumption is not beyond challenge. You should be open to argument. But if it's only the one tiler's opinion against the others, it would be unwise to take it. This is not just 'going along with the crowd', it's giving due weight to expert consensus.

The onus of proof places greater demands on dissenters than on majority opinion, because it is usually rational to assume that majority opinion reflects the judgement of the most competent judges on the basis of the most comprehensive evidence. It doesn't mean dissenters are always wrong and should be dismissed, but it does explain why it is not narrow-minded groupthink to be extra-cautious before accepting what they say.

There are times when the onus of proof lies not on dissenters but upholders of the status quo. In politics and public policy, for instance, Janet Radcliffe Richards argues that 'if a policy causes some clear harm, you start with the presupposition that it's unjustified until proved otherwise, and challenge its supporters to defeat that presumption.' Whatever so-called experts say, if a policy is causing evident harm, the onus of proof has to be on those defending the policy.

This is a challenge to conservatives who assume that the onus of proof is always on reformers and never on defenders of the status quo. Their view is that because change always brings risks of unintended consequences, it always requires a stronger case than doing nothing. I think Radcliffe Richards shows why you can't apply this principle of caution blindly and universally. If the status quo evidently causes a harm, then the onus of proof flips and falls more on conservatives than reformers.

My favourite example are the bans that used to be placed on many women having traditionally male jobs, such as being a firefighter. Because this causes an evident social harm, in that it excludes half of the workforce from certain professions, the onus of proof is not on reformers, who may be the minority, but on those who wish to defend the status quo. Once you make that challenge, it can't be met. For instance, one of the key arguments used was that some jobs require a degree of physical strength that women don't have. But as Radcliffe Richards argued, this is nonsense: if physical strength is the criterion, then there should be a physical strength test for the job, not a sex one.[3]

Radcliffe Richards argued that cases like these show that 'most arguments in ordinary life seem to work on the basis of starting with the conclusion you want to defend and then inventing a justification for it.' Indeed, she found it 'astonishing' how often it turned out that well-worn arguments defending established, discriminatory practices were 'straightforwardly spurious'. Often 'the premises don't support the conclusion, or are manifestly invented for the purpose of reaching the conclusion. It's amazing how many familiar views you can dispose of in this way.'

It is not always easy to agree where the onus of proof lies. In the context of a public health emergency, for example, the onus of proof on pharmaceutical companies to show that a treatment or vaccine is safe may not be as strong as it usually is. Nonetheless, the habit of asking where the onus of proof lies is a helpful one which often has a surprisingly clear answer.

When reaching our conclusions, however, our reliance on expert others is unavoidable. The price we must pay for the benefit of learning from other people is that we have to trust some as reliable sources and cannot verify everything they say for themselves. This invites the question: 'How do we know which experts to trust when we do not have the expertise to judge their expertise?'

I have proposed a process of 'epistemological triage': an assessment of how to rank claims to expert knowledge.[4] First, you look at the domain of claimed expertise: is this an area in which we have grounds to believe anyone can be an expert, and if so, to what degree? If you have been dragged into Covid-denial conspiracy theories, for example, you'll come across claims that the virus isn't real. We have every reason to believe that there are robust domains of relevant expertise here that can settle this: virology, public health, medicine, hospital management, and so on.

Having established that there is a domain of expertise, stage two is to find out who the relevant experts are. A lot of Covid deniers cite experts, but often these are not experts in the relevant domains. It may seem impressive that a theory is backed by a physicist or a chemist, but virology and medicine are specific fields and there's no reason why someone who studies the Higgs-Boson should understand why people fall ill with respiratory diseases. Given the relevant domains of expertise, the right experts are virologists, public health officials, doctors, hospital managers.

This sounds obvious when spelled out, but it is remarkable how often we treat 'an expert in such-and-such' as an expert, period. Think how often the media reports a 'scientist says' without saying what kind of scientist she is, or even whether what she's talking about is a scientific issue. 'Scientist says we have no free will' is my favourite and most hated example, because free will is not something that science can or cannot show exists. In more mundane matters, your electrician may be the expert on your electrical system but not necessarily on interior decoration or ergonomics, so be careful before you defer to her choice of fittings and their placement. An economist may know which employment policies are most likely to lift GDP but clueless about how they affect communities and worker well-being. A doctor can tell you the prognoses of different forms of treatment but not whether your priority is maximising the quantity or quality of the rest of your life.

Rejecting deference to undifferentiated expertise is essential for countering the recent decline of respect for experts of all stripes, rooted in the new populist mood which is distrustful of elites of any kind. Jacques Rancière agrees with the populists that the arrogance of elites who despise the masses is a threat to democracy. But the problem is not expertise per se, rather what Rancière calls 'the monopoly of expertise, the idea that there is only one expertise'. This kind of elitism is undemocratic precisely because it rejects the need for a democratic society to make its decisions on the basis of a plurality of expertise.

If there is a domain of expertise, and there are relevant experts, stage three of our triage is to ask whether the particular expert in question is to be trusted. With the 9/11 conspiracy, stage three of the triage is easy: the relevant experts almost all agree that the collapse did not require controlled explosions, and there is simply no reason to distrust them.

But sometimes we need to be more careful. Take the theory that autism was caused by the combined mumps, measles and rubella (MMR) vaccination. Medical science is a legitimate domain and Andrew Wakefield was the right kind of person to be an expert: a physician and academic who had a good publishing record. His paper falsely linking MMR and autism was even published in a top-ranked, peer-reviewed journal, *The Lancet*. Superficially, he passed the test.

On closer examination, it is clear that Wakefield's claims exceeded his expertise. His paper not only explicitly said that no causal link had been found between the vaccine and autism, it was based on a study of only twelve parents. It was in a press conference and a news release that Wakefield went further and called for a suspension of the MMR jab, something his peers denounced. As we've already seen, where there is recognised expertise, the onus of proof is always on the dissenters to show why everyone else is wrong. Wakefield didn't provide that proof.

Even if his peer-reviewed paper had come to a stronger con- clusion, one research study is not enough to establish anything in science. We often read of how a paper 'shows' that such- and-such is true, but almost always it only merely 'suggests' that it might be. Any novel finding should always be treated as a sign that more work is needed until it is corroborated by other studies.

As time went by, it became even clearer that Wakefield was not to be trusted. Other researchers contradicted his find- ings and it transpired that the subjects for his study had been recruited from a group of parents intending to file a lawsuit against MMR manufacturers, and that much of the funding had also come from a body with an interest in litigation. The case shows that there is a very practical need to inoculate our- selves against bad thinking.

The triage method helps us to decide whom to trust, how much, and about what. If the claim is about astrology, you have very good reasons to suppose there is no expertise, except in the sense of knowing about astrology's history and how it is supposed to work. The opinion of an astrologer on the course of the future is worth no more than that of a random pub bore. If a claim is about diet, remember that although there is some expertise, our knowledge is still very incomplete. Whatever the issue, seek out the best people and writings in any given field, not random figures, or the ones with the biggest book sales or YouTube followings.

Sometimes it is not clear whether a domain admits of genuine expertise. Many have the appearance of respectability since they have membership associations, accreditations and qualifications. But look closely at the claims and you often find they are worth little. To choose a deliberately borderline example, it may sound impressive that someone is an NLP (Neuro Linguistic Programming) Master Practitioner, but since NLP is an unregulated profession, all this shows is that the practitioner has successfully completed the paid-for training licensed by a usually profit-making organisation that uses the NLP brand. To judge the value of this, you have to look more closely at what NLP is and whether its claims stand up. This requires looking at the assessments of other psychotherapy professionals, which in turn requires some kind of assessment of the credibility of psychotherapy itself. (I'll leave you to draw your own conclusion about NLP. Consider it homework.) There's no way to get to the bottom of this conclusively, even with a lifetime's study. At every stage, you have to take a certain amount on trust and rely on your own judgement.

This might seem unsatisfactory, but as Onora O'Neill says, 'the idea of the trust-free life seems to me a really quite childish illusion.' For O'Neill there is no 'magic way of leading your life where you get guarantees and proofs and so you never have to trust'. She offers the mundane example of buying a car. 'As I'm very inexpert I do have to rely on somebody. Who? Why? Do I have a guarantee that they are perfectly objective? ... I think what you always get is imperfect evidence so you have to place your bets this way or that way.'

Deference to expertise is necessary and desirable, but it should never be automatic and uncritical. There are many pseudo-experts and even the real ones should not be taken as absolute oracles. Many of us have people we deeply respect and look up to, but we should be prepared to question even them. Respect experts, admire individuals, but never be an acolyte.

How to think for yourself, not by yourself

- Engage with other people and ideas.
- If you've got any kind of intellectual problem, try to solve it collectively, not by yourself.
- Seek constructive criticism of your own ideas.
- Look beyond your own interest, discipline or culture. Engage respectfully but not uncritically.
- If you can't ask them, try to imagine what other people you respect would think.
- Don't assume you're immune to groupthink. Nobody is.
- Don't get all your information from the same source, or those with a similar stance.
- Be loyal to people, not ideas.
- Don't be partisan.
- Avoid cluster thinking: assuming that certain ideas have to go together when each has its own independent justification.
- Reject false dichotomies, which reduce complex issues to bogus binary choices. Often an either/or hides a neither or a both.
- Ask where the onus of proof lies. Where there is established knowledge and expertise, it is usually on the dissenter. Where there is evident harm, it is on the person defending the causes of that harm.
- Choose the experts you listen to by first asking if there is a genuine domain of expertise, then establishing who the experts are, and then checking the credentials of any particular expert you consult.

II

ONLY CONNECT

> No one can begin by being perfect – there is
> much one cannot understand in life at first.
> In order to attain to perfection, one must
> begin by failing to understand much.
>
> FYODOR DOSTOEVSKY, *The Idiot*

Slavoj Žižek has an interesting take on the contradictions of liberal multiculturalists. 'On the one hand, they elevate and idealise the other. But on the other hand, the moment you touch the topics of homosexuality, women's rights and so on, they are horrified at the other.' He thinks the word 'tolerance' often masks a deeper hostility. 'When they say, "Let's tolerate each other" what it usually practically means is "Let's stay away enough from each other."' He is scathing about the way in which liberals idealise the traditions and practices of other cultures while never feeling bound to follow the traditions and practices of their own. 'This is not just self-denigration, false respect for the other. It's that secretly you really privilege yourself. That is to say, you perceive others as constrained by their particular identity, whereas you are truly universal. Your very tolerance is your secret privileged, universal position.'

At moments like these, Žižek warrants his reputation as one of the most interesting and provocative thinkers of his time. For me, it all goes wrong when he tries to give his analysis a theoretical underpinning:

> In Lacanian terms this pure individual would be the pure symbolic individual and what Lacan calls the hard core of phantasy, object small (a) [*objet petit a*] and so on would be that more, that is, as it were, in Kantian terms the pathological remainder. In a Kantian sense, you cannot have a pure non-pathological personality subject. You need a minimum of pathology for solidarity to function. I think in psychoanalysis you can do this, that all the problems are at this level, of tolerance and of intolerance. You fall in love because of object small (a); at the same time this is what annoys you in the other, and you are afraid of getting too close to the other.

There are many problems with Slavoj Žižek, not least his incontinent verbosity. For me the biggest is his imposition of a Lacanian psychoanalytic framework on everything he says. This adds weight and depth to his observations and analyses only in the sense that it makes them longer and burdens them with crippling baggage.

Even if you think Žižek is an extreme or bad example, I hope to persuade you that much harm is done to clear thinking by forcing our ideas and arguments into theoretical pigeonholes. We should make connections between ideas to see the wider picture. Theories are important explanatory tools and of course we should formulate and study them. But more often than not, being wedded to one theory and using it to connect everything is an obstacle to good thinking, not a help.

Theories are often put centre stage in philosophy, the history of which reads like a history of -isms. Any introductory book or course will try to acquaint you with the meanings of empiricism, rationalism, utilitarianism, Platonism, existentialism, Confucianism, Daoism, pragmatism and so on, along with the odd -ology, like phenomenology and deontology. In Indian philosophy you'll be given a list of the orthodox and heterodox schools, including Nyāya, Sāṁkhya, Yoga, Vedānta, Buddhism, Jainism, Cārvāka, and Ājīvika. In these catalogues of -isms, the different positions are cleanly divided and it's a matter of determining which one has got it right.

Yet most of the philosophers who are put into these categories don't neatly fit them. Take the standard distinction between empiricists and rationalists. Textbooks will tell you empiricists believe that knowledge is grounded in our experience of the world while rationalists believe that we can discover a large class of important truths by the operations of reason alone, unaided by observation. On that basis, how would you categorise the following two philosophers, whom we have already encountered?

Philosopher A adopted a method of universal doubt after observing that sense perception often deceives us. He studied human anatomy and in one of his works included a drawing showing how the flames from a fire stimulate nerve endings in the hand that transmit the sensation of heat to the brain. He argued that the basis of all certain knowledge is awareness of our own self, as this is the only observation we can be certain that we are not mistaken about.

Philosopher B argued that you cannot argue from statements of fact to statements of value as an argument that includes an 'ought' in its conclusion but no 'ought' in its premises is invalid. He also argued that our belief in cause and effect is not grounded in any observation of causation in the world. He thought that certainty was only possible when reasoning about the 'relations of ideas': in other words, when the truths in question were logical rather than empirical.

You'll have guessed which is which because I obviously set it up as a trick question to prove a point. Philosopher A is the great 'rationalist' Descartes – sounding here like an empiricist, while Philosopher B is the empiricist David Hume – sounding here like a rationalist. Of course, I cherry-picked my examples, but I didn't select obscure, marginal ones. They are some of Hume and Descartes' most central ideas.

There are real differences in their approaches that justify categorising them as rationalists and empiricists. But it is not usually helpful to foreground these labels. In practice, both reasoned from experience and used forms of logical analysis. What matters most is whether they used the right kinds of arguments at the right times, and drew the right conclusions.

It should also be remembered that many of these labels are given retrospectively, or at least made more important and clear-cut after the event. In their time, many philosophers were just trying to work things out and were not bothered about which team they belonged to. Kierkegaard, for instance, is known as the father of existentialism, but if he was, he didn't even know the name of his philosophical child, since he pre-dates the term's first use. The materialists Locke and Hume would no doubt have been surprised to find that they have been lumped together as empiricists with the eighteenth-century

Irish philosopher George Berkeley, who argued that reality was essentially mental in nature.

Sometimes, labels are used not only anachronistically but wildly inaccurately. The most commonly abused such term is 'postmodern', which seems to be applied to any philosopher who was remotely sceptical about Truth with a capital T. It's common for Nietzsche to be called a postmodernist when he was writing a century before the term even existed. It's disconcerting to see people like Steven Pinker do this, in the very process of arguing for the importance of truth and reason.[1] Like 'neoliberal' and 'capitalist', 'postmodern' is a term used so loosely in public discourse that it has lost all meaning.

Unfortunately, a contemporary philosophical training sometimes encourages the slapping-on of labels. Students are assigned essays in which they have to apply a particular theory to a particular issue, such as by outlining a utilitarian view on euthanasia. This encourages the idea that there is *a* utilitarian view on such issues when there is in fact a lot of diversity among utilitarians. This isn't just an undergraduate error. The moral philosopher Roger Crisp said that 'People rather enjoy the cut and thrust of philosophical debate,' and this encourages them to place themselves on one side of an argument with clearly defined opponents. 'What worries me is when you get people writing in journals as if those distinctions are clear-cut and there's a consensus on what they amount to.'

The contemporary British political philosopher Jo Wolff identifies a general methodological principle that guards against taking refuge in an -ism. 'Generally, if someone has thought hard and long about an area and they're intelligent to start with and they're thinking in depth and they present an articulated body of thought, it's very unlikely that it's all going to be wrong,' says Wolff. 'The most common mistake people make is to have got part of the truth and to think they've got all of it.'

I'm no Marxist, for example, but I would be an idiot not to see that Marx made many astute observations and analyses. Nor am I a neoliberal, but that doesn't mean I should ignore everything that has been said about the efficiency of markets. Yet it is all too easy to become so enamoured of one way of looking at the world that everything is forced through the same lens. For example, Iain McGilchrist's *The Master and His Emissary* attributes many developments in human history to the different functions of the right and left hemispheres of the brain. It seems McGilchrist is the master and his many readers have become his emissaries, because I have lost count of the number of people who enthusiastically tell me about why left- and right-brain differences explain pretty much everything. (Spoiler alert: they don't.) There is a lot of truth in McGilchrist's work but it is not the whole truth, a master theory of everything. The same is true of Shoshana Zuboff's ideas about surveillance capitalism, Chomsky's analysis of the state manufacturing of consent, Naomi Klein's theory of disaster capitalism, Thomas Piketty's theories about the relationship between ownership of capital and inequality. All explain some things, none explain everything.

Another reason to avoid signing up to sharply demarcated intellectual teams is that it encourages a mentality of competition when the most fruitful work often arises by bringing seemingly opposed sides together. The historian of ideas Jonathan Israel approvingly told me about Marcelo Dascal, a Brazilian-born Israeli philosopher and linguist, who argued that 'The way concepts are formulated in the context of debate has an inherent tendency, as history and experience show, to create polarities and dichotomies around which the discussion unfolds.' In Dascal's view, the greatest innovations in thought occur when great minds have looked for ways to 'de-dichotomise the rigid polarities that had been created by transcending the framework within which the debate had been posed'.

This de-dichotomisation relies on forms of 'soft rationality' which try to 'soften the iron logic of the polarity that has formed'. It would be better if dichotomies did not become so rigid that they needed softening. Hence I advocate 'Ismism': a justified prejudice against the excessive reliance on -isms. Our attachments to any kind of idea should be cautious and critical.

Although it is a mistake to force all our ideas together into one neat -ism, we can't just leave them completely unconnected. Our beliefs form a set and that set should be as consistent as possible, without doing violence to the parts. Too much systematising is stifling, too little anarchic.

Twentieth-century Anglophone philosophy is a case in point. It became so sceptical of grand metaphysical systems that it went too far the other way. 'When I was in Oxford,' recalls John Searle, 'the term "piecemeal" was a term of praise.' This is understandable. In the history of philosophy there seems to be an inverse correlation between the intricacy and size of a system and its credibility. Kant, for example, was brilliant but I believe nothing worth taking from his work requires the convoluted edifice of his 'architectonic' system, his tables of categories and judgements, and so on. Spinoza and Hegel are still worth reading, although few buy into their full-blown metaphysical systems.

Still, as Rebecca Goldstein says, philosophers' ideas do fit together. 'Dan Dennett has a certain kind of philosophical profile, very different from Tom Nagel's, and if you know one of their views you could probably deduce the others.' If you look back at all the great philosophers, their ideas added up to a coherent overall picture. 'Hume very much had a general theory, Locke had a general theory, even Berkeley in his way had a general theory,' says Searle. 'So I think that in intellectual life you should never be just satisfied with bits and pieces of information and understanding. You want to know how it all hangs together.'

Searle is right. We just need to be on our guard against joining dots that aren't actually connected, to force a more complete explanation than we are equipped to offer. Bernard Williams never fell for this temptation. He recalls as 'one of the nicest things ever said about my philosophy' a remark that 'it was liberating, because it stopped people having to think within a certain box where something seems absolutely essentially connected to something else.' In other words, although it may seem a weakness of Williams's philosophy that it didn't join lots of dots, its great strength was that it showed how others had joined them incorrectly.

Philosophy's twentieth-century emphasis on the piecemeal was part of a broader reductionist trend in Western thinking. The success of science was a triumph of reductionism, in which the workings of nature were understood by breaking them down into their smallest parts. Other disciplines took note and followed suit. But this reductionist method has limits, even in science, where a lot of the growth areas are now looking at how complex systems work.

In philosophy and other non-scientific disciplines, reductionist approaches have crowded out holistic ones. (It doesn't help that the word 'holistic' has come to be associated with complementary medicine and dubious spiritual hocus-pocus.) Mary Midgley and Iris Murdoch were two philosophers who never made this mistake. Midgley says, 'I think that [Iris and I] share the thought that it's terribly important to see the whole and that one is usually deceiving oneself if one says "x is only y."' She doesn't deny that 'Sometimes there's good reason to attend only to y,' just that there are also often very good reasons not to.

Reductionist explanations not only privilege parts over wholes, they also tend to overestimate the power of single explanations. But every theory has its scope and limits. Even a 'theory of everything' in physics would not be a theory of everything in any normal sense. It would not even fully explain biology, meteorology or psychology, let alone ethics or art.

The most extreme form of reductionism taken seriously today is scientism. Alex Rosenberg defines scientism as 'the exaggerated confidence in the findings of science and the unreasonable belief that its methods can answer all questions'. As that definition suggests, scientism is usually a term of abuse and few apply the label to themselves. Rosenberg is an exception. He wants to reclaim the term and make it a positive. 'I'm ready to endorse that definition of scientism if you remove the words "exaggerated" and "unreasonable".' He believes that 'the methods of science are the only reliable ways to secure knowledge of anything.' This means that any belief that cannot be tested by the methods of science can't be knowledge and should be seen as mere opinion. Morality and aesthetics are no more than expressions of approval or disgust. Politics is just a practical means of running a society. The 'meaning of life' has no meaning. Scientism suggests that most of philosophy is just an empty word game.

Scientism offers us an impoverished and narrow vision of human rationality. It can only sound plausible by sneaking in the unreasonable demand that reason only concern itself with what is maximally objective and verifiable. It asks what indubitable objective facts morality rests on, finds none and rejects the whole enterprise. But why should the only things that matter, and the only things we can reason about, be the things that can be settled by plain appeal to the facts alone? That claim would be an assertion, one which is itself not based in any facts. 'Only hard facts matter' is not a matter of fact but of values.

Scientism also underplays the role of fact in non-scientific enquiry. Morality is not like science, but it is not mere opinion either. Consider the facts that 'race' is not a meaningful biological category, that women and men are on average equally intelligent, that animals feel pain, that a zygote has no central nervous system, that economic policies have certain consequences, and so on. All of these facts have evident moral significance. Morality is not as straightforwardly amendable to reason as science, but that does not mean it lies beyond rationality altogether.

Not all advocates of scientism reject morality. The neuroscientist Sam Harris takes the other option, arguing that morality can be entirely grounded in science. Harris argues that as long as we agree that human well-being matters, in time neuroscience will tell us everything we need to know about how to maximise it. This is incredibly simplistic. The fundamental claim that human well-being is what matters is non-scientific, since science tells us nothing about what should matter for us. Even if we were to somehow overlook this, Harris assumes a consensus that just isn't there. As Patricia Churchland explained, Harris's view is 'pretty optimistic – or pessimistic, depending on your point of view. Different people even within a culture, even within a family, have different views about what constitutes their own well-being. Some people like to live out in the bush like hermits and dig in the ground and shoot deer for resources, and other people can't countenance a life that isn't in the city, in the mix of cultural wonderfulness. So people have fundamentally different ideas about what constitutes well-being.'

Scientism, like all forms of reductionism, succeeds in joining the dots only to the extent that it massively reduces the number of dots that it decrees need to be joined, only selecting those that are similar and near to each other. Putting everything together is more difficult than this because it requires us to link distant dots of different kinds. In such cases, links need to be weaker, more tentative and always breakable.

Scientism is right that theories should be based on facts. Unfortunately, many people base what they take as facts on their theories. They fall under the spell of a theory and become blinded to any evidence of experience against it. The purity and simplicity of a theory is preferred to the messiness and complexity of reality, even when it obviously fails to fit it.

I remember being stunned many years ago when a libertarian political philosopher assured me that free markets worked because the economist Ludwig von Mises had proved they did *a priori* – meaning by pure logic alone. Von Mises thought that economics was one part of a 'general theory of human action' that he called praxeology. This has a 'Formal and Aprioristic Character', being 'anterior to any actual instance of conception and experience'.[2] The evidence-free certainties of von Mises buttress the libertarians' simple prescription for a strong economy: unregulated free markets as the best mechanism for delivering human prosperity and happiness.

Although von Mises is still revered by many libertarians, in recent decades his star has fallen along with all forms of classical economics that don't attend enough to how people actually behave. Economists are belatedly accepting that human beings are not dispassionate calculating machines that make decisions according to their own best interests, but are swayed by all sorts of desires, values and biases – some good, some bad. That's one reason why stock markets are so volatile: sometimes a collective irrational exuberance leads traders to believe growth will never end, and at other times raw fear leads them to sell and run.

Keeping theory in its place and giving evidence and experience the last word is more difficult than it might sound. Even those who sincerely believe that they have followed the evidence to arrive at their theories often end up more attached to the theories than to the observations they rest upon. To put it another way, observations can give rise to theories which people then give more credence to than observations.

We have seen an interesting example of this during the Covid-19 pandemic. Many governments, keen to make sure their policies would actually work, embraced behavioural science to gain insight into the effects of implementing different restrictions. The UK government, which had created its own Behavioural Insights Team in 2010, repeatedly justified delaying or removing lockdowns and restrictions on the grounds that their experts' advice suggested people wouldn't comply. As Health Secretary Matt Hancock said in June 2021, 'The clear scientific advice at the time was that there was a need to have these tools like lockdown at your disposal but also that the consequences and the costs of lockdown start immediately and, critically, the clear advice at the time was that there's only a limited period that people would put up with it.' Evidence-based psychological mechanisms cited to justify claims like these included 'optimism bias' (people assume other people will get ill, not them), 'reactance' (the desire to do the opposite of what we feel we are being coerced to do), and 'behavioural fatigue'.[3]

In fact, it turned out that most people were very willing to restrict their behaviour, with surveys consistently showing greater public support for restrictions than there was in the government itself, which seemed bizarrely wedded to an *a priori* notion of what the Great British love of freedom required.

There is a dispute about whether the behavioural scientists got it wrong, the government was distorting their message, or some blend of the two. (The term 'behavioural fatigue' seems to have been invented by the government and has no source in textbooks or its own Behavioural Insights Team.[4]) Whatever precisely happened, the episode contains a warning. When people are strongly motivated to reach a conclusion, they are easily persuaded that it is supported by evidence-based theories, even when the evidence is weak. Yet again we have an instance of people not paying enough attention to the dissimilarities between the case in hand and past experience. Behavioural science is a young discipline and it should never have been taken as an authoritative source of predictions about public behaviour in unprecedented circumstances. It was given too much weight because weight was needed and it looked like the only source.

As we've already seen, learning from the past requires paying close attention both to the precedents and to the current situation. The two key questions are: are there genuine precedents? Are there any important differences between those precedents and the current case? And when answering these questions, we have to be mindful that the world is incredibly complex, and we should be on our guard against assuming that we can discern the most important patterns.

I've also become convinced that theory is more of a hindrance than a help in ethics. I reject the widespread assumption that when trying to work out the morally right thing to do, we should first decide what our overarching moral principles are and then try to apply them to the case in hand. A utilitarian would ask: which action will result in the greatest happiness of the greatest number? A Kantian: which of the possible ways of acting could I honestly and consistently say would be the right way for anyone to act in the same situation, not just me? A Confucian: would this act impose on others what I would not wish for myself? And so on. In this kind of 'applied ethics' you take your ethical theory and then apply it to specific cases.

This theory-first approach is doomed to real-world failure because we don't agree on which theory to apply. As Janet Radcliffe Richards says, 'There is nothing so useless, as far as I can see, as telling a doctor that if you're a Kantian you do this and if you're a utilitarian you do that – even supposing there were agreement among either Kantians or utilitarians.' This approach also obscures the fact that in moral reasoning, as Roger Crisp says, 'often when you get down to brass tacks there's a lot more common ground than people realise' and they 'tend to converge on various conclusions. In environmental ethics, for example, most people think that we are wrecking the environment in ways which we shouldn't be and they're coming out with arguments why we should stop.'

Jo Wolff thinks that one reason not to be too wedded to one ethical theory is that each one identifies something important about our moral lives – our flourishing, our rights, our capacities to choose, our social relations – and we need to take them all into account, not decide which one trumps the others. Any comprehensive understanding of ethics 'has to take all of those things into account and this gives us a complicated, messy theory,' says Wolff. That 'might lead us into problems and conflicts, but it doesn't seem to me that we could abandon any of these perspectives'.

Moral theories can give us useful questions to ask, such as: do I have a right to do this? Am I causing unnecessary harm? Would I be fulfilling my responsibilities? Is it fair? Is it equitable? But the function of these questions is to direct our attention to aspects of a problem which can only be properly addressed by carefully considering it from all angles.

One philosopher who recognised this was Mary Warnock. As chair of both the UK government's Committee of Enquiry into the Education of Handicapped Children and Young People in the 1970s and the Committee of Inquiry into Human Fertilisation and Embryology in the 1980s, she showed how engaged philosophers can make real contributions to public life and policy. 'I still maintain that even in academic moral philosophy it is extremely valuable to understand what the facts on the ground are,' she said. 'It's situational ethics, if you'd like to give it a name.'

To see the power and importance of a situational approach, take a decision to go to war or not. This is an unusual area of ethics in that there is surprisingly wide agreement about principles. Just war theory has roots in Christianity and Islam but is now largely secular. It divides the moral justifications for war into two categories: *jus ad bellum* (just reasons to go to war) and *jus in bello* (justice in the conduct of war). Although there are variations in how these are formulated, most include a small number of key principles. The tests of *jus ad bellum* are that the war is a proportionate response, fought in a just cause, with the right intention, with a probability of success, by a competent authority, and only as a last resort. Once a war is under way, the three tests of *jus in bello* are that attacks are only on legitimate targets, all force is proportionate and necessary, and that prisoners of war are treated fairly.

It's hard to argue with any of these principles. But it is, of course, very easy to argue about whether they are satisfied in any particular case. One side's legitimate insurgency is another's terrorist group; one side's proportionate actions are another's over-reaction or the under-reaction of appeasement; war is very rarely literally the last resort, but you can argue it is the last *reasonable* resort if waiting any longer carries the serious risk of an even bloodier conflict, or victory to the unjust side.

In my 2002 book *Making Sense: Philosophy Behind the Headlines*, I used the example of the Second Gulf War to show how the philosophy of just war theory can help us decide on its morality. I cautioned against paying too much attention to the political rhetoric and urged us to look at the substantive arguments for and against. In the final paragraph of that chapter, I said: 'What is needed to move from these theoretical considerations to a decision on whether to support the war or not are the facts about the threats, risks, intentions and consequences of the various options available. [. . .] At that point, the philosopher needs to retire and let others come to their final judgements.'

ONLY CONNECT

Twenty years on, it sounds to me as though I was saying that all the work of moral reasoning happens at a theoretical level and adding in the evidence is a separate task, one that anyone can do. I now think that is wrong. Moral reasoning about any concrete case must concern itself with the facts from the beginning. The form of moral reasoning which says 'First establish your principles and then apply them' is fundamentally, dangerously wrong.

It is telling that in *Making Sense* I came to no conclusion about the morality of the Second Gulf War. At the time this seemed to me like appropriate authorial humility: my job was not to make a moral judgement but to give readers the tools to come to their own conclusions. I was also trying to avoid the kind of overconfidence a philosophical training can give you. This is what Ray Monk identified as the cause of Bertrand Russell's often naive pronouncements about politics. 'You can't adopt the kind of arrogance that Russell adopted and say, "I've thought about the most difficult problem that there is, and so working out who should be the next president of the United States should be a piece of cake." It doesn't work like that.'

But I wasn't just trying not to be arrogant. I had simply come to no clear conclusion. The arguments seemed to me to be much more finely balanced than most people in my social milieu – who were almost all fervently against – believed. Part of the reason, I now think, is that many arguments being made against the war were philosophically weak. These bad arguments captured my attention too much: I was noticing all the many weaknesses in the case against war and not its few key strengths. This is a hazard of a philosophical training. We are taught to pick holes and find weaknesses more than we are to construct good arguments. Professional scepticism becomes the habit of distrusting whatever the dominant argument happens to be.

249

Now, I think that instead of starting by thinking about just war theory and then applying it, I should have begun by examining the facts as closely as possible. On the one hand there were many uncomfortable truths that critics of the war underplayed. Saddam Hussein was a murderous dictator who had fought a devastating war with one neighbour and invaded another. The world had every reason to think he had chemical and biological weapons because Iraq had both biological and nuclear weapon programmes in the 1980s and he had used chemical weapons in the 1980–88 war with Iran and against Kurds and Ma'dan (or Marsh Arabs) in his own country. Plus, he had repeatedly frustrated the work of UN weapons inspectors. He was a destabilising force in the world's most volatile region. The prospect of many more years of his rule was an awful one.

But on the other hand, history has shown time and again that to go to war always results in massive casualties and that the possibility of establishing a peaceful, democratic state in its aftermath is extremely difficult, especially in a country that does not have existing and well-established democratic institutions and that is riven by sectarian divisions. In short, waging war was almost certain to result in disaster; not waging war would permit the extension of terrible tragedy.

You could feed this data into the framework of just war theory and analyse whether Saddam Hussein's aggressions gave just cause for war, whether success was probable and so on. Indeed, breaking down the arguments in these ways could have been extremely helpful. Analysis is a powerful tool to focus attention. But at bottom, you don't need a theory or a complex moral argument to reach the conclusion that going to war was a dangerous, high-stakes gamble that the United States and its allies did not have to take.

Thinking too much about theory risks obscuring this, as something could have been said in favour of every test of just war theory. The cause – removing a murderous tyranny – was just; the legitimate authority claimed was a UN resolution; the fighting parties were legitimate democratic states; the stated intentions were good; civilians would be spared as much as possible; the Geneva convention would be followed; and so on. As for the probability of success, the US and UK were confident and they were supposedly the people armed with the best information.

I think the Second Gulf War is a a good and terrible example of the need in moral reasoning to start with the facts and use theory to help analyse it, rather than starting with principles and trying to apply them. Theory-first approaches detract our attention from what is primary – how things are – and divert it towards what is secondary – how we think about them.

Sometimes when we're trying to fit the pieces of a mental jigsaw together, we think, think, think and think again and seem to hit a brick wall. Is it possible to think too much? If by thinking we mean fully conscious, step-by-step analysis, then the answer is certainly yes. To think well we have to make sure we do all the other things that oil the engine of thought. Most obviously, we need to exercise, try to get enough sleep, avoid too much time in intoxicated stupors or hangovers.

The need for more than just mental labour is evident in Mason Currey's delightful book *Daily Rituals*, which describes the habits of 181 artists and intellectuals. Each is different, but the majority have regular routines and only work three to five hours a day. Making time for the mind to wander or empty seems to be essential, which is why I never feel guilty about heading off for a stroll or a coffee after having done a few hours' work in the morning, as I am about to do now.

Currey's book is also strong counter-evidence against the romantic idea that drugs are cognitive enhancers. Jackson

Pollock, for example, was a dipsomaniac but his best work was produced in one of his more sober periods. Most of the time when people are high they talk bullshit that merely seems profound to them at the time. Hallucinogens can generate profound feelings of connection and oneness, but this doesn't translate into useful knowledge claims. The scant examples of major ideas that have been drug-induced should not be taken as evidence that intoxication is generally a good thinking aid.

The reason drugs *sometimes* help is that they encourage the mind to work on an intuitive rather than a rational level, opening up the possibility of making new and fruitful connections. This unleashing of imagination does not supplant reason but feeds it. It leaves the rational mind with the job of testing and honing ideas, not coming up with them. Indeed, this is imagination's main role.

Where these ideas come from is often a mystery. As the Argentinian novelist Guillermo Martínez asks, 'The way that you reach the truth in mathematics, for example, or the way a new novel comes to your thoughts – is it just coming out from a leap or is it something that comes step by step? Do you see a kind of inspiration which is the end of some hidden reasoning?' Even when we have been thinking hard about something, when an answer comes it often just seems to pop into our heads. I think we rarely have the feeling of a conclusion literally being generated by a deductive process. Rather, we see if the idea is supported by a good argument *after* we've had it. That suggests good thinking requires creating the conditions for mental processing to go about its work in the background, not just having the skills for analysing arguments when they are at the front of our minds.

Genevieve Lloyd is a philosopher who appreciates that 'the operations of intellect and imagination are inseparable.' Reason 'involves the capacity for critical reflection on, and transformation of, received patterns of thought' and this in turn requires the imagination to conceive of alternatives.

Sometimes it makes sense to use non-rational, even irrational processes as tools to fire our imagination and in turn feed our reasoning. This is the intriguing suggestion the humanist writer Philip Pullman made when he created the character of a rational scientist, Mary, who would consult the *I Ching*. Pullman told me he did not believe that the *I Ching*, tarot cards or anything like them reveal the truth. But 'What I do think they do is give us a usefully random set of notions which can free the creative part of our minds, the bit that's not rational, to find things that we otherwise wouldn't find.'

Pullman says Mary is 'bright enough not to be bounded by her rationality'. That's a wonderful phrase. Or to put it another way, our rationality should draw on more than that which is purely rational. Intuition, imagination and speculation can all enrich our rational selves.

How to make the right connections

- Beware of all kinds of -isms and -ologies. They are better used as tools of classification, not as fundamental distinctions.
- Let theory follow fact, not facts made to fit with theory.
- Be especially sceptical of ethical theories. Don't just apply them to real world problems. Attend first to the specifics of the situation and use theories and principles only as tools to help you think about it. Check theories and their limitations through the lens of reality.
- Don't mistake an important part of the truth for the whole of it.
- Try to de-dichotomise rigid polarities, not harden them.
- Join the dots that really are linked. Don't force false connections.
- Don't just analyse things in terms of their parts. Look for holistic explanations of how the whole works.
- Avoid scientism. It is self-defeating since the claim that the only genuine truths are scientific is not a scientific one.
- Use your imagination to generate ideas and hunches for the rational mind to analyse.
- Give the mind time to rest, wander and go about its work in mysterious, unconscious ways.

12

DON'T GIVE UP

Through error you come to the truth! I am
a man because I err! You never reach any
truth without making fourteen mistakes
and very likely a hundred and fourteen.

FYODOR DOSTOEVSKY, *Crime and Punishment*

The virtues of persistence and resilience are widely lauded. Stories of how people brushed off failure to eventually triumph are the favourite folk stories of our time. Philosophy has a few of its own. One paper by David Chalmers and Andy Clark was rejected from three major journals before finally being accepted by *Analysis*. That paper, 'The Extended Mind', subsequently became one of the most discussed in the philosophy of mind.

But persistence in thinking is not a virtue because it will inevitably lead you to eventual triumph. Rather, the refusal to give up is a commitment to keep living an intellectually engaged life even in the absence of final answers. For *Homo sapiens*, thinking is part of what it means to live a fully human life and not just a means to an end.

I heard something like this eloquently expressed around twenty years ago when Jonathan Rée gave a talk on Kierkegaard, of whom he said: 'The point was not to be a philosopher, but to *become* one.' As usual, I remember little of the detail of the talk but this core idea made an impression, whether or not it exactly matches the stamp that made it. Rée had hit upon something fundamental about philosophical thinking. It is an activity, a process, a journey with directions but no destination. To think you've reached its end, that you have it all worked out, is in effect to give up, to pretend you've achieved the impossible.

If we can only ever be in the process of becoming a philosopher, then, as A. C. Grayling says, 'To claim to be one is an act of temerity. It's an accolade that somebody else might give you if you merit it.' In that sense, 'There are plenty of genuine philosophers, people who live philosophically and thoughtfully, who have never studied philosophy, never taught it, never been near a university.' Conversely, there may be some professional philosophy teachers who are not philosophers at all.

So to think like a philosopher is continually to be becoming a philosopher. It requires never giving up, never ceasing to ask questions, never settling. For some this might sound like a cause for despair. But we all know what it means to rest in peace. To be restless is to be alive.

As we have seen, much of this incessant philosophical thought is concerned with resolving aporias, beliefs that make sense individually but which collectively contradict each other. One reason why this process never ends is that these aporias are not all simply out there waiting to be fixed. In the process of thinking hard we actually create them. As Simon Critchley says, 'Philosophy should be about the cultivation of certain

forms of paradoxes in the face of what passes as common sense.'
No wonder that thinking often seems to create two new questions for every one it answers.

Not only are new aporias always springing to life, many philosophers have argued that, once generated, not every aporia can be solved. Kant formulated four 'antinomies': contradictions which inescapably arise when we attempt to understand ultimate reality. We find ourselves compelled to believe that the universe had a beginning *and* that it is eternal; that every object has a smallest part *and* that there are no such fundamental parts; that everything has a cause *and* that some things must be without cause; that there is at least one necessary being *and* no necessary being. Thomas Nagel argued that we cannot reconcile free will with an objective view of the universe and that we have to apply a kind of 'double vision', sometimes viewing ourselves from within as free agents and sometimes from without as cogs in the cosmic machine. Colin McGinn maintains that the problem of consciousness can never be solved, because every species has limits to what it can comprehend. Cats can't understand cryptocurrencies, and humans cannot understand how consciousness is possible.

Daniel Dennett believes that for some issues at least, many of his philosophical colleagues are too quick to declare a problem irresolvable. 'My first suspicion when people say that these problems are intractable is that they are happy they are intractable, they want to keep it that way. [...] This is sometimes transparent, as is the case with the problem of consciousness. You have people like McGinn and Fodor saying, "This is insoluble – go play tennis."'

Knowing when you've gone down an intellectual cul-de-sac is an important skill. Sometimes we really do need to admit defeat. But more often, the best response to a seeming dead end is not to give up altogether but to stop trying the same failed approach again and again. If it looks like you've hit a brick wall, there are two possibilities. One is that it's not as solid, high or long as you think and you haven't found your way over, through or around it. The other is that you need to retrace your steps and try another alleyway. An impasse is often a sign that you are thinking about a problem in the wrong way, not that you shouldn't be thinking about it at all.

But often we don't ever get to an answer that we think satisfactorily wraps everything up. Sometimes there are more-or-less good answers, but they fall short of explaining everything and tying up every loose end. Moral reasoning is usually like this. Very little is clear-cut. Many get frustrated with this, but according to T. M. Scanlon, 'To do any kind of serious philosophy you have to have a high tolerance for frustration and incompleteness: things don't become philosophical questions if they can be answered pretty easily.' As Derrida once said, 'If things were simple, word would have got around.'

Sometimes, no matter how acute our critical thinking skills are, we cannot answer the questions that bug us. It happens even to the greatest philosophers, perhaps especially to them. David Hume wrote that his 'intense view' of the 'manifold contradictions and imperfections in human reason' so 'heated my brain, that I am ready to reject all belief and reasoning, and can look upon no opinion even as more probable or likely than another'. He found himself 'confounded with all these questions' and imagined himself 'in the most deplorable condition imaginable, inviron'd with the deepest darkness, and utterly depriv'd of the use of every member and faculty'.[1] Although he found that 'reason is incapable of dispelling these clouds', fortunately, 'nature herself suffices to that purpose, and cures me of this philosophical melancholy and delirium.' Getting on with life eases the anxiety. 'I dine, I play a game of back-gammon, I converse, and am merry with my friends; and when after three or four hours' amusement, I wou'd return to these speculations, they appear so cold, and strain'd, and ridiculous, that I cannot find in my heart to enter into them any farther.' Life can't wait for all the answers, and nor does it need to.

Some, however, are unwilling to abide in uncertainty. In a culture in which technology promises to measure everything, bogus certainty and precision are to be found everywhere. There is no evidence to suggest that 10,000 steps a day is the key to fitness, but many of us have been fooled into thinking it is and as a result count every step we take. The flavanols in cacao may indeed 'help maintain endothelium-dependent vasodilation, which contributes to normal blood flow', but can we really believe the European Food Safety Authority when it says that we should eat 200mg of cocoa flavanols a day?[2] And why do weather apps continue to give hourly forecasts several days ahead when we all know these will have changed numerous times by the time the actual weather comes round? In each of these cases there is a bogus precision which suggests a fake certainty. It would be more honest to reflect the real uncertainties with less precise advice: keep active, eat modest quantities of dark chocolate if you like it, and be aware there could well be some rain on Thursday at some point.

One reason honesty loses out is that, as psychologists have shown, we like certainty. We tend to be more credulous and trusting of people who convey certainty and distrustful of those who seem doubtful. Psychologists such as Elizabeth Loftus tell us we get this exactly the wrong way round. In court cases, for example, witnesses who express certainty about what they have seen tend to be more believed, but confidence is an unreliable indicator of accuracy. It's really difficult to overcome this bias. Although I know what psychology says about this and loathe arrogance and overconfidence, I still find it harder to believe someone is wrong when they express their views with complete conviction. Because it seems harsh to judge anyone as either dishonest or gravely mistaken, I find it more comfortable to think that maybe they are just right.

Our attraction to certainty is mirrored by our dislike of uncertainty. We often stick with something we don't really want because we prefer it to the risks of change. This preference for the 'devil you know' can be sensible prudence, but it can also reflect an unwarranted bias against uncertainty. For example, should you quit your job or stick it out? The consequences of quitting are usually uncertain, while you have a clear idea of what will happen if you don't. If your job is OK, that may be reason enough to stay put. But if you really hate your job, unless the uncertainties of quitting are potentially disastrous, why not quit? Often the answer is simply that uncertainty itself is frightening. Maybe philosophy can help tame this 'incertophobia', an excessive fear of uncertainty. Even when philosophy provides answers, they're not definitive ones. It is a great teacher of the art of living with uncertainty, without final answers, without closure.

How much we are drawn to certainty and precision as individuals probably has a lot to do with temperament. But we can change. Hilary Putnam, for instance, felt the attraction of certainty but had the wisdom to resist its charms. Although he disliked 'the limits Wittgensteinians put on philosophy', he said many of Wittgenstein's 'criticisms of the traps we fall into seem to me profoundly right'. Some of them come from 'a misplaced belief that systematicity must be possible', what he calls a 'philosopher's *must*'. His resistance to these imperatives to make our ideas neatly ordered tracked his rising appreciation of context sensitivity. Real clarity requires attending to the specific details of each problem or phenomenon. But the quest for certainty tends towards a one-size-fits-all über-explanation, a grand theory of everything.

Stuart Hampshire echoed this when he talked about logic as a form of 'convergent reasoning' in which 'anyone who is competent in the subject will accept the conclusions of the theorems you arrive at. That's that.' For example, 'Bertrand Russell in his autobiography said that when he read Euclid he suddenly emerged into a world which he found perfect because results are proved, there's no argument.' But 'It's the essence of practical problems that it's never "that's that" in that sense. Reasoning which is really working is reasoning that can go wrong, where you take a risk. You do everything you can do to get it right, but maybe you don't get it right, or maybe it's not clear what getting it right actually is.'

Time and again we find that the yearning for certainties, for universal validity, for principles that will cover all eventualities, turns out to be quixotic. Take the philosophy of science. Pretty much every scientist agrees that no description of 'the scientific method' captures all that scientists actually do. 'I'm sceptical that there can ever be a complete overarching theory [of scientific method] simply because science is about rationality,' says physicist Alan Sokal. 'Rationality is always adaptation to unforeseen circumstances – how can you possibly codify that?' Philosophers who believe they can fully prescribe the scientific method fail to recognise that 'the world is just extremely complicated.' They project their ways of thinking on to scientists so there is 'too much formal logic and too little reasoning that is close to what scientists actually do in practice'.

Some are disappointed that a rational life leaves so much uncertain and so many loose ends. The dream of enlightenment turns out to be the reality of a bit less darkness. But disillusion is often the result of starting out expecting too much. A. C. Grayling says there is often a false assumption that 'If reason was so wonderful, things should be perfect.' No wonder that when things evidently aren't perfect, the conclusion drawn is that reason is not so wonderful. 'I think that's a mistake,' he says. He takes the example of rival satellite television systems in the UK, Sky and BSB. Sky's worse technology prevailed, but that doesn't mean anyone was acting irrationally. There were more factors involved than the efficacy of the technology, such as affordability, programme choice, and which was the better investment. All these were driven by rational considerations. 'Very often reason might result in the third-best or the tenth-best of something,' says Grayling, 'but it is still the outcome of reason, and it is still probably considerably better than just leaving it up to whoever happens to be strongest, or to chaos or to chance.' Reason doesn't guarantee optimal decisions or outcomes, not least because it always relies on fallible humans to use it. Still, it remains the best tool we have for making sense of the world.

Paradoxically, sometimes the more we understand, the less things seem to make sense. I remember several years ago when I gave my first talk on my book on free will. The first questioner stood up and said, 'I came here this evening because I wanted to understand free will better. After hearing your talk, I understand it even less.' Maybe I just didn't give a good talk. But if I had done better, he might still have made the same complaint, and my reply would still have been a good defence. I told him that before we sit down to think hard about things, we often have only vague and fuzzy ideas. They seem to make sense only because we haven't interrogated them and exposed their problems and contradictions. In such a pre-reflective, vague state it seems obvious what free will is and that we have it. It seems obvious that knowledge is different from belief and we all know the difference. But when we start to think about these issues, in bringing the picture into sharper focus, we also find that it is much more complicated than we thought. And so *greater clarity brings greater complexity*, and, initially at least, greater confusion.

Ideally, we move beyond this and clarity allows us to make sense of what seems paradoxical or contradictory. But it would be unwise to always expect this to happen, and if it doesn't we still benefit from being clearer than we were. This was, I think, the great virtue of one of Britain's best twentieth-century philosophers, Bernard Williams. After reading him I often feel I understand things better. But if someone were to ask me what Williams's position was, I wouldn't have an answer.

When I met Williams I asked if that description of his work would please him. 'Yes,' he replied. 'In general I guess that's because I think that philosophy starts from realising we don't understand our own activities and thoughts.' What he focused on was 'suggesting and opening up ways in which we might get a better hold of them'.

Some found this approach too negative. His old tutor, Dick Hare, would tell him: 'You knock all this stuff down, what do you put in its place?' Williams's answer was 'In that place I don't put anything. That isn't a place anything should be.'

I'm with Williams. People sometimes complain that they look to philosophy for answers but end up only getting more questions. This is somewhat unfair. Making progress in our thinking does not necessarily mean getting to a right answer. It can be enough to reject a wrong one or come up with a better question. Donald Davidson once said of his friend and colleague Willard Van Orman Quine that he 'encouraged me to think that it was possible, maybe not to get anything right in philosophy, but it was definitely possible to get something wrong. Uncovering mistakes in philosophy is about the only thing that we can actually count on.'

'Clarification is a process, not a state,' says Ray Monk. 'A really good tutorial session, a really good seminar, is when the students come with something which is bothering them and they leave the room slightly clearer about what that is than before. But they haven't achieved any final state.'

Jesse Norman connects this to Keats's idea of negative capability, which he describes as 'the ability not to rush to judgement, to hold a topic in front of you until its lines become clear and until it becomes intellectually or practically tractable'. Keats described negative capability as the ability to be 'in uncertainties, mysteries, doubts, without any irritable reaching after fact and reason'. Keats would be wrong if he was suggesting we shouldn't reach for facts and reason at all. The problem is with '*irritable* reaching' in which our discomfort leads us to grope too desperately, too quickly. As Norman says, 'At the moment there is an enormous array of incentives, which range from the economic to the psychological, to cut too early. [. . .] It's a very rare person who has the intellectual self-discipline and the practical authority to be able to maintain that distance.'

Philosophers – and I suspect all of us – tend towards one of two different objectives: clarity and certainty. Ray Monk gives the contrasting examples of Wittgenstein and Russell:

> The hope that was being thwarted in Wittgenstein's case was the hope of achieving complete crystalline clarity, and the hope that was being thwarted in Russell's case was the hope of achieving complete certainty. I think there's something revealing in that contrast about why we do philosophy. Do we want absolutely certain foundations for everything we believe, as Russell did; or do we feel a bit muddled, a bit confused, and we want this confusion dispelled?

I think that after more than two millennia of seeing which approach is more fruitful, it is clear if not certain that the clarifiers have won. Neither goal is absolutely attainable. Complete clarity is as impossible as complete certainty. But if you seek greater clarity, you can always get a bit more. If you want certainty, however, you will always fall short. Although we colloquially talk about achieving 'greater certainty', certainty admits of no degrees: you either have it or you don't. The only certainty we have is that certainty of any interesting kind isn't possible.

The call to give up on certainty and aim for greater clarity can seem a depressingly modest ambition, leading to disappointing results. As Janet Radcliffe Richards says, 'That's the trouble with philosophy. Once you get something clear it looks obvious.' But if that's true, then without clarity the obvious is hiding in plain sight. Go looking for certainty and you risk missing what's under your nose while in search of a fantastical fiction.

One domain in which the pursuit of absolutes and certainties is fatal is politics. Politician and philosopher Jesse Norman rejects 'what Pascal would call *l'esprit géométrique*, the geometrical idea that somehow political ideas are *a priori* workings out of a certain rational ideal through human action'. He traces this back to Plato's *Republic*, in which the ruler class is 'distinguished by their knowledge of abstract universals'. This contrasted with the Aristotelian approach to politics which is grounded in experience and sees politics as more of a pragmatic, problem-solving enterprise. 'If you look at the issue of how to govern,' says Norman, 'it turns out that the Aristotelian approach is a far better one.'

Because politics is the art of compromise, a means of managing competing interests and values, it is impossible for it to be governed by anything other than a somewhat messy set of agreements and accommodations. Politics without disagreement requires dictatorship. Whenever a government has sought to rule by applying an absolute ideal of its conception of justice, the result has been tyranny and disaster.

As the leading communitarian critic of liberalism Michael Sandel says,

The idea in the back of our heads that there could be a frictionless public sphere is destructive of democratic delib- eration, because when we force underground or sweep under the rug some of the deepest substantive moral views that people have and claim that we've been neutral, that over time generates resentment, cynicism and a sense that people have been dealt with in bad faith, that their views have not been taken seriously.

The striving for consensus which can be productive in sci- ence has no place in politics. Sandel again:

I'm not sure that consensus should be the overriding aim. We live in pluralist societies fraught with disagreements about conceptions of the good life, about morality and religion, and also about justice and rights. [...] I think what we should aim at is to get as close as we possibly can to a just society. But there will always be disagreements as a practical matter about what justice requires, about what rights need to be respected, about what the common good consists in.

If there is one thing all reasonable people should agree on it's that reasonable people will continue to disagree. As the envir- onmental philosopher Dale Jamieson says, 'People can believe a lot of different things without being irrational. They can feel a lot of different ways without being completely insensitive.' But that doesn't mean that there's no point in reasoned dialogue or trying to share experience. 'There are better and worse things to think, and more and less sensitive ways to feel. Part of what life in community is about is forging shared values.' The society that talks, listens and thinks together lives together, harmoni- ously if not entirely happily.

Awareness that nothing can ever be perfectly resolved is one reason why many of the best writers and creatives are reluctant to declare a work finished. Completion is often determined by an arbitrary time constraint that compels them to hand the work in. For some, this perfectionism leads them to produce comparatively little, but of the highest quality. Janet Radcliffe Richards, for instance, has written only two books, twenty-one years apart, and both are brilliant. Derek Parfit announced himself with a seminal paper in 1971 and took another thirteen years to produce a book, and a further twenty-seven to publish the two-volume sequel.

It wasn't until she was in her eighties that Philippa Foot published her first and only monograph, *Natural Goodness*, a magnum opus as rich as it is slim. Yet, with characteristic honesty, she remained very aware that she had still left a lot under- or unexamined. For instance, she said: 'I don't know what to say about happiness and flourishing. It is possible that we really have two concepts of happiness: the sense in which the wicked can flourish and there's another sense in which they cannot.' She said that 'It's important that anyone who reads that book realises that there is a gap in it' and that 'it's something I want to work on.' Foot was not being modest, just clear-sighted. Academics of all stripes tend to be aware of what they do not yet understand, what still needs to be done.

Perfectionism brings its own problems and there are advantages in declaring a work done even when you know there is room for improvement. But no one does good work if they believe that typing the final full stop means their work is as good as it ever could be. David Hume, for example, wrote quite a lot but in later life he was mostly revising old works for new editions. For him, definitive versions didn't exist. Scientists regularly incant 'more research is needed', as though it were a sacred obligation. The philosophical equivalent of this is the almost ritual announcement that certain questions are or should be 'the topic of another paper'. Every thinker should remember that more thought is always needed. 'The last word' can only ever be the last word to date, not the final one.

Another way of not prematurely closing down enquiry is to remain open to ideas that make no sense to you. For Simon Glendinning, being baffled seems to be a major motivator. 'I've found myself drawn to trying to understand things which I don't understand and other people have refused to read on the grounds that they couldn't understand it.' Hence his painstakingly close readings of the likes of Heidegger, Wittgenstein and Derrida, thinkers for whom he has an 'openness to their difficulty, obscurity that others refuse to give'.

This is another instance of the principle of charity, which we encountered earlier. Glendinning says that his attitude reflects 'a kind of well of good will which I have to difficult writing, which is something about me thinking these people are much cleverer than I am'. The risk of this is that if you are *too* charitable you spend too much time on ideas that don't deserve it. Glendinning accepts that 'there are cases where that well of good will is not as deserving as I may initially give it.' But it is better to err on the side of charity than dismissal. Whether or not those you don't understand are cleverer than you, they are almost certainly clever. The idea that there is no merit at all in their work is implausible.

Time is limited, so I'm not convinced we should actively prioritise the work of people we find difficult or bonkers. But we should at least dip in from time to time and keep the door open. I have found Heidegger, for example, to be somewhat portentous and needlessly obscure. Nonetheless, through secondary commentaries I've found some of his ideas, such as those concerning our relationship to technology, to be worth my attention and I'm sure there are others. Derrida has also generally been out of my orbit and often mocked by people within it. But since reading Glendinning on Derrida I've seen great sense in his iterative view of language, and Peter Salmon's brilliant biography confirmed that he is no charlatan.

It is dispiriting how often you hear people dismiss the likes of Derrida and Heidegger on the basis of false hearsay and caricature. You won't hear such things from Anthony Gottlieb because the most important lesson he learned from his years as a journalist was 'not to trust anything or anybody. Check, check and check again.' This served him well when he was writing his history of Western philosophy. 'It's quite remarkable how much of what gets into print, especially in journalism but also, I've found, in books, is wrong, just because people copy what they've seen elsewhere.' We should check our own thinking at least as thoroughly.

For practical purposes, we often have to declare a project or a line of enquiry over and move on. The deadline for this book looms and although I hope to have narrowed the gap between how good it is and how good it could conceivably be, a lifetime would not be enough to close it completely. Keeping things open is often not a practical option, but it is still a valuable state of mind. Even when we have to shut an intellectual door, we should remember where it is, in case we ever need to open it again.

The ceaselessly questioning life of the mind might sound like too much hard work. There is a sense in which it certainly isn't easy. The deeply philosophical writer Michael Frayn once said, 'I've spent my life in severe intellectual difficulties and can see no hope of ever getting out of them.' His choice of the word 'hope' is interesting, since one of his most quoted lines comes from his screenplay for *Clockwise*: 'It's not the despair, Laura. I can stand the despair. It's the hope.' In the film, hope is a torment, as it keeps the protagonist hanging on for a salvation that never comes.

Hope is often essential. But it is a curse if that hope can never be satisfied. If we live in the hope that we will one day be able to work everything out, that all of life will make sense and all mystery will be dissolved, we are setting ourselves up for frustration and disappointment. We need to learn to live with the loose ends, even perhaps to enjoy them, as Frayn does. He told me about a conversation he had with Jonathan Bennett about what made them happiest in life and Bennett said that it was 'being in severe intellectual difficulties'. I've heard a lot of advice about what makes you happy in life, but I'd never heard that one before.

Perhaps Bennett was a bit weird. I tend to agree with Ray Monk when he said, 'Philosophy doesn't make you happy and it shouldn't. Why should philosophy be consoling?' But 'happy' is a slippery word. If we take it to mean a feeling of pure, radiant contentment, it is fleeting and more likely to be found when sitting before a plate of delicious food than it is with a copy of Kant's *Critique of Pure Reason* open before you.

Sometimes we take 'happiness' to mean 'satisfaction', but even this needs to be understood carefully. If we mean satisfied in the sense of feeling fulfilled, complete, then that too is elusive and not to be found by thinking hard. But if by satisfaction we mean the feeling that this is enough, it is satisfactory, then I think satisfaction can be found by a life in which we think deeply about things, without resolution.

Not everyone needs to live this way. The unexamined life can be worth living too. I think that what makes any life feel like it is worth living is *engagement*. This can be wordless, as it is for some who work the land or live in constant contact with the natural world. For others it is social, being engaged with other people. For yet others it is creative: making things, arts or crafts. Thinking hard is just another way to engage more deeply with the world. It expands our mental horizons, opens up ways of understanding that we could never have imagined. Making more sense of the confusing buzz of events can be a way to make us feel more at home on our perplexing planet.

You might think this sounds too optimistic. Doesn't a cold, hard look at the world just reveal a cold, hard world? I don't think so. Whenever we understand something more deeply, more of reality is revealed to us and its wonder only increases. Scientists who look beyond appearances to the fundamental forces behind them are often left in awe, not dismay. 'Every time science has displaced us from the centre of things it has given back far more in return,' says the neuroscientist Anil Seth.[3] Similarly, the physicist Carlo Rovelli wrote: 'Every time that something solid is put into doubt or dismantled, something else opens up and allows us to see further than we could before.'[4]

It is true that not everything we discover is positive. Unlike science, philosophy concerns itself with the normative: how things ought to be, not just how they are. This opens a gap between the ideal and the actual which can be a source of disappointment. But how we react to that is up to us. In French existentialism, the absurdities of life were the cause of anguish, abandonment and despair. In British existentialism, they caused laughter. By 'British existentialism' I mean the work of Monty Python. In the films *The Holy Grail* and *The Life of Brian*, Python ridiculed the idea that human life was driven by some higher, transcendental purpose. Rather, we just muddle through, often enduring cruelty and mockery. Yet the films were comedies. We can only laugh because it's not all grim. 'Laughter is in a great many cases a recognition of our falling short from an ideal,' said Roger Scruton. 'If we didn't have ideals, humour would all be black.'

Being prepared for questions to go unanswered, for greater clarity without absolute certainty, and for correcting more mistakes than getting right answers should not mean giving up. Jean-Paul Sartre said that 'one need not hope in order to undertake one's work.' In other words, since no guarantees are ever given in life, we have to act without them. You don't have to believe in the inevitability of eventual success to try; you just need *not* to believe in the inevitability of failure.

But perhaps the strongest argument for persisting with the often frustrating, confusing and difficult process of thinking as best we can is that we really *ought* to do so. There is an uncontroversial sense in which reasoning involves 'oughts'. Whenever we encounter a strong argument, there is a sense that we *should* accept its conclusion. This 'ought' of reasoning is often assumed to be different from the 'ought' of ethics. I don't think it is. We ought to think well because, when we do so, we see more clearly what we ought to think. And if we don't think well, and don't see what we ought to think, we often end up believing what we shouldn't. Reasoning as well as we can is not just a practical means to an end. It is an ethical imperative.

How to keep going

- See thinking as part of a never-ending process of growth, not a means of achieving final wisdom.
- Accept that you will always be accompanied by unsolved intellectual problems and that new ones always arise to take the place of any you manage to see off.
- When you reach an impasse, it could be because you've been following the wrong path. Try retracing your steps and approaching the issue from a different angle.
- Life can't and should not wait for all major uncertainties to be resolved. Get on with it.
- Resist the allures of certainty, bogus precision and overconfidence.
- Learn to overcome incertophobia. Uncertainty is too ubiquitous to be scary. Cultivate the capacity to be comfortable with uncertainties, mysteries and doubts.
- Accept the limits of schematisation and formalism. Not everything can be reduced to a rule or method.
- If you don't exaggerate the power of reason you won't be disappointed with it. It is the worst method for getting at the truth except for all those others that have been tried.
- Seek greater clarity, being aware that in the short term it might reveal more complexity and therefore bring even more confusion.
- Don't try to force consensus when dealing with people's desires, preferences and values. Balance differences, don't try to erase them.
- You don't have to be a perfectionist to maintain an awareness that better is always possible and that nothing is ever definitively completed.

- Remain open to what you don't 'get' or understand.
- Don't forget the satisfactions of a reflective life. Thinking about the world is one of the profoundest ways of engaging with it.

CONCLUSION

Above all, avoid falsehood, every kind of
falsehood, especially falseness to yourself.
Watch over your own deceitfulness and
look into it every hour, every minute.

FYODOR DOSTOEVSKY, *The Brothers Karamazov*

Lurking unstated in the background to this book has been
Aristotle's incredibly useful doctrine of the mean, a version of
which is also found in Confucius. This says that for almost every
virtue, there is not an opposite vice but an excess and a deficiency.
Generosity is the mean between profligacy and tightfistedness,
understanding between lack of sympathy and indulgence, pride
between self-hatred and arrogance.

The same applies to the virtues of thinking, as we've seen
time and again. You can be too precise as well as too vague,
if that precision is bogus. You can be too understanding of a
view you disagree with as well as too dismissive. You can think
too much for yourself or too little. That is why every piece of
advice comes with a warning not to slavishly follow it: follow

the argument wherever it leads but don't follow it to absurdity; question everything but not always; define your terms but don't think all terms can be defined. The virtues of thinking require balance and judgement, and for every way of erring there is an equal and opposite way of going wrong. We can apply any critical-thinking rule to excess or not enough, depending on the context. The doctrine of the mean is a kind of meta-principle that we should bear in mind at all times.

It is not, however, the skeleton key that unlocks the power of reason. A fundamental claim of this book is that there is no algorithm for thinking well, no single method that can be applied, no one P-factor. Nonetheless, it can be useful to have some kind of aide-memoire, a general framework to hold all the various elements of good thinking together.

When I tried to come up with something pithy, I found myself describing a kind of process. I say 'kind of process' because in practice it's not neatly linear and it has to be applied sensitively according to the context, not mechanically. Unfortunately, its four parts do not create a nice acronym. Instead, the first letters of *Attend, Clarify, Deconstruct, Connect* form the name of Australia's finest rock band, AC/DC. This is somewhat ironic since the group are not known for their intel-lectualism. Perhaps it's a useful reminder that there are some things you should not think about too much.

ATTEND

The first ingredient is both the first step in reasoning well and a necessary component of every move that follows. I can't empha-sise enough how important it is. Pretty much every piece of advice in this book could be described as an exercise in attention: attend to the evidence, to what matters, to the steps in your reasoning, to the unstated assumptions, to the language you use, to what other experts and disciplines have to contribute, to the tricks of the mind, to your own biases and temperament, to your ego, to the wider picture, to the seductions of a grand theory, and so on.

If this sounds like hard work, that's because it is. Rigorous thinking is largely a matter of effort and application. We have evolved to be 'cognitive misers' using as little mental energy as we need to get us the next meal and the next offspring. It's easier not to think and if we must, it's more fun if we do so lacka-daisically, tossing off opinions around a boozy dinner table or spitting out hot takes on social media. No one is blameless, but there is an important difference between those who strive to do better and those who don't, those who push their intelligence to the limits and those who stay within them.

CLARIFY

One of the most important things close attention allows us to do is to get more clarity. It's probably not an overstatement to say that most error is the result of failing to have a clear enough pic-ture of what it is you're thinking about. You need to understand what the problem really is and not just assume you or others already get it. What really matters? What is at stake? You need to clarify what the relevant facts are, as well as what the concepts in play mean. You need to clarify how the argument is struc-tured, whether it is a deduction, an induction, an abduction, or some combination of these. Greater clarity is usually the most we can hope for in our reasoning, and if we don't start with as much of it as possible we're unlikely to end with much more.

DECONSTRUCT

You've paid attention, you've tried to see things as clearly as possible. Now is the time to deconstruct, to make any necessary distinctions, to pull aspects of the issue apart. Some of this is formal: how exactly does the argument progress? Is each step robust? Some is conceptual and linguistic: is there more than one meaning hiding behind one word? Do we need to coin a special word or phrase that is more precise than the concepts to hand? Have we lumped together ideas that need not, or should not, be part of a single package? Some deconstruction is empirical: which facts are important and which are incidental, misleading, or just red herrings? Some is psychological: how much of what seems plausible is what I want to believe is true, and am I rejecting anything merely because I don't like it? Everything needs to be unpicked with great care.

CONNECT

Attending, clarifying and deconstructing are all essential elements of good thinking. But by themselves all they leave you with is a collection of unassembled parts, neatly laid out but useless as they are. At some stage, you've got to try to put the pieces together. How complete a structure you'll be able to make, only time will tell. But if you don't even try to join at least some of the dots, nothing has been truly constructive.

Putting the pieces together requires, of course, close attention. Connections may not be obvious. You might be convinced that an organic vegan diet is the most ethical, but you may not have realised that without animal manures, the vast majority of organic farms couldn't function. Myth-busting might sound like a good idea if you don't know that the psychological research suggests it tends to entrench the very myths it aims to debunk. We should always be slow to enthusiastically get behind exciting-sounding ideas without thinking through their implications.

Making connections benefits from the social dimensions of reasoning. If you don't read widely, you'll miss knowledge from other domains that relates to the issues you're thinking about. If you don't talk about your ideas with smart people, you miss out on the surprising connections that they might make.

The building stage of thinking things through has to be done very carefully, with humility and patience. I think it's right that three of the four elements of AC/DC are primarily to do with thinking things through and only the last mainly about drawing conclusions. For if you could sum up the key to good thinking in one imperative it would be *Don't jump to conclusions*. Crawl to them, on your hands and knees, slowly checking every step of the way. In a world which promises everything quickly and easily, thinking must be hard and slow.

GLOSSARY OF KEY CONCEPTS

Cross-referenced terms in bold

Abduction
Argument to the best explanation. All other things being equal (*ceteris paribus*), the best explanations have a combination of simplicity, coherence, comprehensiveness and testability.

Accuracy
One of Bernard Williams's two primary 'virtues of truth', alongside **sincerity**. When the insistence on accuracy leads, truth tends to follow.

Ad hominem fallacy
Arguing against the arguer rather than the argument, the person rather than the position. It can be important to know who is making an argument, but it never by itself tells you if the argument is a good one.

HOW TO THINK LIKE A PHILOSOPHER

Affirming the antecedent

A valid form of **deductive** argument: If x, then y; x (the antecedent), therefore y. For example, if this sausage is made of tofu, then it is suitable for vegans. This sausage is made of tofu, therefore it is suitable for vegans.

Affirming the consequent

An invalid form of **deductive** argument: If x, then y; y (the consequent), therefore x. For example, if this sausage is made of tofu, then it is suitable for vegans. This sausage is suitable for vegans, therefore it is made of tofu. (False: it could be made of seitan, textured vegetable protein or many other things.)

Aggregation fallacy

The false belief (usually an implicit assumption) that if something is good, the more of it the better.

Aporia (or apory)

Two or more contentions that individually seem to be true but are collectively inconsistent. An example strangely neglected by philosophers is that Stevie Wonder is a musical genius *and* he made the risible 'I Just Called to Say I Love You'.

A posteriori

From experience. Science, for example is *a posteriori*, in contrast to . . .

A priori

Prior to experience or without recourse to it. Mathematics, for example, is *a priori* because to know that 2+3=5 you only need to know what the numbers and symbols mean.

Attention economy
The contemporary consumer environment in which organisations are constantly competing with each other to gain our attention, usually to monetise it. They're doing well because we often give ours away cheaply.

Availability heuristic or bias
The tendency to base our judgements on the evidence that is most recent or salient rather than that which is most strong and relevant.

Begging the question
Assuming in one or more **premises** of an argument that which the argument is supposed to be demonstrating.

Behavioural fatigue
A piece of bogus social psychology invented by the UK government to justify delaying the introduction of restrictions during the Covid-19 pandemic. A reminder that not everything that looks like proper science really is.

Biting the bullet
Accepting a counter-intuitive or implausible consequence of an argument or a position. Not to be done lightly.

Category mistakes
Thinking of something as one kind of thing where it is another, or not a kind of thing at all.

Ceteris paribus
All other things being equal. A useful and underused qualification for a wide range of statements.

Change blindness
The strange tendency we have not to notice changes to our physical environment, if our attention is directed away from where the change is happening, or if we never attended to it in the first place.

Cluster thinking
The tendency to assume that logically and/or **empirically** distinct beliefs necessarily go together, and that to believe one requires you to believe the others, or to reject one requires rejecting the others. A tempting piece of **cognitive miserliness**.

Cognitive empathy
The ability to understand the reasoning of another, in contrast to *affective empathy*: the ability to share their feelings.

Cognitive misers
Humans are cognitive misers because we seek to expend the minimum amount of mental energy we need to get us through the day and so adopt **heuristics**, or shortcuts, many of which are misleading.

Conceivability arguments
Arguments that reach a conclusion about what is the case on the basis of what can be coherently conceived. Mostly inconceivably bad.

Conclusion
Something you shouldn't jump to. A conclusion in a **valid deductive** argument should follow by necessity from the **premises**.

Confirmation bias
The tendency to notice and remember evidence that supports your view and to ignore or forget anything that challenges it. Also known as myside bias.

Consistency
A desirable state which is achieved when beliefs do not contradict each other.

Cui bono?
Who benefits? A useful question to ask because it alerts us to vested interests. But by itself the answer tells us nothing about an argument's **soundness**.

Dead cat strategy
The tactic of saying something outrageous or dramatic, irrespective of its truth or relevance, in order to detract attention from something that is causing us difficulties. Very popular with politicians.

Deduction
An argument which attempts to reach a **conclusion** that follows by necessity from the **premises**.

Echo chambers
Real or virtual spaces in which we only ever hear opinions that are the same as or close to our own. They are not new: most neighbourhoods, newspapers, clubs and associations have tended to be echo chambers.

Empirical
Based on evidence. Science is empirical, maths and logic are not.

Enthymemes
Premises that are unstated and often assumed. Often worth spelling out.

Error theory
An explanation for why an argument or a point of view that is wrong is nonetheless believed by otherwise sensible people.

Faffing about
The core of good thinking: check your Facts, pay Attention, and ask what Follows.

Fallacy of the complex question
A question that does not allow anyone to answer it directly without forcing them to admit something that they might not want to. For example, why are you such a jerk?

Fallacy of domestication
Interpreting an idea in such a way as to change it into one which is closer to one that is more familiar. A common crime in cross-cultural thinking.

Fallacy of equivocation
To mistakenly or deliberately misuse a word with an ambiguous meaning in one of its inappropriate senses. For example, accusing someone of discrimination in the negative sense when they are merely being discriminating, in the sense of recognising a real distinction.

Fallacy of the telling slip
Assuming that a slip of the tongue or a careless remark reveals the truth about what someone is really like, more than the entirety of how they usually speak and behave.

False dichotomy
A binary choice that doesn't have to be made. For example, some say that you cannot be both in favour of making some forms of disinformation illegal and in favour of freedom of speech. But is it possible to believe that freedom of speech is conditional on not abusing that freedom to cause harm?

Genetic fallacy
Rejecting an argument or a belief because of its questionable origins when those origins are not relevant to its truth. Bad people sometimes have good ideas.

Heuristics
Mental shortcuts or rules of thumb that save us the effort of thinking too much. We can't live without them, but they often lead us astray.

Iff
'If and only if' or the biconditional. The logics of if and iff are very different, so it's worth being clear which you mean. See **affirming the antecedent** and **affirming the consequent**.

Implicit bias
Unconscious prejudice, which can also affect those who are victims of the bias, as they tend to internalise societal norms.

Incertophobia
Fear of uncertainty. A measure of intellectual immaturity.

Induction
Arguments from experience. They are never **deductively valid** but we couldn't survive without them.

Intonation
Something that makes a great deal of difference to how we understand many beliefs. Imagine someone saying, 'Without God, morality is down to human beings alone' in a calm and relaxed manner, and someone else saying it in panicked terror. Same belief, different worlds.

Intuitive and reflective beliefs
Intuitive beliefs are ones we really feel to be true in our bones and which affect our behaviours accordingly. Reflective beliefs are ones we say are true if asked, but they don't necessarily impact our feelings and actions in the way you might expect. Someone might reflectively believe they shouldn't have another beer but not feel any discomfort when they do.

Ismism
A justified prejudice against -isms, -ologies and all attempts to divide how people think into overly neat schools of thought.

Is/ought gap
The logical distinction between statements of facts and statements of values. No **valid deductive** argument **premised** on facts can have a **conclusion** about values. But that does not mean facts have no bearing on matters of value.

Groupthink
The tendency of opinion within a group to converge to such an extent that saying or thinking anything different becomes extremely difficult.

Holistic explanations
Explanations that are based on and account for the way a whole system is and behaves. Contrasts with **reductionism**.

Logocentrism
A way of understanding that prioritises words or concepts.

The maverick's paradox
Mavericks do the right thing when they follow the evidence and the arguments, not the crowd; but when they do so, most are led to the wrong conclusions.

The mean
The virtue that lies between an excess and a deficiency, in ethics and in reasoning. You can be too vague or too precise; demand logical validity when that would be asking too much or accept less when it isn't; give up too easily or carry on too stubbornly.

Meaning as use
The idea that meanings of words are not usually strictly specifiable in definitions but are to be found in how they are used.

Meta-induction
Reasoning from general precedents about 'this kind of thing' rather than on the basis of the specifics of the case in hand. Useful when there is insufficient specific information but lots of evidence about 'this kind of thing'.

Myside bias
See **confirmation bias**.

Naturalistic fallacy
Arguing from the naturalness of something to its rightness or goodness. A natural mistake to make.

Ockham's Razor
The principle that you should not posit more entities than are necessary to explain something. More generally, the principle that, *ceteris paribus*, simpler explanations are preferable to more complex ones.

Onus of proof
Something worth establishing. In any disagreement, is the onus more on one side than the other to prove their point? Generally, the onus of proof is on people who advocate something that causes evident harm, or which goes against expert opinion.

Optimism bias
A not-universal human tendency to expect the best, or at least the better.

Premise
Statements (or propositions) which form the basis of arguments. They need to be established as true by experience or by other **sound** argument.

Principle of charity
When considering an argument or a belief, consider the best version of it that you can imagine. Otherwise any rejection may be premature.

Psychologising
Attributing a person's beliefs or actions to usually hidden psychological motives. Almost always speculative, generally to be avoided, including by therapists.

Redefinition, high and low
High redefinition changes the use of a word to make its application narrower than would reasonably be expected. For example, saying that a real friend should risk going to jail to avoid their partner finding out about an affair unreasonably raises the bar on friendship. Low redefinition makes the application of a word wider than would reasonably be expected. Calling someone a murderer because they didn't donate a lot to an emergency appeal, for example, is stretching it.

Reductio ad absurdum
An attempt to show that a belief is wrong by arguing that it logically leads to an absurd conclusion. For example, if you believe that it's OK to suspend judgement about climate change because it isn't 100 per cent proven, then you should suspend judgement on everything, because nothing is certain. That's crazy, so you must be wrong about your reasons for suspending judgement on climate change.

Reductionism
Explanations based on breaking something down to its smallest components. Powerful in science, but not appropriate in cases when breaking things down removes just those things that need explaining. For example, you can't explain the beauty of a photograph by examining it at the level of individual pixels.

Regression to the mean
The tendency of many systems to return naturally to a state of equilibrium. A failure to take this into account leads people to attribute bogus causes for things like the end of a winning streak, or recovery from an illness.

Scepticism

Scepticism comes in many forms and degrees. Methodological scepticism is doubting everything as part of a process of trying to establish what is most certain. Pyrrhonian scepticism is a universal suspension of belief on the grounds that nothing can be known. Mitigated scepticism, as advocated by David Hume, advocates balancing the fact that nothing is certain with a realistic assessment of the things we must accept to be true.

Scientism

The belief that only beliefs that are scientifically verifiable are meaningful. Scientism is not scientific.

Semantic slide

A deliberate or accidental slippage where the meaning of a word comes to change into something similar or closely related but importantly different. For example, 'awesome' slid over time from meaning 'inspiring of awe' to 'quite good'. Not every example is as harmless.

Significance

A slippery term. Something is statistically significant if it is unlikely to be the result of an error. Whether it is significant in any other sense is different. There may be a statistically significant difference in health outcomes between two behaviours, for example, but it might be so small that it makes no difference to how you act. If not eating your favourite food on average extended your life by a month, would you stop eating it?

Sincerity

The other of Bernard Williams's two primary 'virtues of truth', alongside **accuracy**. Sincerity requires communicating beliefs to other people in an honest way, and genuinely being a truth seeker.

Situational ethics

Small-case situational ethics emphasises the need to attend carefully to the specifics of any given moral dilemma and not to crudely apply general principles. Not to be confused with Joseph F. Fletcher's Christian Situation Ethics, sometimes called Situational Ethics.

Slippery slope

When accepting one apparently good or acceptable thing inevitably leads to another bad one. Slippery slopes are generally more psychological than logical and they are also often not as inevitable as those warning about them claim.

Social epistemology

The study of the social basis of knowledge acquisition and justification.

Sorites paradox

The paradox that a series of small changes which individually make no significant difference collectively do. Losing one hair doesn't make you bald, but keep losing them one by one and you'll get there. A demonstration of the fact that many concepts have fuzzy borders.

Sound

A **deductive** argument is sound if it is **valid** and its **premises** are true.

Stipulative definitions

A definition which we do not claim captures the pre-existing meaning of a word but which defines it as we wish to use it for a specific purpose. These are acceptable when we are clear we are using terms of art, but not when we pretend that we're merely describing the one true meaning.

Straw man fallacy
Defeating a weak version of an idea or argument, often one that opponents don't actually maintain, rather than a stronger one.

Testimonial injustice
When people's testimony is not given due weight, usually because the testifier is not given sufficient status.

Thought experiments
Hypothetical situations which are designed to elicit intuitions and so clarify key factors at play in our reasoning. Not to be confused with actual arguments.

Transcendental argument
An argument of the structure, 'Given that this is evidentially true, this must also be true.' If Rembrandt's self-portraits are works of genius, then Rembrandt must be a genius.

Tu quoque
You too. Not a decisive argument against a position, but an indicator of inconsistency in the arguer. For example, if someone says you are immoral for eating meat but they eat meat, *tu quoque*! But that doesn't mean it isn't immoral to eat meat. It just means they are a hypocrite.

Valid
A **deductive** argument is valid if its conclusion necessarily follows from its **premises**. But that does not necessarily make it **sound**. If you have any sense, you'll now go and buy all the rest of my books. You have some sense, therefore you will now go and buy all the rest of my books. Valid but, alas, not sound.

THE INTERVIEWEES

This book draws on interviews with philosophers and other philosophical folk I have conducted over the last two decades. This cast list tells you more about them, when and for what they were interviewed, and where to start if you're interested in finding out more about how they think. These are personal recommendations and may not be the works they are best known for, which are easy enough to discover for yourself. Interviewees' books which might be challenging for the general audience are flagged with the warning sign Φ, perhaps sometimes unfairly: it's hard to know what some find difficult and others don't.

Many of the interviews were for *The Philosophers' Magazine* (*TPM*) during my 1997–2010 editorship. In that period women were still woefully under-represented in philosophy, especially at the top, and the situation has been improving only gradually since. This imbalance is unfortunately reflected in this list, as is the relative lack of ethnic diversity. To appreciate the improved diversity in philosophy, check out the videos of the Royal Institute of Philosophy on YouTube from when I became Academic Director in 2019, or the Institute's *Thinking Hard and Slow* podcast.

Many of these interviews were edited and anthologised in *What Philosophers Think* and *What More Philosophers Think*, edited by myself and Jeremy Stangroom (Continuum, 2005 and 2007). Several were interviewed for the book *New British Philosophy: The Interviews*, again edited with Jeremy Stangroom (Routledge, 2002).

Kwame Anthony Appiah is a political and moral philosopher with interests in cosmopolitanism and African intellectual history. Interviewed in *TPM* issue 53, 2nd quarter 2011. Start with: *The Lies That Bind: Rethinking Identity – Creed, Country, Color, Class, Culture* (Profile Books, 2018).

Joan Bakewell is a broadcaster and writer who has spent her career engaging with intellectuals. Interviewed in *TPM* issue 72, 4th quarter 2005. Start with: *The Centre of the Bed: An Autobiography* (Hodder & Stoughton, 2003).

Simon Blackburn has worked mainly in ethics and the philosophy of language. Interviewed in *TPM* issue 15, 3rd quarter 2001 with a version in *What Philosophers Think*. Start with: *Truth: A Guide for the Perplexed* (Penguin, 2005).

David Chalmers is a philosopher of mind best known for his work on the problem of consciousness. Interviewed in *TPM* issue 43, 4th quarter 2008 and *Prospect*, online, February 2022. Start with: *Reality+: Virtual Worlds and the Problems of Philosophy* (Penguin and W. W. Norton, 2022).

Patricia Churchland is a neurophilosopher working on the philosophy of mind and the neural foundations of morality. Interviewed in *TPM* issue 61, 2nd quarter 2012 and *Prospect*, November 2019. Start with: *Touching a Nerve: Our Brains, Our Selves* (W. W. Norton, 2013).

Tim Crane is a philosopher of mind who is also interested in the nature of belief. Interviewed in *New British Philosophy*. Start with: *The Meaning of Belief: Religion from an Atheist's Point of View* (Harvard University Press, 2017).

Roger Crisp is a moral philosopher. Interviewed in *New British Philosophy*. Start with: *The Cosmos of Duty: Henry Sidgwick's Methods of Ethics* (Oxford University Press, 2017).Φ

Simon Critchley's areas of work include continental philosophy, philosophy and literature, psychoanalysis, ethics and political theory. Interviewed in *TPM* issue 40, 1st quarter 2008. Start with: *Infinitely Demanding: Ethics of Commitment, Politics of Resistance* (Verso, 2007).Φ

Daniel Dennett is a philosopher of mind. Interviewed for *TPM* issue 6, 2nd quarter 1999 and issue 30, 2nd quarter 2005. Also interviewed for my book *Freedom Regained: The Possibility of Free Will* (Granta, 2015). Start with: *Intuition Pumps and Other Tools for Thinking* (Penguin and W. W. Norton, 2013).

Roger-Pol Droit is a philosopher who has written a lot on issues of daily life. Interviewed for *TPM* issue 34, 2nd quarter 2006. Start with: *How Are Things? A Philosophical Experiment with Unremarkable Objects* (Faber & Faber, 2006).

Michael Dummett was a philosopher of language. Interviewed for *TPM* issue 15, 3rd quarter 2001 with a version in *What Philosophers Think*. Start with: a deep breath. His philosophy is extremely dense. But he also had a deep interest in the history of Tarot and wrote *A History of the Occult Tarot* with Ronald Decker (Duckworth, 2002).

Jerry Fodor mostly worked in the philosophy of language. Interviewed for *TPM* issue 49, 2nd quarter 2010. Start with: *LOT 2: The Language of Thought Revisited* (Oxford University Press, 2008).Φ

Philippa Foot was one of the most insightful and important moral philosophers of the twentieth century. Interviewed for *TPM* issue 21, 1st quarter 2003 with a version in *What More Philosophers Think*. Start with: *Natural Goodness* (Oxford University Press, 2001).

Michael Frayn is a novelist, playwright and the author of two works of philosophy. Interviewed for *TPM* issue 47, 4th quarter 2009. Start with: his masterpiece, the play *Copenhagen* (1998), adapted into a TV film in 2002.

Simon Glendinning specialises in European philosophy. Interviewed in *New British Philosophy*. Start with: *The Idea of Continental Philosophy* (Edinburgh University Press, 2006).Φ

Anthony Gottlieb is a journalist and the author of a two-volume history of Western philosophy. Interviewed for *TPM* issue 16, 4th quarter 2001. Start with: *The Dream of Reason: A History of Philosophy from the Greeks to the Renaissance* (Penguin, 2016).

A. C. Grayling is an academic and prolific public philosopher. Interviewed for *TPM* issue 26, 2nd quarter 2004 with a version in *What More Philosophers Think*. Start with: *The Challenge of Things: Thinking Through Troubled Times* (Bloomsbury, 2016).

John Harris is a bioethicist and philosopher. Interviewed for *TPM* issue 13, 1st quarter 2001 with a version in *What*

Philosophers Think. Start with: *Enhancing Evolution: The Ethical Case for Making Better People* (Princeton University Press, 2007).Φ

Sam Harris is a neuroscientist and philosopher. Interviewed for the *Independent*, 11 April 2011. Start with: *Waking Up: Searching for Spirituality Without Religion* (Simon & Schuster/ Transworld, 2014).

Jonathan Israel is a historian of ideas. Interviewed for *TPM* issue 43, 4th quarter 2008. Start with: *A Revolution of the Mind: Radical Enlightenment and the Intellectual Origins of Modern Democracy* (Princeton University Press, 2011).

Dale Jamieson is a philosopher who works primarily on environmental ethics and animal rights. Interviewed for *TPM* issue 3, 3rd quarter 1998. Start with: *Reason in a Dark Time: Why the Struggle Against Climate Change Failed – and What It Means for Our Future* (Oxford University Press, 2014).

Anthony Kenny has worked in the philosophy of mind, ancient and scholastic philosophy, the philosophy of Wittgenstein and the philosophy of religion. Interviewed for *TPM* issue 37, 1st quarter 2007. Start with: *Brief Encounters: Notes from a Philosopher's Diary* (SPCK, 2019).

Kobayashi Yasuo is one of the leading intermediaries between European and Japanese philosophy. Interviewed for my book *How the World Thinks: A Global History of Philosophy* (Granta, 2018). Where to start: very little has been translated into English but there are essays in English and French in *Le Cœur/ La Mort* (University of Tokyo Centre for Philosophy, 2007).Φ

Christine Korsgaard is a philosopher who has worked on issues of moral philosophy, practical reason, agency, personal identity and human/animal relations. Interviewed for *TPM* issue 58, 3rd quarter 2012. Start with *Self-Constitution: Agency, Identity, and Integrity* (Oxford University Press, 2009).Φ

Oliver Letwin is a former Conservative member of the British Parliament and philosophy PhD. Interviewed for *TPM* issue 32, 4th quarter 2005. Start with: *Hearts and Minds: The Battle for the Conservative Party from Thatcher to the Present* (Biteback, 2017).

Alexander McCall Smith is a bestselling novelist and former professor of medical law. Interviewed for *TPM* issue 29, 1st quarter 2005 with a version in *What More Philosophers Think*. Start with: Any book in *The Sunday Philosophy Club* series.

Tony McWalter is a former Labour member of the British Parliament and holder of a BPhil in Philosophy. He participated in a round-table discussion for *TPM* issue 17, 1st quarter 2002 with a version in *What More Philosophers Think*. Start with: admiring a doer, not a writer.

Howard Marks was an international cannabis smuggler. Interviewed for *TPM* issue 54, 3rd quarter 2011. Start with: his autobiography, *Mr Nice* (Vintage/Secker & Warburg, 1996).

Michael Martin's main focus has been the philosophy of perception. Interviewed in *New British Philosophy*. Start with: you'll have to wait as his website says he is 'forever finishing a book on naïve realism in the theory of perception, titled *Uncovering Appearances*'.

Guillermo Martínez is an Argentinian novelist and short story writer. Interviewed for *TPM* issue 37, 1st quarter 2007. Start with *The Oxford Murders* (Abacus, 2005).

Mary Midgley is best known for her work on science, ethics and humanity's place in the natural world. Interviewed for *TPM* issue 7, 3rd quarter 1999. Start with *Beast and Man: The Roots of Human Nature* (Routledge, 1978; revised edition 1995).

Ray Monk is a philosophical biographer. Interviewed for *TPM* issue 14, 2nd quarter 2001 and in *New British Philosophy*. Start with: *Ludwig Wittgenstein: The Duty of Genius* (Vintage/The Free Press, 1990).

Stephen Mulhall is a philosopher whose interests include Wittgenstein, Post-Analytic Philosophy and film and philosophy. Interviewed in *New British Philosophy*. Start with: *On Film*, 3rd edition (Routledge, 2015).

Mylo (Myles MacInnes) is an electronic musician and producer. Interviewed for *TPM* issue 36, 4th quarter 2006. Start with: his breakthrough album, *Destroy Rock & Roll* (2004).

Jesse Norman is a philosopher and Conservative member of the British Parliament. Interviewed for *TPM* issue 55, 4th quarter 2011. Start with: *Edmund Burke: The Visionary Who Invented Modern Politics* (Basic Books, 2013).

Martha Nussbaum is a moral and political philosopher whose best-known work concerns human capabilities and the philosophical importance of the arts and humanities. Interviewed for *TPM* issue 5, 1st quarter 1999 and issue 11, 3rd quarter 2000.

Start with: *Not For Profit: Why Democracy Needs the Humanities* (Princeton University Press, 2010).

Onora O'Neill is a moral philosopher and a crossbench member of the House of Lords. Interviewed for *TPM* issue 21, 1st quarter 2003 with a version in *What More Philosophers Think*. Start with: *A Question of Trust: The BBC Reith Lectures 2002* (Cambridge University Press, 2002).

Michel Onfray is a French philosopher and founder of the Université populaire (People's University) de Caen. Interviewed for the *Times Higher Education Supplement*, 3 August 2007. Start with: *In Defence of Atheism: The Case Against Christianity, Judaism and Islam* (Serpent's Tail, 2007).

Philip Pullman is a novelist. Interviewed for *TPM* issue 24, 4th quarter 2003 with a version in *What More Philosophers Think*. Start with: *The Good Man Jesus and The Scoundrel Christ* (Canongate, 2010).

Hilary Putnam was one of the foremost figures of twentieth-century analytic philosophy, contributing to the philosophies of mind, language, mathematics and science. Interviewed for *TPM* issue 15, 3rd quarter 2001 with a version in *What Philosophers Think*. Start with: *The Threefold Cord: Mind, Body, and World* (Columbia University Press, 1999).Φ

Janet Radcliffe Richards is a philosopher who is best known for her work in bioethics. Interviewed for *TPM* issue 3, 1st quarter 2001 with a version in *What Philosophers Think*. Start with: *Human Nature After Darwin: A Philosophical Introduction* (Routledge, 2000).

Jonathan Rée is a philosopher and historian. He participated in a round-table discussion for *TPM* issue 17, 1st quarter 2002 with a version in *What More Philosophers Think*. Start with: *Witcraft: The Invention of Philosophy in English* (Allen Lane, 2019).

Alex Rosenberg is a philosopher of science and a novelist. Interviewed for a Bristol Festival of Ideas event at Foyles book-shop on 23 February 2012 and edited for the season 2, episode 6 of the microphilosophy podcast, 'Science as a Guide to Life'. Start with: *The Atheist's Guide to Reality: Enjoying Life without Illusions* (W. W. Norton, 2012).

Michael Sandel is a moral and political philosopher. Interviewed for *TPM* issue 48, 1st quarter 2010. Start with: *The Tyranny of Merit: What's Become of the Common Good?* (Farrar, Straus and Giroux/Allen Lane, 2020).

Ziauddin Sardar is a scholar, writer, broadcaster, futurist, cultural critic and public intellectual. Interviewed for *TPM* issue 48, 1st quarter 2010. Start with: *A Person of Pakistani Origins* (C. Hurst & Co., 2018).

T. M. (Tim) Scanlon is one of the most important moral and political philosophers working today. Interviewed for *TPM* issue 41, 2nd quarter 2008. Start with: *Why Does Inequality Matter?* (Oxford University Press, 2018).Φ

Roger Scruton wrote widely on political philosophy and aesthetics. Interviewed for *TPM* issue 42, 3rd quarter 2008. Start with: *A Political Philosophy: Arguments for Conservatism* (Continuum, 2006).

John Searle is a philosopher of mind and language. Interviewed for *TPM* issue 8, 4th quarter 1999 with a version in *What Philosophers Think*. Start with: *Mind, Language and Society: Doing Philosophy in the Real World* (Basic Books, 1998).

Peter Singer is probably the most famous moral philosopher in the world and an advocate of animal rights. Interviewed for *TPM* issue 4, 4th quarter 1998, with a version in *What Philosophers Think*, and issue 47, 4th quarter 2009. Start with: *Ethics in the Real World: 82 Brief Essays on Things That Matter* (Princeton University Press, 2016).

Alan Sokal is a physicist whose spoof paper parodying 'post-modern' science and technology studies caused an international sensation. Interviewed for *TPM* issue 4, 4th quarter 1998, with a version in *What Philosophers Think*, and issue 41, 2nd quarter 2008. Start with *Intellectual Impostures*, with Jean Bricmont (Profile, 1999), published in America as *Fashionable Nonsense: Postmodern Intellectuals' Abuse of Science* (Picador, 1999).

Peter Vardy is a philosopher of religion who has written dozens of books for high-school students. Interviewed for *TPM* issue 10, 2nd quarter 2000, with a version in *What Philosophers Think*. Start with: *The Puzzle of God* (Routledge, 1997).

Nigel Warburton is a philosopher and author of some of the most popular introductions to philosophy of recent decades. Interviewed in *New British Philosophy*. Start with: *A Little History of Philosophy* (Yale University Press, 2011).

Mary Warnock was a moral philosopher, bioethicist and member of the House of Lords. Interviewed for *TPM* issue 7, 3rd quarter 1999 with a version in *What Philosophers Think*, and issue 20, 4th quarter 2002 with a version in *What More Philosophers Think*. Start with: *Making Babies: Is There a Right to Have Children?* (Oxford University Press, 2002).

Bernard Williams was one of the leading moral philosophers of his generation. Interviewed for *TPM* issue 21, 1st quarter 2003 with a version in *What More Philosophers Think*. Start with: *Ethics and the Limits of Philosophy* (Routledge, 2006).

Timothy Williamson is the Wykeham Professor of Logic at the University of Oxford, one of the most prestigious positions in the discipline. Interviewed for *TPM* issue 45, 2nd quarter 2009. Start with: *Tetralogue: I'm Right, You're Wrong* (Oxford University Press, 2015).

Jonathan (Jo) Wolff is a political philosopher. Interviewed in *New British Philosophy*. Start with: follow him on Twitter @ JoWolffBSG.

Tony Wright is a former Labour member of the British Parliament and a political theorist. Interviewed for *TPM* issue 46, 3rd quarter 2009. Start with: *British Politics: A Very Short Introduction*, 3rd edition (Oxford University Press, 2020).

Slavoj Žižek draws crowds every other philosopher can only dream of. Interviewed for *TPM* issue 25, 1st quarter 2004 with a version in *What More Philosophers Think*. Start with: Astra Taylor's documentary *Žižek!* (2005).

NOTES

INTRODUCTION

1 'Transferable skills' has a webpage all to itself on the Cambridge Philosophy website: www.phil.cam.ac.uk/curr-students/ugrads-after-degree-folder/ugrads-trans-skills

I. PAY ATTENTION

1 René Descartes, *Principles of Philosophy*, (1644) Part One, Section 9, in *Selected Philosophical Writings*, trans. John Cottingham, Robert Stoothoff and Dugald Murdoch (Cambridge University Press, 1988), p. 163.

2 David Hume, *A Treatise of Human Nature*, (1739) Book 1, Part 4, Section 6.

3 David Hume, 'Letter from a Gentleman to His Friend in Edinburgh: containing Some Observations on A Specimen of the Principles concerning Religion and Morality, said to be maintain'd in a Book lately publish'd, intituled, A Treatise of Human Nature, &c.' (1745).

4 Edmund Husserl, *Logical Investigations* (second edition 1913).

5 Edmund Husserl, *The Crisis of European Sciences and Transcendental Phenomenology* (1936).

6 https://youtu.be/bh_9XFzbWV8

7 https://youtu.be/FWSxSQsspiQ

8 https://youtu.be/vJG698U2Mvo

9 Plato, *Theaetetus*, 173d–174a.

10 *The Listener*, 1978.
11 Leah Kalmanson, 'How to Change Your Mind: The Contemplative Practices of Philosophy', The Royal Institute of Philosophy, the London Lectures, 28 October 2021. https://youtu.be/OqsO2nNrUiI

2. QUESTION EVERYTHING (INCLUDING YOUR QUESTIONS)

1 *Behind the Curve* (2018), dir. Daniel J Clark.
2 Immanuel Kant, *Critique of Pure Reason*, (1787) A548/B576
3 A. M. Valdes, J. Walter, E. Segal and T. D. Spector, 'Role of the gut microbiota in nutrition and health', *BMJ* 2018; 361:k2179 doi:10.1136/bmj.k2179

3. WATCH YOUR STEPS

1 'We're told we are a burden. No wonder disabled people fear assisted suicide', Jamie Hale, *Guardian*, 1 June 2018, https://www.theguardian.com/commentisfree/2018/jun/01/disabled-people-assisted-dying-safeguards-pressure
2 https://www.scope.org.uk/media/press-releases/scope-concerned-by-reported-relaxation-of-assisted-suicide-guidance/
3 https://www.unep.org/resources/report/unep-food-waste-index-report-2021
4 One of the favourite questions of BBC Radio's highly recommended *More or Less* programme.
5 https://www.eu-fusions.org/index.php/about-food-waste/280-food-waste-definition
6 Household Food and Drink Waste in the United Kingdom 2012, https://wrap.org.uk/sites/default/files/2020-08/WRAP-hhfdw-2012-main.pdf
7 Food surplus and waste in the UK – key facts, 2021, https://wrap.org.uk/resources/report/food-surplus-and-waste-uk-key-facts
8 https://www.usda.gov/foodwaste/faqs
9 Steven Pinker, *Rationality* (Allen Lane, 2021), p. 225

4. FOLLOW THE FACTS

1 David Hume, *An Enquiry Concerning Human Understanding* (1748/1777), Section X, 'Of Miracles'.

2 William Paley, *Natural Theology or Evidences of the Existence and Attributes of the Deity* (1802).
3 *An Enquiry Concerning Human Understanding*, Section XI, 'A Particular Providence and a Future State'.
4 G. Gigerenzer, 'Out of the frying pan into the fire: Behavioral reactions to terrorist attacks', *Risk Analysis*, April 2006; 26(2):347–51, doi: 10.1111/j.1539-6924.2006.00753.x. PMID: 16573625.
5 B. F. Hwang, J. J. Jaakkola and H. R. Guo, 'Water disinfection by-products and the risk of specific birth defects: A population-based cross-sectional study in Taiwan', *Environmental Health*, 2008; 7(23), https://doi.org/10.1186/1476-069X-7-23
6 Jo Macfarlane, 'Chlorine in tap water "nearly doubles the risk of birth defects"', *Daily Mail*, 31 May 2008.
7 There's a good account here of 9/11 conspiracy theories debunked: David Oswald, Erica Kuligowski and Kate Nguyen, *The Conversation*, https://theconversation.com/9-11-conspiracy-theories-debunked-20-years-later-engineering-experts-explain-how-the-twin-towers-collapsed-167353

5. WATCH YOUR LANGUAGE

1 Ludwig Wittgenstein, *Philosophical Investigations* (1953) §38.
2 Confucius, *Analects*, Book 13, Chapters 2–3, in James Legge, *The Chinese Classics Vol. 1*, (Oxford University Press, 1893), p. 102.
3 Thanks to Patrick Greenough for identifying the source.
4 Ludwig Wittgenstein, *Philosophical Investigations* (1953), p. 43.
5 https://www.globallivingwage.org/about/what-is-a-living-wage/
6 https://www.livingwage.org.uk/what-real-living-wage
7 *Shurangama Sutra*, Chapter 2, http://www.buddhanet.net/pdf_file/surangama.pdf
8 Ludwig Wittgenstein, *Tractatus Logico-Philosophicus* (1922) §7.

6. BE ECLECTIC

1 David Hume, *A Treatise of Human Nature*, (1740) Book 3, Part 1, Section 1.
2 *Cosmopolitan*, July 2013.

7. BE A PSYCHOLOGIST

1 Anil Seth, *Being You: A New Science of Consciousness* (Faber & Faber, 2021).
2 See Kahneman's magnificent *Thinking, Fast and Slow* (Farrar, Straus and Giroux, 2011).
3 Steven Pinker, *Rationality: What It Is, Why It Seems Scarce, Why It Matters* (Viking, 2021), Preface.
4 Hugo Mercier and Dan Sperber, *The Enigma of Reason* (Harvard University Press, 2017).
5 David Hume, *An Enquiry Concerning Human Understanding* (1748/1777), Section V, Part I.
6 S. L. Beilock, R. J. Rydell and A. R. McConnell, 'Stereotype threat and working memory: Mechanisms, alleviation, and spillover', *Journal of Experimental Psychology: General*, 2007; 136(2): 256–76, https://doi.org/10.1037/0096-3445.136.2.256
7 https://beingawomaninphilosophy.wordpress.com/2016/04/28/its-the-micro-aggressions/
8 A. C. Grayling, 'A booting for Bertie', *Guardian*, 28 October 2000.
9 Rachel Cooke, interview, Amia Srinivasan: 'Sex as a subject isn't weird. It's very, very serious', *Guardian*, 8 August 2021, https://www.theguardian.com/world/2021/aug/08/amia-srinivasan-the-right-to-sex-interview

8. KNOW WHAT MATTERS

1 Robert Heinaman, 'House-Cleaning and the Time of a Killing', *Philosophical Studies: An International Journal for Philosophy in the Analytic Tradition*, 1983; 44(3): 381–9, http://www.jstor.org/stable/4319644
2 Nicholas Rescher, 'Importance in Scientific Discovery', 2001, http://philsci-archive.pitt.edu/id/eprint/486
3 Jerry Fodor, 'Why would Mother Nature bother?', *London Review of Books*, 6 March 2003.
4 For a fuller account of my take, see *Freedom Regained* (Granta, 2015).
5 https://twitter.com/nntaleb/status/1125726455265144832?s=20
6 https://drug-dev.com/management-insight-antifragile-nassim-taleb-on-the-evils-of-modern-medicine/

9. LOSE YOUR EGO

1 David Papineau, 'Three scenes and a moral', *The Philosophers' Magazine*, Issue 38, 2nd Quarter 2007, p. 62.
2 https://bostonreview.net/articles/ned-block-philip-kitcher-misunderstanding-darwin-natural-selection/
3 David Hume, 'Whether the British Government inclines more to Absolute Monarchy, or to a Republic', in *Essays, Moral, Political, and Literary*, Part 1 (1741, 1777).

10. THINK FOR YOURSELF, NOT BY YOURSELF

1 https://www.philosophyexperiments.com/wason/ I think a problem with the experiment is the ambiguity between 'if' and 'if and only if'.
2 See David Hume, *A Treatise of Human Nature*, (1739).
3 Janet Radcliffe Richards, *The Sceptical Feminist: A Philosophical Enquiry* (Routledge, 1980).
4 See *A Short History of Truth* (Quercus, 2017).

11. ONLY CONNECT

1 Steven Pinker, *Enlightenment Now* (Penguin/Viking, 2018).
2 *Human Action: A Treatise on Economics* (Ludwig von Mises Institute, 1949, 1998), p. 33.
3 See Anne-Lise Sibony, 'The UK Covid-19 Response: A behavioural irony?', *European Journal of Risk Regulation*, June 2020; 11(2), doi:10.1017/err.2020.22
4 https://www.bi.team/blogs/behavioural-insights-the-who-and-Covid-19/

12. DON'T GIVE UP

1 David Hume, *A Treatise of Human Nature*, (1739), Book 1, Part 4, Section 7.
2 Really. https://www.efsa.europa.eu/en/efsajournal/pub/2809
3 Anil Seth, *Being You: A New Science of Consciousness* (Faber & Faber, 2021), p. 274.
4 Carlo Rovelli, *Helgoland*, (Allen Lane, 2021), p. 168.

CREDITS

EDITOR	Bella Lacey
COPY-EDITOR	Linden Lawson
PROOFREADER	Kate Shearman
COVER DESIGN	James Jones
MARKETING	Simon Heafield
SALES	Noel Murphy and Rosie Morgan
PUBLICITY	Lamorna Elmer
INTERNATIONAL RIGHTS	Isabella Depiazzi
PRODUCTION	Sarah Wasley
MANAGING EDITOR	Christine Lo
LITERARY AGENT	Lizzy Kremer
LITERARY AGENT'S ASSISTANT	Maddalena Cavaciuti
EXISTENTIAL SUPPORT	Antonia Macaro

BOOKSHOP SALES

UK: Kellie Balseiro, Sam Brown, Luke Crabb, Sarah Davison-Aitkins, Richard Evans, Richard Fortey, Sue Jackson, Rosy Locke, John McColgan, Mel Tyrrell, Jeremy Wood. Export: Amelie Burchell, Viki Cheung, Mallory Ladd, Bridget Lane.

SUPPORTERS

Phil Alsop, Vladimir Antimonov, Valerie Bosworth, John Boyd, Paul Breach, Mark Cohen, Susan Costello, Harry Davies, Paul Devine, Matt Evans, James Flux, Elisabetta Geromel Lister, Timo Hannay, Carlien Hillebrink, Spencer Hyman, Rune Isene, Carol Jefferson-Davies, Dan Kettmann, Kris Krimel, Michael Lawton, Michael Leigh, Janet Lentzos, Robert Little, Rosmarie Maran, Marilyn Mason, James Nathan, Brian Pagano, John Park, Keith Robinson, Magdalena Rogier, Bill Singleton, David Sutherland, Windsor Viney, Anthea Windsor, Frank Yeary.

WRITTEN BY

Julian Baggini